**Zahera Harb** is a Lebanese journalist and academic. She teaches media studies for the Department of Culture, Film and Media at Nottingham University. She has more than ten years' experience as a journalist in Lebanon, working for Lebanese and international media organisations. She started as a news reporter and distinguished herself in the coverage of war operations in the battlefield in south Lebanon. She is a member of the consultancy team of Thomson Foundation, UK, conducting media training for Arab journalists in and outside the Arab World. She is also a review editor for *Journal of Media Practice*.

*To the late Lebanese prime minister, Rafic Hariri.*

*Without his support, pursuing a PhD and telling this story would never have become reality*

*and*

*To my late tutor, Geoff Mungham.*

*Without his guidance, I would not have come to this new understanding of propaganda in my work as a journalist*

# CHANNELS OF RESISTANCE IN LEBANON

## LIBERATION PROPAGANDA, HEZBOLLAH AND THE MEDIA

Zahera Harb

I.B.TAURIS
LONDON · NEW YORK

Published in 2011 by I.B.Tauris & Co Ltd
6 Salem Road, London W2 4BU
175 Fifth Avenue, New York NY 10010
www.ibtauris.com

Distributed in the United States and Canada
Exclusively by Palgrave Macmillan
175 Fifth Avenue, New York NY 10010

Copyright © 2011 Zahera Harb

The right of Zahera Harb to be identified as the author of this work
has been asserted by her in accordance with the Copyright,
Designs and Patent Act 1988.

All rights reserved. Except for brief quotations in a review, this book, or any
part thereof, may not be reproduced, stored in or introduced into a retrieval
system, or transmitted, in any form or by any means, electronic, mechanical,
photocopying, recording or otherwise, without the prior written permission
of the publisher.

ISBN:   978 1 84885 120 7 (hb)
        978 1 84885 121 4 (pb)

A full CIP record for this book is available from the British Library
A full CIP record is available from the Library of Congress

Library of Congress Catalog Card Number: available

Index produced by Gerard M-F Hill of Much Better Text

Printed and bound in Great Britain by TJ International Ltd,
Padstow, Cornwall

# CONTENTS

| | | |
|---|---|---|
| *Acknowledgements* | | vi |
| 1 | Introduction | 1 |
| 2 | Propaganda: Definitions and Techniques | 5 |
| 3 | Ethnography and Journalism Culture | 32 |
| 4 | Overview of the Arab–Israeli Conflict | 55 |
| 5 | The Media in Lebanon | 92 |
| 6 | Tele Liban Coverage, April 1996: Grapes of Unity Facing Grapes of Wrath | 113 |
| 7 | Liberation Media: Hezbollah and Al Manar, 1997–2000 | 173 |
| *Reflection: Achieving Liberation Propaganda* | | 228 |
| *Notes* | | 235 |
| *Bibliography* | | 241 |
| *Index* | | 261 |

# ACKNOWLEDGEMENTS

I would like to express my appreciation and gratitude to Professor Terry Threadgold, without whose academic and personal support, advice and constructive comments I would not have produced this book. My sincere and warm thanks go to her. Equally, I am grateful to Dr Karin Wahl-Jorgensen, who tailored my work with her invaluable criticism, comments and suggestions.

I would like to thank Thor Ekevall and Gerard M.-F. Hill, who dedicated their time and energy to helping me with my work.

My appreciation and gratitude also go to Philippa Brewster of I.B.Tauris, Professor Nick Hewitt, Professor Roger Bromley, Professor Catherine Davis and Dean Allan Ford of Nottingham University for offering me personal and institutional support in getting this book published.

A big thank you goes to my family – my mum Khadijah, my dad Yousef and my brothers Salam and Tarek – who waited a long time for the birth of this work. The same goes to my friends and colleagues in the UK, back home and overseas: your love, encouragement and support were invaluable, though you are far too numerous to mention (it would take pages).

Finally, many thanks to all those who dedicated their time and effort to help me with my research – and particularly to all Lebanese journalists: you are the heroes of my story. Thank you.

# 1

# INTRODUCTION

On 18 April 1996, I was there.

Children, women and old people lay in dozens, beheaded and eviscerated. They thought that sheltering inside the United Nations headquarters in the village of Qana might save their lives from indiscriminate Israeli shelling over their villages, but it did not. One hundred and six innocent souls were crushed.

I remember how drastic and horrendous the scene was. I remember the villagers of Qana shouting at the camera, waving their hands in every direction, asking us to film and tell the world what the Israeli army had done to the innocents, to their loved ones. I remember standing among the scattered bodies of guiltless people paralysed by the horrors of what I was witnessing and the civil defence rescuers screaming at us to continue filming. I remember the UN soldier sitting in one corner and crying over a child he was playing football with before the Israeli bombs fell.

These strong memories have remained ever present in my mind, even today, years after the massacre took place. They are now part of a collective memory shared by most Lebanese citizens and journalists.

Israel occupied south Lebanon for over 22 years between 1978 and 2000.[1] In April 1996, Israel launched a massive assault on Lebanon, aimed at uprooting the Lebanese resistance, mainly from Hezbollah ('Party of God'). The Israeli army caused massive destruction and committed massacres, killing and injuring hundreds of Lebanese civilians. For 16 days I was positioned in south Lebanon, reporting Israeli assaults on the villages and cities of the south for Lebanese state-run television, Tele Liban.

We journalists played an important role in bringing people together, uniting them behind their fellow citizens in the south and in support of the resistance fighters against the Israeli occupation forces. Broadcasting live images of the shattered, innocent bodies of the Qana victims brought solidarity among Lebanese people to a climax. It was only when the war ended that I realised how we journalists were perceived as 'heroic' in the Lebanese press and among the Lebanese people.

At the time I felt that I had simply fulfilled my duty as a journalist to report and inform the public about what was really happening in south Lebanon. The nationalism and patriotism in my reporting seemed to me and my colleagues to be part of our role as professional journalists, but later I realised that it was that patriotic and nationalistic approach that made our coverage of the events in the south seem 'heroic'.

In the view of the Lebanese public, being 'heroic' was not inimical to the idea that our coverage was professional and it is still remembered as such. Roula Abdallah, of the daily *Al Mustaqbal*, wrote on 29 March 2007: 'Zahera and her colleagues raised the audiences' confidence in the Lebanese media to inform, [and] without the need to quote international agencies like Reuters or AFP' (Abdallah 2007: 8).

What seemed to be the first national media campaign to have brought Lebanese people together in solidarity against a foreign occupation force was followed later by a more structured media campaign conducted by Al Manar TV, the television station affiliated to Hezbollah, the main armed resistance force in south Lebanon. Al Manar's media campaign came to dominate the broadcasting environment of the country. They labelled themselves 'the Resistance Channel' and had one aim in mind: making liberation of south Lebanon from Israeli forces achievable.

## The rationale of this book

Between April 1996 and May 2000, when the Israeli army withdrew from south Lebanon, public figures emphasised the positive role that Lebanese television stations played in achieving liberation.

Hassan Nasrallah, Secretary General of Hezbollah, told Al Manar journalists afterwards that, if it had not been for Al Manar, the resistance would not have achieved the liberation. The late Lebanese Prime Minister, Rafic Hariri, praised the role the Lebanese media played in leading the country towards liberation – and it was then that I felt the need to address questions about the role that we, the Lebanese journalists, played in achieving that liberation.

The most poignant question to me was whether our media campaigns – for that was how we, and other commentators later, saw them – could be labelled as propaganda, a term that is usually pejorative and can have sinister undertones.

If so, what kind of propaganda was it? Did it match up with models of twentieth-century propaganda discussed in the West? Did it meet all the same criteria, techniques and principles? If it was propaganda, then what defined 'our propaganda'?

The aim of our media campaigns – both Tele Liban and Al Manar – was to help in achieving liberation of our land from a foreign occupation force. Thus the propaganda we conducted, if shown, was propaganda with the aim of liberation and could be given the name 'liberation propaganda'.

Alongside our unease that we might be accused of producing 'propaganda', there emerged a clear sense that we, the journalists, were deeply proud of the 'objective coverage' we delivered between 11 April 1996 and 25 May 2000, Liberation Day. Nonetheless, what kind of objectivity were we adhering to? How do journalism's norms and values fit with certain kinds – or any kind – of propaganda? Does objectivity apply in a propaganda campaign and what kind of objectivity would it be?

This book seeks to address these questions by exploring Lebanese media coverage, using the following as case studies:

1. How Tele Liban covered the events of April 1996, by close examination of prime-time news programmes.
2. How Al Manar covered major military incursions and encounters between the resistance and the Israeli occupation forces in south Lebanon between October 1997 and May 2000.
3. What press commentaries said about the above coverage.

As well as the case studies themselves, there are interviews with journalists, heads of news, editors and chairmen involved in the coverage during those five years.

This study is a qualitative investigation into Lebanese journalism's culture and its performance in relation to the Israeli forces' aggression against Lebanon and their encounters with the Lebanese resistance. Necessarily, the tale of how Lebanese journalists did their job is narrative and retrospective. Because this concerns a culture under threat, this study also uses the methodologies of ethnography to examine that aspect. The framework is a story about journalism told by a journalist, yet one who is using academic tools to tell it; this study is therefore self-critical and reflective.

Conceptually and politically, this study extends to questions that reporters face all over the world, because I examine Lebanese journalism culture and performance within the framework of war propaganda. As stated later, the objective here is to restore propaganda as a distinct generic entity (O'Shaughnessy 2004) and to claim a new understanding for it in the context of two conditions: foreign occupation and the struggle against that occupation.

To identify the characteristics of a more positive interpretation of propaganda, this study explores the historical, cultural, organisational and religious contexts in which the Lebanese television outlets and journalists studied here operated and how these contexts shaped their news values. This involves looking at particular genres of journalism, but as positive forms of propaganda. The study will also briefly draw upon examples from the July 2006 war, during which similar contexts existed.

This book suggests a definition, a set of characteristics and an understanding of liberation propaganda. What makes it original in the field of propaganda is that no other academic literature has been found on media campaigns operating in the same context: foreign military occupation and the struggle against that occupation.

# 2

## PROPAGANDA: DEFINITIONS AND TECHNIQUES

> Propaganda must be defined by reference to its aims.
> (Bartlett 1942: 6)

Barlett's approach to propaganda hardly matches the way other scholars define what propaganda is or how we can identify it (see Ellul 1965; Taithe and Thornton 1999; White 1939; Jowett and O'Donnell 1999). As this chapter aims to demonstrate, as long as propaganda has existed, people have seen it in various quite different terms, with some positive but mostly negative connotations attached to it. No one could claim to give a definitive description.

By looking at the work of prominent scholars on the issue, I want to illustrate how propaganda takes different definitions and forms in different political, social and cultural circumstances. I do not claim to cover here all that has ever been written on the issue, but I present and analyse the history, definitions and principles of different notions of propaganda as seen by scholars throughout the twentieth century and at the beginning of the twenty-first. I particularly wish to think about the meaning of the word and its connotations, both negative and positive, historically and in the literature. Using various researchers' approaches, my aim is to develop an understanding of different kinds of propaganda, especially in liberation contexts.

There are clearly different kinds of liberation movements. Since the beginning of the twentieth century, around the world, there have been insurgencies self-consciously aiming to resist or throw off a dominant foreign power (Hungary, Vietnam), liberation movements targeting imperial or colonial rule (Algeria, South Africa), indigenous liberation movements against nation-state formations (Native Americans in the USA and Mexico, ethnic groups in the Balkans) and of course nation-states resisting invasion.

However, although my discussion of propaganda is informed by the whole variety of liberation contexts, it is the Lebanese situation I am interested in and working towards. A wider understanding allows us to explore whether the media campaigns in Lebanon (against the Israeli occupation of part of its southern territories) match any of the concepts of propaganda illustrated here – and, if they do, how far and in what way.

## History and definitions

There is a tendency to think of propaganda as a relatively recent development and to associate it with the appearance of modern media, yet it has an extremely long history. Thousands of years before the invention of mass media in the modern sense, ancient civilisations could use the communication channels of their own era with skill and effect (Thomson 1999: 1). Hatem (1974: 54) went further, saying that propaganda has been with us in one form or another throughout recorded time.

Ancient and mediaeval understandings of the term were very different from those of today (Taithe and Thornton 1999), leaning towards the idea of proselytisation. In its strictest definition, propaganda meant the activities of a papal body, the *Sacra Congregatio de Propaganda Fide* (ibid: 1). Indeed, the term 'propaganda' did not exist until 1622. In this context, it simply meant 'extension, increase or enlargement' (Currey, quoted in ibid: 63).

### Bartlett, Kontler, Doob and White

Political propaganda in the twentieth century was generally first developed by the state, within its own borders, for its own inhabitants. Nevertheless, external propaganda soon gained similar importance; and its neglect, as Bartlett (1942: 7) argued, might run any such group into serious danger. Bartlett was writing when Nazi propaganda was at its climax during the Second World War. This was the time when Goebbels, the mastermind of Nazi propaganda, made it clear that 'objectivity has nothing in common with propaganda, nothing in common with truth' (quoted in Thomson 1999: 4). Goebbels' statement dismisses any form of propaganda that is not related to deception. Such a negative model of propaganda is not appropriate to this book, which seeks to focus on the more positive definitions of propaganda.

As I have mentioned, the term propaganda did not see widespread use until the early twentieth century, when it was used to describe the persuasion tactics employed during the First World War and those later used by the 'totalitarian regimes'. In this context, Laszlo Kontler charted early uses of a negative understanding of propaganda, defining it as the attempted supremacy of an overpowering ideology (in Taithe and Thornton 1999: 14). This is also important to my argument here. I want below to differentiate good and bad, defensive as opposed to offensive, and integrative rather than subversive, forms of propaganda.

Propaganda came to be defined as the dissemination of biased ideas and opinions, often through the use of lies and deception. However, as scholars began to study the topic in more detail, many came to realise that propaganda was not the sole property of 'evil' and totalitarian regimes, and that it often consists of more than just clever deceptions. Leonard W. Doob was one scholar who revisited his own definition of propaganda and rejected any clear-cut definitions:

> Leonard W. Doob, who defined propaganda in 1948 as 'the attempt to affect the personalities and to control the behaviour of individuals towards ends considered unscientific or of doubtful value in a society at a particular time' (p. 390), said in a 1989 essay 'a clear-cut definition of propaganda is neither possible nor desirable' (p. 375). Doob rejected a contemporary definition of propaganda because of the complexity of the issues related to behaviour in society and differences in times and cultures.
>
> (Jowett and O'Donnell 1999: 4)

The word propaganda has changed to mean mass suggestion or influence through the manipulation of symbols and the psychology of the individual. As Pratkanis and Aronson put it, propaganda has become:

> The communication of a point of view with the ultimate goal of having the recipient of the appeal come to 'voluntarily' accept this position as if it were his or her own.
> (Pratkanis and Aronson 1991: 9)

In 1939, A.B. White explained that political propaganda had (during the 1920s and 1930s) become the chief internal weapon of governments, employed not only to persuade a sufficient number of people that a particular course of action was expedient or right, 'but to keep whole populations in a complete, and, it is apparently hoped, a perpetual emotional subjection' (White 1939: 11). Thus, as White described, the object of the propaganda carried on by many governments in that period was to induce great masses of people to think alike and in the way desired by those governments (White 1939: 23).

By 1942, F.C. Bartlett adopted almost the same definition of political propaganda – as a process that aims, either wittingly or unwittingly, at producing whole nation groups in which all individuals think, act and feel alike – 'which has profound consequences'. However, Bartlett (1942: 14) went further by asserting that propaganda could only achieve its purposes in tandem with censorship:

> The propaganda that Bartlett identified appeals to a particular pride in a group or race, to the emotions and sentiments attached to strong symbols, to fear and anxiety, to the urge for dominance or submission, to greed and envy, or to what passes as legitimate social and political ambitions.
> (Bartlett 1942: 24)

## Ellul

In his famous book *Propaganda: The Formation of Men's Attitudes* (1965/1973), Jacques Ellul speaks of several kinds of propaganda. He first divides propaganda into two kinds: political propaganda and sociological propaganda. For Ellul, the first involves techniques of influence employed by a government, a party, an administration or a pressure group, with a view to changing the behaviour of the public.

> The choice of methods used is deliberate and calculated; the desired goals are clearly distinguished and quite precise,

though generally limited. Political propaganda can be either strategic or tactical. The former establishes the general line, the array of arguments, the staggering of the campaigns; the latter seeks to obtain immediate results within that framework (such as wartime pamphlets and loudspeakers to obtain the immediate surrender of the enemy).

(Ellul 1965/1973: 62)

He defines sociological propaganda as a means to penetrate a whole society and engage every member of society in a particular ideological culture (ibid: 64).

Ellul also identifies eight other kinds of propaganda, starting with the propaganda of agitation, an often subversive propaganda that has the stamp of opposition.

[Propaganda of agitation is a] propaganda led by a party seeking to destroy the government or the established order. It seeks rebellion or war. At that moment the subversion is aimed at the enemy, whose strength must be destroyed by psychological as well as physical means, and whose force must be overcome by the vigour of one's nation.

(ibid: 71)

He then moves on to talk about the propaganda of integration, where each member should be an organic and functional fragment of the society in which they are 'perfectly adapted and integrated'. It involves members that must share the stereotypes, beliefs and reactions of the group; each 'must be an active participant in its economic, ethical, aesthetic, and political doing'.

Propaganda of integration thus aims at making the individual participate in his society in every way. It is a long-term, self-reproducing propaganda that seeks to obtain stable behaviour, to adapt the individual to his everyday life, reshape his thoughts and behaviour in terms of the social setting.

(ibid: 75)

The kind of liberation propaganda I define below involves aspects of both of these: subversive and integrative propaganda. This is because those who are committed to the process of liberation are also almost always totally socialised and integrated into the political action that is their particular form of liberation, while also subversively acting for the nation against the perceived enemy.

Ellul suggests the conditions that are required for propaganda to thrive. He believes that modern propaganda could not exist without mass communication. By that he means the inventions that produced press, radio, television and motion pictures, or those that 'produced the means of modern transportation and which permit crowds of diverse individuals from all over to assemble easily and frequently' (ibid: 89).

We could update his argument by adding the internet, mobile phones and many other forms of information technology that have become available since 1989. All these factors are directly relevant to the kind of propaganda I want to focus on below, which is crucially connected to the operations of the media and the behaviours of practising journalists in wartime.

But, for Ellul, political circumstances are also immediate and effective catalysts for mass propaganda (ibid.). He insists that propaganda can only develop in a modern society if it is also a mass society, which for him is a society with considerable population density in which local structures and organisations are weak, while flows of opinion are strongly felt, people are grouped into united and influential collectives, the individuals are part of these groupings and a certain psychological unity exists (ibid: 93).

For Ellul, mass society is characterised by uniformity. Members of a mass society share the same material life, the same preoccupations, the same mythical beliefs and the same prejudices. The individuals making up the mass in the grip of propaganda may seem diversified, but they have enough in common for propaganda to work on them directly. 'Without the mass to receive propaganda and carry it along, propaganda is impossible' (ibid: 95). He argues this further by considering that 'from mass society emerge the psychological elements most favourable to propaganda: symbols and stereotypes' (ibid: 94). Also, Ellul puts primary importance on the feeling of 'togetherness' for propaganda to be effective psychologically and sociologically (ibid: 95). As I will argue later, a unified mass society or group and the feeling of togetherness are essential to the propaganda I describe below.

In 2002 Nancy Snow, the author of *Information War* (2003), interviewed Konrad Kellen, who translated Ellul's book *Propaganda* (from French into English) and wrote the introduction to the American edition. Kellen said of Ellul that 'the greatest contribution to the literature on propaganda was his proposition that propaganda is most effective when it is least noticeable' (Snow 2003: 22). Snow related Ellul's proposition to present-day American war propaganda, which I discuss later in this chapter.

## Whaley and Lasswell

Barton Whaley (in Lasswell et al. 1980) saw deception and psychological manipulation as characteristic features of propaganda. He identified different terms used of propaganda when applied to the international arena: psychological warfare, political warfare, international political communication and public diplomacy. Nevertheless, by whatever name, by whichever groups, propaganda (for Whaley) seeks to influence the behaviour of one or more foreign groups, ranging from the general public to particular elites.

He considers deception to be an important element – sometimes the dominant element – of such efforts to control or influence (Whaley in Lasswell et al. 1980: 341).

> I treat deception as information designed to manipulate the behaviour of others by inducing them to accept a false or distorted presentation of their environment – physical, social, or political. So defined, deception is a special psychological mode of both communication and power. In terms of communication it is disinformation, that is, information intended to mislead.
> (Whaley in Lasswell et al. 1980: 340)

Harold Lasswell, the American pioneer of propaganda studies in the 1930s, defined propaganda as 'the management of collective attitudes by the manipulation of significant symbols' (in Thomson 1999: 1).

As Thomson points out, the Institute of Propaganda Analysis (founded in 1937) defined propaganda in very similar mode as 'the expression of opinion or actions by individuals or groups deliberately designed to influence the opinions or actions of other individuals or groups with reference to determined ends' (Thomson 1999: 1).

## Thomson

The definition adopted by the Institute of Propaganda Analysis introduces a deliberate aspect to propaganda, which Oliver Thomson contests:

> First of all, there is the question of whether propaganda always has to be deliberate or planned, excluding, as Lasswell did, what he called the 'unpremeditated contagion of ideas'.
>
> (ibid: 1)

He believes it is unwise to insist on the words 'deliberate' or 'systematic' in any definition of propaganda, recognising as Ellul did (see above) the importance of sociological or integrative propaganda and refusing to tie the definition of propaganda down to merely deliberate or planned forms. He states that too many great movements of mass persuasion have begun and continued without any master plan, that much of what is legitimated by the media, and becomes the staple 'common sense' or dominant myths of a society, is in fact propaganda (Thomson 1999: 8).

According to Thomson, as in the definitions discussed above, a second problem with the definition of propaganda lies in the common assumption that mass persuasion is only propaganda when it uses untruth with deception or emotional manipulation (Thomson 1999: 3). He believes that any definition of propaganda that emphasises a reliance on untruth would be naïve and would exclude too many important campaigns of mass persuasion that did not have to resort to any deception.

Thomson recognises the existence of non-negative forms of propaganda and sees news, information and facts as potentially constituting a major component of such propaganda (ibid: 4). This fits with the understanding of propaganda I want to develop below and is helpful here to my arguments. Using similar arguments, Thomson defined propaganda very broadly as 'the use of communication skills of all kinds to achieve attitudinal or behavioural changes among one group of people by another' (ibid: 5).

## NATO and others

Equally broad definitions have achieved some influential currency. Both Wright (1991: 73) and Tugwell (1987: 409) use the definition established by NATO: 'Any information, ideas, doctrines or special appeals disseminated to influence the opinion, emotions, attitudes, or behaviour of any specified group in order to benefit the sponsor either directly or indirectly'.

According to Miller (1994), this is not in principle a partisan definition, but in the work of counter-insurgency theorists it is applied only to enemies of the West. Such writers are apparently unable to conceive that Western governments might also engage in special appeals to their own benefit, and so discussions of the media strategies of Western governments as forms of propaganda are few indeed (Miller 1994: 72).

The activities of Western governments are referred to as 'counter-propaganda' or 'spin' or 'media management' (Wright 1991: 207; Alexander et al. 1990: 24, quoted in Miller 1994: 70), never as 'propaganda'. Accordingly, Miller agrees with Robins et al. (1987: 8, quoted in Miller 1994: 72) that propaganda is a 'matter of the politics of information'. This position ultimately leads Miller to argue that propaganda is just a small part of the media information strategies of all governments.

What is important for my argument here is that these theorists, taken together, bring together the operations of the media, the question of power, the issue of information warfare and the common sense of everyday life, within the framework of a broad definition of 'propaganda' which is about influencing public opinion in ways that the influencer believes to be positive or good.

## Hatem

On the other hand, Mohammed Abdel-Kader Hatem (1974) begins with the negative view of propaganda, and argues for a narrower concept of it: that is, to view it as the dissemination of information from concealed sources or with concealed objectives.

> Motives are difficult to designate and record, and can be reported only indirectly since they are subjective states, and the discussion of motives usually involves evaluation. Yet a motive of devious manipulation, and its evaluation, must enter into what most social scientists (as well as the common man) have defined as propaganda.
> 
> (Hatem 1974: 56)

Hatem refused to connect propaganda completely to dishonesty or harm, even though 'the present century provides examples enough of its calamitous results in the hands of a group prepared to distort truth' (Hatem 1974: 59). In his defence of 'honest propaganda', Hatem points out that selectivity in terms of material need not operate against the public interest, provided the selection employed does not suppress essential facts, however injurious to its case, but rather reveals truths which might be hidden. One of the examples he gives is when a party in opposition justifiably concentrates its propaganda effort on publicising information that the dominant group has been at pains to conceal (ibid: 59).

Again, we find the theorist returning to the idea that, for those in opposition (that is, without power), propaganda may actually be a positive way of challenging the status quo. This too will be useful to my arguments about liberation propaganda.

According to Hatem, the compulsions towards 'honest propaganda' are especially strong in the realm of international affairs, where timing is often critical, where many key facts are available as classified information known only at the highest level, where the consequences of a wrong decision are incalculable and where in any case the pre-existence of propaganda-conditioned reflexes properly calls for counter-propaganda to supply world opinion with the means of effecting a balanced judgement – in other words, to bring to light an adequate selection of facts and essential considerations which would otherwise remain hidden (ibid: 63).

Hatem believes that counter-propaganda of this kind is a significant issue. He identifies one key example within the Arab–Israeli conflict.

> The Arab–Israeli confrontation ... admirably illustrates this function, in a situation in which the Zionist party to the conflict has for decades exploited its greater access to the mass media to mould much of world opinion in a manner favourable to its cause. The interests of truth and objectivity demand the presentation of the facts in their totality, and consequently demand the most effective and widest publication of the Arab case. It is in circumstances like these that public relations, in alliance with honest propaganda, exercise their most valuable function by bringing before world public opinion the truth in its most complete yet

assimilable form. This is the essence of information for justice and peace.

(Hatem 1974: 63)

Discussing counter-propaganda during confrontations and conflicts, Hatem adds that since any political act may influence mass opinion, regardless of the means employed, an important part of total policy is the calculating and managing of psychological effects. Thus, when aimed at an enemy during wartime, propaganda is identified as 'psychological warfare' (ibid: 58). It is significant here that propaganda has begun to merge in terms of definition with public and media relations so that it begins to become possible in certain circumstances to define a media campaign as propaganda.

## Taylor

The work of Philip Taylor demonstrates how propaganda needs to attain a higher level of sophistication in implementing it to win over an audience (in Taithe and Thornton 1999: 12). Taylor considers that, in the struggle for power, propaganda is an instrument to be used by those who want to secure or retain power just as much as by those wanting to displace them. He says 'for the smoke to rise there must first be a spark which lights the flame. Propaganda is that spark' (Taylor 1995: 5).

Taylor, like Hatem (1974), believes that propaganda can be used for 'good purposes', just as it can be abused. He assumes that it is those good reasons and causes behind propaganda that should be the legitimate objects of moral and critical analysis and judgement, not the propaganda itself.

Thus, according to Taylor, if the history of propaganda in the twentieth century appears to be largely a history of abuse, it does not follow that this has always been, and always will be, the case (ibid: 6). Taylor has provided his own definition of propaganda as the communication of ideas designed to persuade people to think and behave in a particular way (ibid.).

> By propaganda, then, I mean the deliberate attempt to persuade people to think and behave in a desired way. Although I recognise that such propaganda [might be] accidental or unconscious, here I am discussing the conscious, methodical and planned decisions to employ

techniques of persuasion designed to achieve specific goals that are intended to benefit those organising the process.

(Taylor 1995: 6)

Taylor's recognition of accidental or unconscious propaganda is similar to the understandings of sociological or integrative propaganda (see above) in acknowledging the fact that symbols and deeds can have unintended meanings that cannot be controlled by those who author them, and that the generally-held understandings of a society or social group may not have been planned or deliberately constructed by anyone. On the other hand, this does not stop people making very conscious and deliberate decisions to attempt to control and manage meanings. It is the latter process that Taylor is most interested in.

## Jowett and O'Donnell

In their 1999 book, Jowett and O'Donnell dismiss the idea of accidental or unplanned propaganda. They identify propaganda as the deliberate, systematic attempt to shape perceptions, manipulate cognitions and direct behaviour, to achieve a response that 'furthers the desired intent of the propagandist' (ibid: 6). They assume that the purpose of propaganda is to send out an ideology to an audience that has a related aim:

> Whether it is a government agency attempting to instil a massive wave of patriotism in a national audience to support a war effort... (or a leader showing his strength or a company marketing a product,) a careful and predetermined plan of prefabricated symbol manipulation is used to communicate an objective to an audience.
>
> (ibid: 3)

They adopt Combs and Nimmo's (1993) view of propaganda as 'an indispensable form of communication' and 'a major form of public discourse' (quoted in Jowett and O'Donnell 1999: 5). Based on this, their definition of propaganda focuses on the communication process and, most specifically, on the purpose of the process (ibid: 6). They seek to understand and analyse propaganda by identifying its characteristics and they place it within communication studies 'to examine the qualities of context, sender, intent, message, channel, audience, and response' (ibid: 5).

If propaganda devices can be spotted by analysing media messages, then for Jowett and O'Donnell propaganda fall into three categories:

> Propaganda is also described as white, grey, or black, in relationship to an acknowledgement of its source and its accuracy of information White propaganda comes from a source that is identified correctly, and the information in the message tends to be accurate...Black propaganda is credited to a false source and spreads lies, fabrications, and deceptions. Black propaganda is the 'big lie', including all types of creative deceit...Grey propaganda is somewhere between white and black. The source may or may not be correctly identified, and the accuracy of the information is uncertain.
>
> (ibid: 12–15)

According to Jowett and O'Donnell (1999), national celebrations, with their 'overt patriotism and regional chauvinism, can usually be classified as white propaganda' (ibid: 21). As I demonstrate later in this chapter, their definition of white propaganda is useful to the understanding of propaganda I want to develop in this book.

Jowett and O'Donnell also make reference to another dimension of propaganda, Doob's (1948) 'sub-propaganda', where they believe the propagandist's task is to spread an unfamiliar doctrine, for which a considerable period is needed to build a frame of mind in the audience tending towards acceptance of the doctrine (Jowett and O'Donnell, 1999: 22).

## Taithe and Thornton

Beyond this, Taithe and Thornton (1999) present an extreme classification of propaganda. For them, 'Propaganda is about life and death and this choice is never better exemplified than in time of war, when the choice is indeed between staying at home and going to the front' (ibid: 15). However, they believe propaganda is often most fully discussed in counter-propaganda. 'Denouncing the other's devious techniques and lack of credibility, while displaying similar methods, makes this a paradoxical and in some ways self-undermining process' (ibid: 1). Nonetheless, demonising 'the enemy's' credibility and keeping one's own credibility intact might be achievable in a propaganda campaign, as the cases I am investigating indicate.

Unlike Taithe and Thornton, Herman and Chomsky do not relate propaganda to war specifically. They speak of systematic propaganda 'in a world of concentrated wealth and major conflicts of class interest' (Herman and Chomsky 1994: 1). They believe mass media serve as a system for communicating messages and symbols to the general public. It is their function to amuse, entertain and inform, and to inculcate individuals with the values, beliefs and codes of behaviour that will integrate them into the institutional structures of the larger society. This requires the systemic propaganda mentioned above (ibid.).

> A propaganda model focuses on this inequality of wealth and power and its multilevel effects on mass-media interests and choices. It traces the routes by which money and power are able to filter out the news fit to print, marginalize dissent, and allow the government and dominant private interests to get their messages across to the public..
>
> (ibid: 2)

The raw material of news must pass through successive filters, leaving only the cleansed residue fit to print. The filters fix the premises of discourses and interpretation, and the definition of what is newsworthy in the first place, and they explain the basis and operations of what amount to propaganda campaigns (ibid.). In one way or another this is the relationship between propaganda and censorship identified by Bartlett (1942: 14), but here it is in the hands of big corporations and media moguls. The question of power is central here.

## Propaganda since 2000

However, soon after September 11, the war in Afghanistan in 2001 and the war in Iraq in 2003, Western governments were again in control of the flow of information and media messages to the public. Poignantly, Bernays' (1928) 'vicious propaganda' was given the name 'Public Diplomacy' by the American administration (Snow in Miller 2003: 54). In this we see again how easily the negative and positive

## Propaganda: Definitions and Techniques 19

forms of propaganda transmute into one another. It is all a question of perspective and context. It depends whether you (or the group you represent) are the one who benefits from the propaganda and it is a question of semantics.

In 2001–3 the American and British administrations conducted media campaigns to legitimise the wars in Afghanistan and Iraq as part of the 'war on terror'. Many scholars related these media campaigns to lies, deception and psychological manipulation (see Connelly and Welch 2005; Rutherford 2004; Miller 2003; Rampton and Stauber 2003; Snow 2003). Thus, the term propaganda has been introduced again in the twenty-first century, with the same negative connotations.

> The propaganda war is the most integrated part of the new war on terror; it's the part that is most hidden from view but also the most pervasive ... it is controlled information, not designed for community empowerment or popular education that aims to further the ability of people to think for themselves. American propaganda is the sugar pill that makes sure the bitter truth goes down.
> 
> (Snow 2003: 23)

Rutherford (2004) speaks of war being managed through news media. This is what Connelly and Welch identify as the war for the hearts and minds of the public:

> Modern military campaigns are likely to become struggles of information in the battle for the high ground of public opinion. In such a struggle the management of perception – the battle for 'hearts and minds' – will continue to be about words and pictures and not just about bombs and aeroplanes.
> 
> (Connelly and Welch 2005: xvii)

Nicholas O'Shaughnessy tries, in his book *Politics and Propaganda, Weapons of Mass Seduction* (2004), to analyse the meaning, content and significance of the word 'propaganda' today. He believes that:

> Propaganda is ubiquitous. While such saturation is an obvious and definitive characteristic of totalitarian regimes, in democracies it is more concealed, because it is more sophisticated and naturalised as supposedly objective mass

media communication. [However,] if we do not have labels for phenomena we tend not to recognise them.

(O'Shaughnessy 2004: 224)

He argues that the recognition that new forms of propaganda have arrived, and old ones continue, 'means that the work of propaganda analysis is never complete' (ibid: 244). Yet, in this regard, O'Shaughnessy believes that 'there is no universal "key" to propaganda via either sociology or psychology' and that 'those who look for a universal theory, a code to unlock, search in vain'. He argues that 'the many manifestations of propaganda, styles, appeals, tricks, must be accessed in a ... heterodox way' (ibid: 62).

However, several scholars and institutions through the twentieth century and beyond, including O'Shaughnessy himself, have identified certain characteristics of propaganda. He speaks of myth, symbolism and rhetoric as foundation concepts, and hyperbole, fantasy, emotion, enemies, manipulation, deceit and utopia as key elements (ibid: 3). His concepts and key elements relate to what other scholars have identified as the tools and principles of propaganda.

Before presenting these principles and tools, it is essential that we look at the one academic study[1] that deals with propaganda in a liberation context, which argues for legal control of what it calls 'Liberation Propaganda'.

## Propaganda in liberation contexts

The only use of the term 'liberation propaganda' that I have been able to find actually refers to a very different kind of propaganda from the kind that I want to call liberation propaganda. Gerhard von Glahn (1966) introduced the term in an academic article submitted to the journal *Law and Contemporary Problems*. He refers to 'the so-called "liberation" propaganda' (von Glahn 1966: 553) as a form of Ellul's agitation and subversive propaganda mentioned above (ibid: 562).

The propaganda von Glahn investigated was one conducted by foreign governments in support of local revolutionary groups to achieve domestic change in a foreign country. Domestic change by force is an essential element of the phenomenon von Glahn describes. According to him, this type of propaganda has in its object 'the arousal and abetment of tendencies toward an outbreak of revolutionary violence in another country' (ibid: 553). He adds:

The purpose of such violence may be assumed to be the creation of radical domestic changes, such as a termination of colonial status, the elimination of legal racism, the ending of 'neo colonialism,' or simply the replacement of one governing elite by another.

(ibid.)

Von Glahn studied the case for what he called 'legal control of 'Liberation' propaganda'. He explained that the propaganda he was looking at was that emanating from foreign governments, excluding propaganda conducted by other groups:

> In order to keep this analysis within reasonable bounds, the inquiry has been restricted to propaganda emanating from governments, thus leaving aside similar efforts by private individuals and by groups below the level of national political grouping in single party states such as the Soviet Union.

(ibid: 553)

Von Glahn considers that the phenomenon he is describing represents 'a mortal danger to any government, for it seeks to dissolve the basic cement of loyalty that binds a citizen to his or her government and his community' (ibid: 554). Nonetheless he identifies liberation propaganda as a 'common tool in foreign policy' (ibid: 553).

It is very important here to distinguish this use of the term 'liberation' from the one I want to develop. The propaganda that I am investigating is one that is conducted by domestic governments, alongside domestic liberation resistance movements, with the aim of achieving liberation from a foreign occupying army. Indeed, it could be said that the liberation propaganda I describe is something like a domestic response to von Glahn's externally driven version.

What I want to describe is a propaganda that seeks loyalty, and that binds citizens to their governments and their resistance groups, in their fight against a foreign enemy. It is what Karl von Clausewitz might have called continuation of 'war' by other means (cited in Thomas 1996: xi). It is propaganda of integration; where it is a propaganda of subversion, it is subversive of the activities of a foreign enemy. It is, like most forms of propaganda, context-specific. It borrows some, and rejects other, aspects of the principles and tools of propaganda which are identified in different academic studies in the twentieth and twenty-first centuries. The rest of this chapter lists and explores some of these tools and principles in order to be able to refer to them in later chapters in relation to detailed case studies of forms of propaganda utilised in the Lebanese–Israeli conflict.

## Principles and tools

Shaping perception is usually attempted through language and images, which is why slogans, posters, symbols, and even architectural structures are developed during wartime. How we perceive is based on 'complex psychological, philosophical, and practical habitual thought patterns that are carried over from past experiences'.

(Hayward 1997: 73 quoted in Jowett and O'Donnell 1999: 7)

One of the main propaganda characteristics or principles that Jowett and O'Donnell speak of is shaping perception. Perception for them is the process of digging up information from the world around us, as well as from within ourselves. 'Each individual has a perceptual field that is unique to that person and which has formed and influenced their values, roles, group norms and self-image' (O'Donnell and Kable 1982, quoted in Jowett and O'Donnell 1999: 7).

But what has this to do with propaganda? According to Jowett and O'Donnell, propagandists understand 'that our constructed meanings are related to both our past understanding of language and images and the context in which they appear' (Jowett and O'Donnell 1999: 7). Shaping perception is needed when propaganda is aiming or attempting to rouse an audience to certain ends or attempting to render an audience passive, accepting and non-challenging (Szanto quoted in ibid: 12).

Pratkanis and Aronson add to this idea, explaining that for a propagandist to change old beliefs or to create new ones, he or she has to build on beliefs that already exist in the minds of the audience. A propagandist has to use anchors of belief to create a new belief. They aver that, 'the stronger the belief of a receiver, the more likely it to influence the formation of a new belief' (Pratkanis and Aronson 1991: 31).

Pratkanis and Aronson point out the importance of having an authoritative figure whom people are willing to believe in order to let the message pass through to them. They go back to Aristotle, who wrote on the matter more than 300 years before Christ:

> We believe good men more fully and more readily than others: this is true generally whatever the question is, and absolutely true where exact certainty is impossible and opinions are divided. It is not true, as some writers assume in their treatises or rhetoric, that the personal goodness revealed by the speaker contributes nothing to his power of persuasion; on the contrary, his character may almost be called the most effective means of persuasion he possesses.
> (Aristotle quoted in Pratkanis and Aronson 1991: 86)

They also draw attention to another aspect propagandists should consider while planning for their campaign. They believe that the clear trustworthiness of a person can be increased and the clear bias of the message decreased if the audience is absolutely certain the person is not trying to influence them (Pratkanis and Aronson 1991: 98). In their presentation they stick to this formula: 'When communicators do not appear to be trying to influence us, their potential to do so is increased' (ibid: 99). Besides, they believe the propagandist should consider encouraging the fear aspect, which means making the audience fearful of the [perceived] enemy (ibid: 99). This contradicts what the Lebanese journalists tried to achieve in their media messages to the home front between 1996 and 2000. They did not want their audiences to fear 'the enemy' – they wanted the public to feel fearless and resist 'the enemy', as I show in Chapters Six and Seven.

Hatem, on the other hand, draws attention to the importance of myths and legends in operating propaganda campaigns. He identifies legends as 'modified accounts of past events and historic figures, whereas myths are imaginative accounts of the meaning of life'. Coming down to us from the past as a part of our cultural heritage, myths and legends are adult extensions of the childhood world of fantasy and make-believe. 'Whether the birth of a legend is deliberate or not, the fact remains that masses of mankind live in these images' (Hatem 1974: 77). According to Hatem, the most effective leader-symbols are the national, cultural and group heroes. These are personifications of values, causes and critical events. Their names, pictures and status are a focus for the emotional loyalties of their publics (ibid: 81). As will be demonstrated in Chapters Six and Seven, the late Lebanese prime minister, Rafic Hariri, and Secretary General of Hezbollah, Hassan Nasrallah, were viewed as leader-symbols in the Lebanese context that this book explores.

For Merton (in Jackall 1995), the overall strategy of persuasion makes use of a special social situation in which mass interest and emotions are centred on a national co-operative venture. He assumed varied techniques and devices were employed to move the audience from a state of mind to definite action. 'But these devices of mass persuasion, primarily *technical* in character though they are, have a *moral* dimension as well' (Merton in Jackall 1995: 261).

> The public sacrifice presumably entailed by a daylong stint at the microphone set Smith apart from others who 'only talked but didn't act'. Propaganda of the deed proved persuasive among some who rejected propaganda of the word. Listeners who revealed their profound distrust of the 'power of speech' were moved by the symbolic act.
>
> (ibid: 263)

Merton made it clear that people are moved 'by emotion, by fear and hope and anxiety, and not by information or knowledge'. However, he assumes it may be pointed out that complex situations must be simplified for mass publics and, in the course of simplification 'much that is relevant must be omitted' (Merton in Jackall 1995: 270).

## Goebbels' principles of propaganda

Leonard W. Doob dedicated a whole chapter in Jackal's book *Propaganda* (1995) to the Nazi Propaganda Minister Goebbels' principles of propaganda. He reveals that among the Nazi documents put back together by the American authorities in Berlin in 1945 are close to 6,800 pages of manuscript, presumably dictated by Goebbels as a diary, that cover the period from 21 January 1942 to 9 December 1943 (Doob in Jackall 1995: 190).

> All that is being assumed, in short, is that the manuscript more or less faithfully reflects Goebbels' propaganda

strategy and tactics: it is a convenient guide to his bulky propaganda materials.

(ibid: 191)

Goebbels speaks of 19 principles. All aim to dictate, manipulate and deceive people. Some of these techniques were fully or partly applied in forms of propaganda used in the Lebanese–Israeli conflict, which is the subject matter of this book. Some of them were used by Tele Liban and Al Manar journalists, but the case studies I investigate here show very clearly that these features do not characterise all forms of propaganda.

If we are later to contest this list, it is important to state these principles in detail, as offered by Doob (1995: 193–214), remembering that these are principles of negative propaganda, designed to deceive:

Principle 1: Propagandists must have access to intelligence concerning events and public opinion;
Principle 2: Propaganda must be planned and executed by only one authority;
Principle 3: The propaganda consequences of an action must be considered in planning that action;
Principle 4: Propaganda must affect the enemy's policy and action;
Principle 5: Declassified, operational information must be available to implement a propaganda campaign;
Principle 6: To be perceived, propaganda must evoke the interest of an audience and must be transmitted through an attention-getting communications medium;
Principle 7: Credibility alone must determine whether propaganda output should be true or false;
Principle 8: The purpose, content, and effectiveness of enemy propaganda; the strength and effects of an exposé; and the nature of current propaganda campaigns determine whether enemy propaganda should be ignored or refuted (Doob 1995: 200);
Principle 9: Credibility, intelligence, and the possible effects of communicating determine whether propaganda materials should be censored;
Principle 10: Material from enemy propaganda may be utilised in operations when it helps diminish that enemy's prestige or lends support to the propagandist's own objective;

Principle 11: Black rather than white propaganda must be employed when the latter is less credible or produces undesirable effects;
Principle 12: Propaganda may be facilitated by leaders with prestige;
Principle 13: Propaganda must be carefully timed;
Principle 14: Propaganda must label events and people with distinctive phrases or slogans;
Principle 15: Propaganda to the home front must prevent the raising of false hopes, which can be blasted by future events;
Principle 16: Propaganda to the home front must create an optimum anxiety level;
Principle 17: Propaganda to the home front must diminish the impact of frustration. Goebbels sought to diminish the impact by following two principles: First, inevitable frustrations must be anticipated. Goebbels' reasoning seems to have been that a frustration would be less frustrating if the element of surprise or shock were eliminated. Second, inevitable frustrations must be placed in perspective;
Principle 18: Propaganda must facilitate the displacement of aggression by specifying the targets of the hatred;
Principle 19: Propaganda cannot immediately affect strong countertendencies: instead it must offer some form of action or diversion, or both.

Full reference to these principles and tools appears in Chapters Six and Seven, where they are used to compare Tele Liban and Al Manar journalists' performances. However, they will be used illustratively in the discussion of later data and do not constitute a method for the systematic examination of output.

## Analysis: what the literature says

Bartlett (1942: 131) wrote six and a half decades ago that no accurate measurement of the effects of propaganda was yet possible. Nonetheless, Jackall (1995: 218–222) presents the devices that the Institute for Propaganda Analysis look for in order to detect the existence of propaganda. These constitute a rough mode for analysing the rhetorical devices that characterise an instance of propaganda. They call them 'the seven common propaganda devices'.

## The name-calling device

Here the propagandist appeals to our hates and fears. He does this by giving 'bad names' to those individuals, groups, nations, races, policies, practices, beliefs and ideals that he would have us condemn and reject.

## The glittering generalities device

Here he appeals to our emotions of love, generosity and values like brotherhood, honour, liberty, social justice, public service, the right to work, loyalty and progress, and concepts like democracy, the American way and constitution defender.

## The transfer device

Transfer is a device by which the propaganda carries over the authority, sanction and prestige of something we respect and revere to something the propagandist would have us accept (such as religious leaders).

## The testimonial device

In this device, the propagandist makes use of testimonials. 'When I feel tired, I smoke Camel and get the grandest "lift".'

## The plain folks device

'Plain folks' is a device used by politicians, labour leaders and businessmen, and even ministers and educators, to win our confidence by appearing to be people just like ourselves – 'just plain folks among the neighbours'.

## The card-stacking device

This is a device in which the propagandist employs all the arts of deception to win our support for himself, his group, nation, race, policy, practice, belief or ideal. He stacks the cards against the truth.

## The band wagon device

This is a device to make us follow the crowd, to accept the propagandist's programme *en masse*. Here his theme is: 'Everybody's doing it'.

## Propaganda and emotion

Observe that in all these devices our emotion is the stuff with which propagandists work. The Institute for Propaganda Analysis states that the public are fooled by these devices because they appeal to our emotions rather than to our reason. They make us believe and do something we would not believe or do if we thought about it calmly, dispassionately. The institute's advice in examining these devices is to note that they work most effectively at those times when we are too lazy to think for ourselves (Jackall: 217).

## Thomson: what is it all for?

Thomson (1999) changes the question of how to detect propaganda to: what was it all for? And he provides a rather more detailed account of what to look for in analysing propaganda.

First he divides propaganda into eight main categories, so analysis can be undertaken according to the objectives for which it is used: 'Political, Religious, Economic, Moral, Social, Diplomatic, Military, and Diversionary' (Thomson 1999: 7–12). Then he moves to consider the range of media used in the propaganda campaign: visual arts, photography, music, opera, dance and body language, literature, poetry, theatre, the novel, history, the press and print, leaflet distribution, cinema, radio, television, telephone and internet, and event management (ibid: 13–45). Each alone or combined is related to a particular device of propaganda in order to achieve its effect. These propaganda devices, according to Thomson, range from structural tools to linguistic, musical and visual, which make the task of persuasion easier.

> Rhyme has been recognised for thousands of years as having the capacity to make simple phrases more memorable, more exciting and apparently more significant. There have been numerous rhyming moral or legal codes such as the Norse Havamal and rhyme has been almost universally used to help with behavioural training of the young.
>
> (ibid: 49)

He draws attention to what he calls 'The Dangers of Not Going Far Enough'. He believes in analysing the likely reasons for failure in propaganda campaigns: 'there are three main areas to consider: message structure, media and audience factors' (Thomson 1999: 72). The failure might be related to public resistance to too much propaganda that is obvious or people having difficulty accessing media messages, or there may be some other general irregularities such as the fact that some groups who are very good at internal propaganda (to the home front) are bad at external (propaganda to non-home audiences) (ibid: 73). Thomson also refers to certain factors that have helped improve propaganda performance over time:

> A number of factors, both of message presentation and media usage, have tended to improve propaganda performance down the ages. The value of repetition has been recognised subconsciously from the earliest times, particularly in terms of visual messages on coins or buildings, event management and music. More recently its efficacy for verbal propaganda has been more appreciated.
>
> (ibid: 74)

## Jowett and O'Donnell: how to analyse a campaign

In *Propaganda and Persuasion* (1999), Jowett and O'Donnell give a straightforward chart showing how to analyse a propaganda campaign, looking at ten elements:

- the ideology and purpose of the propaganda campaign;
- the context in which the propaganda occurs;
- identification of the propagandist;
- the structure of the propaganda organisation;
- the target audience;
- media-utilisation techniques;
- special techniques to maximise effect;
- audience reaction to various techniques;
- counter-propaganda, if present;
- effects and evaluation (ibid: 31).

These ten divisions are intended, alongside the other lists and suggestions explored briefly above, to provide checklists of common understandings of what propaganda is – checklists against which to measure and compare the activities in the case studies which are the focus of this book. They will be referred to again in Chapters Six and Seven, but they are not intended to provide any kind of exhaustive analytical methodology.

## Conclusion

In this chapter I have tried to present a brief history of some definitions, principles and analyses of a variety of notions of propaganda, as seen by scholars through the twentieth century and into the twenty-first. I have sought to explore these different definitions and characteristics of propaganda found in the literature to see what basis they provide for developing a model of liberation propaganda that would be adequate to describe the activities of Tele Liban and Al Manar journalists during the Lebanese–Israeli conflict, a model that might be generalised to cover other such situations.

As long as it has existed, different people have seen propaganda in, and identified it by, different terms. Some positive, but mostly negative connotations were attached to it. Few people have seen it as neutral and none could claim to give a definitive description. This study is trying to restore Edward L. Bernays' (1928) argument that 'the fine old word, Propaganda' in itself has certain technical meanings which, 'like most things in this world, are neither good nor bad but custom makes them so' (ibid: 20) – and then to use the word again in a positive sense to describe what might also be called a 'media campaign' or indeed something else.

To reinforce Bernays' point, I adopt Barlett's approach to propaganda, which states that 'Propaganda must be defined by reference to its aims' (Bartlett 1942: 6). Both Bartlett and Bernays have this element of purpose in their definitions of propaganda. However, Bernays' (1928) emphasis is on the word 'systematically' in the process of gaining public support, while Bartlett (1942) uses the phrase 'wittingly or unwittingly', which identifies more accurately the understanding of propaganda that I am arguing for. This fits within the framework of Ellul's propaganda of integration, where 'Propaganda aims at making the individual participate in his society in every way' (Ellul 1973: 75), but this participation can be accomplished even when the campaign is part accidental, part improvised, part an almost unconscious (because professionally trained) response to desperate situations. 'Deliberate' here acquires nuanced, context-specific meanings that do not entirely contradict its apparent opposites, 'automatic' and 'unwitting'.

Nevertheless, by propaganda I mean a campaign that achieves, and was intended to achieve, public support for a national cause or other mission, with mass media being a core tool in disseminating political, social and patriotic messages to the public. In accordance with that, the notion of 'liberation propaganda' this book is investigating is certainly of a media campaign, in this case a campaign that seeks to promote national unity and strengthen support for the resistance groups that are fighting invasion or occupation forces within a sovereign, independent state. Further;

- it is a propaganda of integration, not (internal) subversion;
- it is an 'honest' (Hatem 1974), 'white' (Jowett and O'Donnell 1999) propaganda whose sources and aims are acknowledged;
- it is a propaganda that claims to be based on objective, factual information; and
- it is a propaganda that aims at dismissing fear of the enemy and denouncing the enemy's credibility and abilities, while highlighting the ability and credibility of the resistance groups and their leaders.

This liberation propaganda therefore dismisses Goebbels' assertion that 'objectivity has nothing in common with propaganda, nothing in common with truth' (quoted in Thomson 1999: 4). This propaganda uses national symbols, relating them to the history of the conflict between occupied and occupier, to achieve its goals.

This chapter's objective has been to analyse what has been thought, written and said about propaganda, in preparation for my exploration of this book's case-studies. Drawing on these similarities and differences in concepts and practices of propaganda, I aim in Chapters Six and Seven to illustrate the elements of liberation propaganda and the contexts in which it operates.

The next chapter looks at how ethnography and the methodologies related to it can explore these contexts and help to achieve the suggested new understanding of propaganda. It also tries to establish how different cultural contexts might generate different understandings and implementations of (apparently) the same set of journalistic norms and values. Contextualising norms such as objectivity and neutrality is arguably essential in identifying the putative concept of liberation propaganda, assessing performances of it and distinguishing it from other kinds of propaganda.

# 3

# ETHNOGRAPHY AND JOURNALISM CULTURE

> A new ethnography is a story based on the represented, or evoked, experiences of a self, with others, within a context... Its theme is the persuasive expression of interpreted cultural performances.
>
> (Goodall 2000: 83)

This study is an ethnographically-informed study. Ethnography is the process that I use to conduct a qualitative investigation into the culture of Lebanese journalism and how it performed in relation to the Israeli forces' escalation of conflict against Lebanon and their encounters with the Lebanese resistance.

This investigation adopts Goodall's assessment of ethnography as 'a way of writing the personal experience of the researcher into meaning in ways that serve as analyses of cultures' (Goodall 2000: 126). Cultures are what Goodenough (cited in Wolcott 1995: 86) refers to as the combination of concepts, beliefs and principles of action and organisation of a society. Culture is what 'an ethnographer has found and [what] could be attributed successfully to the members of that society in the context of his [her] dealings with them' (ibid.). This study also recognises the contribution of ethnography to theory development and testing (Hammersley and Atkinson 1983: 24), which is the stage reached by liberation propaganda theory. It will do what Goodall describes as an ethnographer's main task: to 'try to find out why by figuring out how' (Goodall 2000: 127).

The culture of Lebanese journalism and how it performed will be examined within the framework of war propaganda. The objective here is to re-connect what is often simply referred to as media campaigning with the positive meanings of propaganda discussed above and thus to restore to propaganda its potential meaning as a positive and distinct generic entity (O'Shaughnessy 2004). I intend to claim a new understanding for propaganda as it was enacted and performed in the specific context of this study. To try to identify the characteristics of a new interpretation of propaganda, I explore the historical, cultural, organisational and religious contexts in which the Lebanese television outlets and journalists studied here operate and how these contexts shape their professional practice and their news values. My argument will be that particular kinds and genres of journalism realise a positive form of propaganda in this particular context. This positive form of propaganda is what I will call liberation propaganda.

This chapter explains how new forms of ethnography, and the methodologies related to them, are able to explore these contexts to achieve the suggested understanding of liberation propaganda. It will also establish how different cultural contexts are capable of generating different understandings and implementations of the same kinds of professional practice and the same sets of news values.

Given that different interpretations of news values may produce different journalistic performances, contextualising these (El-Nawawy and Iskandar 2003) is arguably essential to identifying the suggested propagandistic performances.

## Ethnography

In *Writing Culture* (1986: 3), James Clifford reviewed ethnography as an emergent interdisciplinary phenomenon. He realised that 'its authority and rhetoric have spread to many fields where "culture" is a newly problematic object of description and critique.' He saw ethnography as a 'hybrid textual activity... [that] traverses genres and disciplines' (Clifford and Marcus 1986: 26).

Clifford's work was a major intervention in ethnography. It was the first twentieth-century collection that drew scholars' attention to the need to critically review the nature and doing of ethnography. Aull

Davies (1999) attributes the development of an extensive postmodern critique of the production of ethnographic texts to Clifford and Marcus (1986), and earlier to Marcus and Cushman (1982). It was in particular the critique of the idea that the ethnographer could ever be (or had ever been) a detached observer of the cultures in which s/he always became embedded in doing his/her work, and the understanding of the ethnographic product (the written-up data or findings) as writing – and thus text/interpretation – rather than objective truth that made an impact on the later theory and practice of ethnography.

After Clifford and Marcus (1986), ethnography was always subjective, always an interpretation, always positioned and inevitably involved or implicated, as well as constructed and able to be deconstructed (see Sanjek 1990; Smith 2005). It was always, like all texts, multiply contextualised; the study of context thus became a key part of it.

Schlecker and Hirsch (2001: 75), following Clifford's understandings, believe that the turn to ethnography in media studies indicates the ambition of researchers to explore multiple contexts, seeking to acquire ever more knowledge about the processes of production of media texts. They consider that 'more contextualization yields more knowledge' and argue that 'ethnography made possible the study of the subject-matters belonging to multiple contexts' (ibid: 78).

However, for Hammersley and Atkinson (1983: 2) ethnography is simply one social research method, drawing on a wide range of sources of information. They consider 'participant observation' similar in meaning to 'ethnography'. Thus 'the ethnographer participates overtly or covertly, in people's daily lives for an extended period of time, watching what happens, listening to what is said, asking questions' (ibid.). Researchers collect in these contexts whatever data are available to shed light on the issues with which they are concerned. This matches the ethnographic process conducted in this research. Some scholars have simplified the description of ethnography and related it to 'any written report that is based on fieldwork' (Werner and Schoepfle 1987 Vol. 2: 42, and attributed to Robert Launay by Wolcott 1995: 93).

Nevertheless, if we adopted this description alone, despite the value of ethnographic accounts as writing, we would be neglecting the different methodologies in ethnographic practice – such as dedicating a period of time in the field to participant observation, taking field notes, writing diaries, collecting records and documents, conducting focus groups and in-depth interviews, and becoming an active participant in the daily life being observed and studied. These are the processes that produce the ethnographer's involvement, and they position the ethnographer as an 'insider': these then are also the processes which must be accounted for in articulating later the position from which the ethnographer writes or speaks. It is this complex and broad definition of ethnography which I am referring to when I speak of this study as ethnographically informed. In the next section I explore different methodological approaches to ethnography.

## Participant observation: fieldwork

Participant observation is usually taken as a typical research strategy – rather than a 'unitary research method' – in that it is always made up of a variety of methods (Aull Davies 1999: 67).

> The hallmark of participant observation is long-term personal involvement with those being studied, including participation in their lives to the extent that the researcher comes to understand the culture as an insider.
>
> (ibid: 71)

There have been several attempts to differentiate the various roles that an ethnographer may take on in field settings. Junker (1960) and Gold (1958) – Gold being cited in Hammersley and Atkinson 1983: 93, in Aull Davies 1999: 72 and in C. Seale 1999: 222 – distinguish four roles: complete participant, participant-as-observer, observer-as-participant and complete observer. Table 3.1 shows what Junker believed to be the 'theoretical social roles' for fieldwork.

**Table 3.1** Fieldwork

| Comparative involvement: subjectivity and sympathy | | Comparative detachment: objectivity and sympathy |
|---|---|---|
| II Participant-as-observer | →→ | III Observer-as-participant |
| ↑ | | ↓ |
| ↑ | | ↓ |
| I Complete participant | | IV Complete observer |

*Source:* Junker 1960: 36, quoted in Hammersley and Atkinson 1983: 93.

Nevertheless, the 'complete participant' might take two forms: covert and overt. The first is when 'the ethnographer's activities are wholly concealed' (Hammersley and Atkinson 1983: 94). The researcher here may join an organisation or group... as though 'they were ordinary members but with the purpose of carrying out research'. The second is when complete participation occurs, 'where the putative researcher is already a member of the group or organisation that he or she decides to study' (ibid.).

Being a member of the 'Lebanese journalists' grouping, the researcher in this study is involved in overt form as a complete participant. I am examining the work of two groups of journalists in two different television institutions at different periods of time. I worked as a journalist for Tele Liban during the period under investigation and had close connections with journalists of Al Manar, who considered me to be 'one of them', reflected in phrases like 'you know what I am talking about'. In particular, both groups were aware of my research aims, which helped to facilitate my conversations, interviews and discussions.

I was granted access to many hours of television archive that covered the two periods under study. When I asked the chairman of Tele Liban (TL), Ibrahim Khoury, for permission to access the TL April 1996 news archive, he responded without hesitation: 'The least we can do is give you access to the coverage you played an essential role in'. The chairman of Al Manar at the time, Muhamad Haidar, received me with words of praise for the role I played in covering the events in south Lebanon in April 1996, when Israel launched its military operation code-named Grapes of Wrath.

However, I had to ask my 'colleagues' from both institutions not to treat my questions as coming from someone who was there and knows, but as coming from a researcher who does not know already and is looking for their answers and opinions on certain issues, attitudes and behaviours. I tried to treat my subject as 'anthropologically strange' (Hammersley and Atkinson 1983: 8), that is, to now distance myself from my earlier insider status and attempt to look at the material they provided from somewhere else. This is of course always a difficult task. The insider position is never actually forgotten by either the researcher or the researched, but it is possible at least to make that insider position less familiar and to take up an additional position, now informed by academic theory, through which to see and hear what is being researched.

This double positioning had two quite different consequences. First, none of the journalists that I approached for an interview refused my request, and access to all the visual and print archives needed for the research was granted to me. I also had discussions and conversations with the journalists interviewed for this research before and after conducting the tape-recorded interviews. Haidar Dukmak, the Hezbollah media co-ordinator at the time, answered all my requests for interviews with personnel in the 'Islamic resistance' media unit.

As Hammersley and Atkinson (1983: 98) argue, being an insider or a complete participant helped me get access to inside information about the world, in ways that brought out other participants' experiences. 'In this way greater access to [other] participant[s'] perspectives may be achieved' (ibid.). Nevertheless, being a complete participant, studying a group I was a member of, made it impossible to achieve complete detachment, and this raises the question of the disadvantages of being a complete participant, and of being a retrospective complete participant, in particular, in conducting fieldwork.

Learning to see what I had experienced at first hand through the lens of academic theory, and then learning to question my informants and my data from that same academic perspective and in ways which refused to allow them any longer to regard me as a complete insider, was one of the major challenges of doing the research. It involved developing a double or hybrid professionalism, as journalist and academic researcher, and learning to challenge the one with the other and vice versa. In doing the research, I therefore remained always both inside and outside, both involved and at something of a distance. That distance was achieved as a result of academic training and the time that had elapsed between the events analysed and the doing of the research.

## Problems and issues

Hammersley and Atkinson speak of the danger of 'going native'. 'Not only may the task of analysis be abandoned in favour of the joys of participation, but even where it is retained bias may arise from over-rapport' (1983: 98). The complete participant might be overwhelmed by the experience of participation itself, so he or she gives more prominence to this experience than to analysis of the data generated by the experience. This would not apply to the case where the researcher is claimed to be a complete participant before the start of the research, as is the case here.

In this research I am in part researching my own professional practice in retrospect. I am doubly positioned here too – as complete participant in the processes and events researched, and then retrospectively as a complete participant looked at from a distance through the eyes of the researcher. This raises again the issue of detachment, but also questions of memory and hindsight.

There might be a tendency among political actors – and reporters sometimes become political actors – to attribute greater coherence to past actions than existed in the actor's mind in the situation at the time. The questions of propaganda and objectivity were not asked by the Lebanese journalists at the time. It was the researcher who presented the journalists with these questions, many years after the events took place. The professionalism of the coverage at the time had as one of its aims the provision of objective reports.[1] Hence, the question of propaganda was not a dominant issue, but the issue of objectivity was indirectly present given that objectivity, as a news value, has been studied in journalism courses in Lebanon. These two issues emerged from my academic attempts to understand what had gone on: they were constructs of the research process, used then to question and explore the professional processes of an earlier period.

Discussing issues of propaganda – as well as objectivity, balance, neutrality, detachment and truth – years after the events was not contested by the journalists; on the contrary, they embraced this opportunity to reflect on their work in covering the Lebanese–Israeli conflict between 1996 and 2000. Propaganda in its negative connotation was dismissed, as the data in Chapters Six and Seven make clear, in particular because it was related (in their understanding) to matters of lying and deceiving. The only person who embraced the word 'propaganda' in his reflection was the chairman of Tele Liban at the time, Fouad Naim, who said: 'If it was propaganda, then it was propaganda of the truth'. Nevertheless, the national aspiration for liberation was asserted by all journalists involved in this study at the time of the events.

It was from the collocation of those two understandings – 'propaganda of the truth' and 'aspiration for liberation' – that I first came to see that what I was analysing was a form of liberation propaganda. I observed this collocation as an active member of the group during the conflict, and later in my analysis of interview and television data. As I present in this book, memories of what happened at the time of the events – including what was done and what the journalists said their intentions were – were an essential part of both the researcher's encounters with the journalists (as subjects of this study) and the researcher's viewing of the recorded tapes of the coverage. An archive of press commentary, on the events themselves and coverage of them, also continually revived those memories – and reinforced or challenged them.

In fact, being both a retrospective complete participant and an academic researcher trying to maintain some distance helped me to verify whether the journalists' responses were genuine (that is, matching my memory of events) or were fabricated, exaggerated or even driven by public and official appreciation of the outcome of their coverage. The important methodology here was something akin to triangulation in social science or multiple positioning in the humanities. It involved constantly checking my own memories and hindsight against the interviews and the press and television archives.

This checking helped to counter the other kind of disadvantage that can arise from participating in the field. Ethnography has sometimes been rejected on the grounds that its data and findings are subjective, mere personal impressions that cannot provide a solid foundation of rigorous analysis. On the other hand, others argue that 'only through ethnography can the meanings that give form and content to social processes be understood' (Hammersley and Atkinson 1983: 2). Moreover, Hertz (1997: 97) refers to the possibility that 'while a foreign researcher runs the risk of being culture blind, an indigenous researcher runs the risk of being blinded by the familiar'. In spite of this, the question of bias and 'going native' and 'being blinded by the familiar' can be countered with the approach of triangulation and self-reflexivity that this study adopts.

## Self-reflexivity

Writings on *self*-reflexivity, in contrast, are more often about finding ways to compel a subject to locate itself and/ or to engage in a certain degree of conscious and critical *self*-reflection. Self-reflexivity is therefore commonly portrayed as an introspective act that solidifies as it identifies a subject.

(Nast 1998: 97)

Nast argues that 'besides involving a re-analysis of the body-as-place', reflexivity 'requires recognising the emotional and material qualities of inter-subjectivity' (ibid: 111). She refers to Keith's analysis of racism in Britain and how it was important for him to bring his anger about racism into his research agenda and writing (Keith 1992). Nast (1998: 107) points out that reflexivity is an embodied process wherein the body is itself a field for registering and negotiating difference. Differences are negotiated and registered in relation to performances in different cultural contexts, associated here with journalism cultures and performances.

On the other hand, Clifford and Marcus (1986: 14) describe self-reflexivity as 'a subgenre of ethnographic writing'. They consider a 'self-reflexive "fieldwork account"' and decide that even if it is seen as 'variously sophisticated and naïve, confessional and analytic', this account 'provides an important forum for the discussion of a wide range of issues, epistemological, existential, and political' (ibid.).

A good example of this is Sasha Roseneil's research project: 'Greenham revisited: researching myself and my sisters' (Roseneil in Hobbs and May 1993). She discusses the process of carrying out research on a socio-political movement and community of which she has been a part. She locates her research in the newly established tradition of 'post-positivist feminist methodology', and focuses particularly on how she has used her own experience and how being an 'insider' has impacted on the research process (ibid: 177). In her work Roseneil gives prominence to the commitment to reflexivity in feminist methodology. She argues that

> [F]eminist methodology aims to highlight and examine the role of the researcher, and demands that the researcher's work be un-alienated labour (Reinharz 1984; Stanley 1990). Based on an epistemology that considers all knowledge to be socially constructed, it begins with the acknowledgement that the identity of the researcher matters. She is unavoidably present in the research process, and her work is shaped by her social location and personal experiences.
>
> (ibid: 181)

Aull Davies, in her book *Reflexive Ethnography* (1999), takes reflexivity from its feminist methodology to a broader definition.

> Reflexivity, broadly defined, means a turning back on oneself, a process of self-reference. In the context of social research, reflexivity at its most immediately obvious level refers to the ways in which the products of research are affected by the personnel and process of doing research. These effects are to be found in all phases of the research process from initial selection of topic to final reporting of results.
>
> (Aull Davies 1999: 4)

Referring to the close relationship between reflexivity and objectivity, she also says 'The two are not identical' (1999: 4). Nevertheless, she argues

> [R]esponses to the difficulties apparently raised by reflexivity frequently involved attempts to ensure objectivity through reducing or controlling the effects of the researcher on the research situation.
>
> (ibid: 4)

Nonetheless, as alluded to earlier, Hammersley and Atkinson (1983: 8) have suggested that, even when the ethnographer is researching a familiar group or setting, the participant observer is required to treat it as 'anthropologically strange' in an effort to make clear the assumptions the researcher takes for granted as 'a culture member'.

> In fact the description of cultures becomes the primary goal. The search for universal laws is rejected in favour of detailed descriptions of the concrete experience of life within a particular culture and of the social rules or patterns that constitute it.
>
> (ibid.)

This does not overcome Bolak's evaluation of problems of one's own representations of the field. He sees these as 'only partial truths and descriptions' (Bolak, in Hertz 1997: 96). Moreover, he makes it clear, drawing on his self-reflexive account of the study he did of urban, working-class households in Turkey, that 'how we represent and account for others' experiences is intimately related to who we are, and the connections needed to be spelled out' (ibid.). Thus, the personal element could not be cast out.

> The story you write will be part of the larger story of who you are, where you've been, what you've read and talked about and argued over, what you believe in and value, what you are compelled to name as significant.
> 
> (Goodall 2000: 87)

Aull Davies (1999) points out that the use of the ethnographer's self to study and understand others occurs most commonly in what she calls 'native anthropology'. She explains that the word 'native' is 'usually interpreted as the representatives of Third World countries or disadvantaged groups in Western societies, [who] carry out ethnographic research on their own people' (ibid: 181).

This gives the ethnographer an insider perspective and claims him or her to be the key informant of the research – see Lal (1996) on her research in India, which led to her 'identity examination' as an American from a South Asian background; Panourgia (1995) on death and the social organisation of dying in the context of modern Athens; Rosaldo (1993) on how his interpretation of Ilongot head-hunting was transformed in response to his own experience of grief following a tragic personal loss.

Working as a television journalist in Lebanon for more than ten years equipped me with the insider perspective. As Clive Seale (1999) put it, I (the researcher) became the primary research instrument and informant. As mentioned earlier, this research is self-reflexive. However, I have to emphasise that the self and the others (Tele Liban and Al Manar journalists) here shared the same cultural, social and political heritage. Thus, studying the performance of other journalists was achieved by studying the self and vice versa, as well as by triangulation with other press and television data and the data of memory and hindsight: for these must become part of the data for analysis in a project of this kind.

## Ethnography and journalism culture

Ethnography is one of the tools to explore cultures. Or, as Wolcott put it, 'culture [is] an explicit conceptual orientation that provides the purpose and rationale for doing ethnography' (Wolcott 1995: 86).

> Culture is an abstraction based on the ethnographer's observations of actual behavior, coupled with insights and explanations of the other 'that is our way,' 'We've always done it like that,' or 'if that happened, I guess my reaction would be …'.
>
> (ibid.)

Here, journalism culture is the object of this ethnographically informed study.

## Zelizer

> Pronouncedly interdisciplinary and self reflexive, the cultural inquiry of journalism employs diverse research perspectives and scholarly tools that are used to variously consider journalism broadly as a culture. 'Culture' itself has many invocations, not all of them mutually exclusive.
>
> (Zelizer 2004: 175–6)

Zelizer presents culture as 'a phenomenon of concerted action that uses conventional understandings to guide members of collectives in doing things in consensual ways' and draws attention to the fact that 'culture is one of the resources journalists draw upon to coordinate their activities as reporters and editors' (ibid.). Alternatively, as Zelizer put it, 'news itself is seen as cultural', a culture that is relative to the actions of the groups and individuals taking part in its production.

In this study, cultural inquiry takes an analytical track where 'journalists are seen both through journalists' own eyes, tracking how being part of the community comes to have meaning for them, and through the eyes of a commentator who queries the self-presentations that journalists provide' (Zelizer 2004: 175–6).

Cultural analysis of journalistic performance is considered here because it emphasises 'the constraining force of broad cultural symbol systems regardless of the details of organisational and occupational routines' (Schudson 1991: 143 cited in ibid: 176). Such analysis moves simultaneously with and against the 'conventional understandings of how journalism works' (Zelizer 2004: 176), acting as a check on the impartiality of the study.

> Cultural analysis of journalism views journalists not only as conveyors of information but also as producers of culture,

who impart preference statements about what is good and bad, moral and amoral, and appropriate and inappropriate in the world.

(ibid: 177)

In addition, cultural analysis considers the 'meanings, symbols and symbolic systems, rituals, and conventions by which journalists maintain their cultural authority as spokespeople for events in the public domain' (ibid: 176).

## Pedelty

Mark Pedelty, in his book *War Stories* (1995), spoke about war correspondents in El Salvador as a community in and of themselves. He referred to the fact that 'they work together, play together, and often live together', but most importantly, 'they share an integrated set of myths, rituals, and behavioral norms' and 'they are a culture as coherent as any in the postmodern world'. He conducted an ethnographic study of this culture, which he described as 'oddly alien and exotic' (Pedelty 1995: 4).

Whereas Pedelty looked into war correspondents' culture in El Salvador, I studied the culture of reporters and editors during certain military operations that began with the Israeli occupation of south Lebanon. However, these reporters share most of the features found in the El Salvadorian correspondents' community. The reporters in Lebanon, too, shared an integrated set of myths, rituals and behavioural norms. They too evinced a distinctive culture, though this might be true of any occupational culture.

However, Pedelty believes that his war correspondents have a unique relationship with terror in that they need it 'to realize themselves in both a professional and spiritual sense, to achieve and maintain their culture identity as war correspondents' (Pedelty 1995: 2). This understanding does not apply to the Lebanese journalists covering the escalation of conflict with Israel. Those interviewed for this research revealed that the sense of terror they experienced was one that Israel imposed on them. What kept them going was a sense of injustice, a sense they all shared. The difference is that the Lebanese journalists were part of the nation under attack. Pedelty's journalists were not.

## News values and objectivity

News values and objectivity are key aspects of the culture that this book is exploring. Journalists' admiration for truth and fact is discussed in earlier scholarly works in tandem with journalistic norms of objectivity, neutrality and balance. Lebanese journalists' interpretations of these values are presented in the coming chapters, which give a prominent place to continuing discussions of the validity of a single understanding of objectivity, which some scholars in the West advocate (Campbell 2004).

Here I present some of these arguments and discussions, trying to put more focus on alternative views of the traditional understanding of objectivity. This section aims to establish how different cultural contexts might generate different understandings and implementations of the same set of news values.

## Objectivity

To start with, the concept of objectivity for its advocates in journalism 'assumes the possibility of genuine neutrality, of some news medium being a clear un-distorting window'; but, as Fowler emphasises, it 'can never be this' (1991: 12). Campbell points out that there is a distinct body of criticism that questions the Western news media's attachment to objectivity (Campbell 2004: 160; see also Pavlik 2001, Bell 1998 and Hall 2001). Campbell divides this body of literature into three kinds:

> First are those who decry objectivity on grounds of it being an impossible goal... Second, are those who regard objectivity as undesirable regardless of whether it can be achieved or not... Third and perhaps the most recent school of thought, are those who decry objectivity on the basis that technology has made the concept unnecessary and redundant.
> (Campbell 2004: 160–1)

In relation to this research, the most poignant of these three categories is the second. Martin Bell, the former BBC war correspondent, explains it thus:

> I am no longer sure what 'objectivity' means: I see nothing object-like in the relationship between the reporter and the

event, but rather a human and dynamic interaction between them.

(Bell 1998: 18)

Kate Adie, former BBC chief news correspondent (1998: 44, quoted in Allan and Zelizer 2004: 3) questions the understanding of objectivity when covering wars, but without labelling it. She says 'the very nature of war confuses the role of the journalist'. She points to the fact that, in having to face the horrendous realities of conflict, 'any belief that the journalist can remain distant, remote, or unaffected by what is happening tends to go out the window in a hurry' (ibid.). Adie admits that 'when faced with the consequences of battle and the muddle of war...I don't have the answers, but I keep on asking questions' (Adie 1998: 54, quoted in Allan and Zelizer 2004: 3).

> I was there to witness... to repeat what I hear, to observe the circumstances, note the detail, and confirm what is going on with accuracy, honesty and precision... (Witnessing was) the only way you can stand by your words afterwards, the only guarantee that you can give your listeners, or viewers, or readers. You saw it, you heard it, you are telling the truth as far as you know.
> 
> (Adie 1998: 46–47, cited in Allan and Zelizer 2004: 5)

According to the Lebanese journalists of Tele Liban and Al Manar interviewed for this research, being an eyewitness, and being one with a commitment to telling the 'truth' and reporting facts, was what characterised their performance while covering the Israeli operation against Lebanon. 'Being an eyewitness' also reflected my own interpretation of what I was doing during my years of war reporting. Our sense of citizenship and patriotism characterised most of the coverage under investigation. And, as Allan and Zelizer (2004: 5) point out, this sense called into question my perception of how best to conduct myself as a reporter.

I was made to judge my performance by trying to match what I had learned in the West about being an 'objective reporter' with what I did on the ground. As Campbell put it clearly, 'in Western nations the principle of objectivity traditionally stands as a fundamental cornerstone of journalistic professionalism and integrity' (Campbell

2004: 153). I was taught that objectivity meant that as a journalist I should adopt a position of detachment, rather than neutrality, toward the subject of reporting. This suggests the 'absence of subjectivity, personalized involvement, and judgment' (El-Nawawy and Iskandar, in Allan and Zelizer 2004: 320).

This confusion kept haunting me while I was trying to formulate a theory capable of framing my own wartime experience. Autobiographies of war correspondents like Jeremy Bowen (2006), Robert Fisk (2006), Fergal Keane (2005), Kate Adie (2002) and Martin Bell (2003), along with John Simpson's (1999) book on the war in Kosovo, eased my confusion, but I was still looking for a theoretical frame to relate to.

Allan and Zelizer address some theoretical aspects of this confusion. They believe that a distinction should be drawn between 'patriotism and militarism' in the work of a war reporter. They believe it is central to the problems of this profession. They point out that a reporter's sense of national identity needs to be considered 'in a way that sheds light both on how it can underpin journalism's strength, while simultaneously recognizing the constraints it can impose of the integrity of practice' (Allan and Zelizer 2004: 4). However, they point out that 'war reporting reveals its investment in sustaining a certain discursive authority—namely that of being an eyewitness' (ibid.).

As I struggled with these issues, the atrocities of September 11 took place. The Arab satellite channels entered the international news market – mainly Al Jazeera, through the coverage of the war on Afghanistan in 2001 and the war on Iraq in 2003 – and were criticised by both the American administration and the British government for not being objective in their reporting (Harb and Bessaiso 2006).

## Context

At that point, the concept of contextual objectivity floated to the surface (El-Nawawy and Iskandar 2002; El-Nawawy and Iskandar, in Allan and Zelizer 2004). The notion of contextualisation was seen as a corrective to some of the limitations related to the notion of objectivity:

> Contextualization demonstrates a situational position, a way by which collectivism among participants within the same 'context'—whether cultural, religious, political, or economic— is realized and engaged. It is precisely this contextualization

that aggravates and complicates the pursuit of 'objective' coverage within the news media setting. Contextualization further confuses attempts at even-handedness and efforts to cover all sides of a story. Particularly in times of war, it is the context within which a reporter operates that makes communication with the 'enemy' unacceptable.

(El-Nawawy and Iskandar, in Allan and Zelizer 2004: 320).

El-Nawawy and Iskandar relate contextual objectivity to the audiences the media is reporting for. They see the theory as 'the necessity of television and media to present stories in a fashion that is ... impartial yet sensitive to local sensibilities' (El-Nawawy and Iskandar 2002: 54). However, they make it clear that objectivity and context should not be the sole priorities. The exclusivity of either is dismissed, and the reporter is placed in 'the gray area in-between the two where fairness and balance are situated' (ibid: 321).

News also has to be new. Bernard Roshco, in his piece 'Newsmaking' (in Tumber 1999: 18), speaks of the significance of three aspects of timeliness when a news story is being considered for publication or broadcasting:

For an item of information to be timely, in the sense employed here, requires the conjunction of: (1) *recency* (recent disclosure); (2) *immediacy* (publication with minimal delay); (3) *currency* (relevance to present concerns). To speak of news as timely information, therefore, is to imply the existence and interaction of a news source, a news medium, and an audience.

(ibid: 18)

The importance of immediacy and recency – as a necessity in gaining public attention – was well acknowledged by journalists and editors interviewed for this research, but the main concern of my research at this point is the concept of currency, which supports the argument of contextual objectivity.

When an editor speaks of exercising 'news judgment' in assessing the 'news value' of a report, he is applying his criteria of currency to the available items of recent information from which a news presentation can be assembled. Currency is the 'local angle' in the broadest sense, which is why emergencies that acutely affect local audiences are a news staple for local media.

(ibid: 19)

Looking at the bigger picture, in his study of *The Power of News*, Schudson argues that news is produced by people who operate within a cultural system that he described as 'a reservoir of stored cultural meanings and patterns of discourse' (Schudson 1995: 14). He sees news as a form of culture that 'incorporates assumptions about what matters, what makes sense, what time and place we live in, what range of considerations we should take seriously' (ibid.).

Similarly, in his book *Television Culture* (1987), Fiske made a clear statement that news can never give a full, accurate, objective picture of reality. He asserted that news should not attempt to do so, for this 'can only serve to increase its authority and decrease people's opportunity to "argue" with it, to negotiate with it' (Fiske 1987: 307). In the same vein, in his book *Media Organization and Production* (2003), Cottle states that studies of the sociology of news production have 'produced an invaluable sociological record and analysis of news production and the forces constraining news output.' According to Cottle, these studies demonstrate how 'in-depth study of news producers, their cultural milieu and professional domains could help to explain the dynamics and determinants of news output' (Cottle 2003: 16).

Schudson (1989) speaks of how journalists he met at conferences were pushed into fiercely defending their conduct:

> [They defend their conduct] on the familiar ground that they just report the world as they see it, the facts, and nothing but the facts, and yes, there's occasional bias, occasional sensationalism, occasional inaccuracy, but a responsible journalist never, never, never, fakes the news.
> (Schudson 1989, in Berkowitz 1997: 7)

The journalists in Schudson's story identified with the notion of 'truth' that most of the Lebanese journalists interviewed for this study were embracing when asked whether they were 'objective' or 'biased' in their reporting.

Discussions around objectivity go back to the nineteenth century, when objectivity was first identified as the professional norm of

American journalists and a 'cornerstone of the professional ideology of journalists in liberal democracies' (Lichtenberg in Curran and Gurevitch 2000: 239). Lichtenberg took her defence of objectivity further, to announce that 'American journalists still embrace it as one of the fundamental norms of their profession' (ibid.). Lichtenberg (quoted by Curran and Gurevitch 2000: 239) speaks of what she calls critics of objectivity – who assert 'that reality is not 'out there'; it is a 'vast production, a staged creation' – something humanly produced and humanly maintained (Carey 1989)':

> Reality, on this view, is 'socially constructed', and so there are as many realities as there are social perspectives on the world. There is no 'true reality' to which objective knowledge can be faithful.
>
> (ibid.)

Gaye Tuchman, in her 1972 study of objectivity as a strategic ritual, states that journalists, like social scientists, deal with objectivity as a safeguard between themselves and their (potential) critics:

> Attacked for a controversial presentation of 'facts', newspapermen invoke their objectivity almost the way a Mediterranean peasant might wear a clove of garlic around his neck to ward off evil spirits.
>
> (Tuchman 1972, in Tumber 1999: 298)

Tuchman says that newspersons, unlike social scientists, 'have a limited repertoire with which to define and defend their objectivity.' She argues that the newsperson must make immediate decisions 'concerning the validity, reliability, and 'truth' in order to meet the problems imposed by the nature of his [or her] task' in processing news.

> The newsmen cope with these pressures by emphasising 'objectivity', arguing that dangers can be minimised if newsmen follow strategies of newswork which they identify with 'objective stories'. They assume that, if every reporter gathers and structures 'facts' in a detached, unbiased, impersonal manner, deadlines will be met and libel suits avoided.
>
> (ibid: 298)

## Partial truths

Soloski assumes that objectivity is the most important professional norm for journalists in the United States. He asserts that objectivity does not exist in news stories as such, but in the behaviour of journalists:

> Journalists must act in ways that allow them to report the news objectively. For journalists, objectivity does not mean that they are impartial observers of events—as it does for the social scientists—but they seek out facts and report them as fairly and in as balanced a way as possible.
> (Soloski 1989, in Berkowitz 1997: 143)

The emphasis on the importance of objectivity as a professional norm, for American journalists in particular, has since been dismissed by other scholars who speak of certain circumstances where 'the media were deemed to be partial', such as in time of war, where not supporting their own country's war efforts might seem 'inappropriate' (Williams 2003: 126). Schudson refers to journalists' consciousness at the height of the Cold War of the risk to national security of reporting and publishing. This, according to Schudson, was transferred into a wave of patriotic fervour in the wake of September 11:

> After September 11, 2001, however, American journalists individually and collectively shared in a wave of patriotic fervor and a deep sense of vulnerability. This led to some serious self-criticism about news stories that detailed the flaws in airport security, the vulnerability of subways to terrorist attack, and the technology of crop dusting. When reporters and editors begin to reasonably imagine that their audiences include mass murderers who seek to inflict as much damage on the country as they can, these journalists, too carry out their work on a wartime footing.
> (Schudson 2003: 164–5)

Schudson (2003: 187) points to the idea that objectivity is vulnerable to external circumstances. He defines three circumstances that might jeopardise American journalists' objectivity: tragedy, public anger and threats to national security.

Williams (2003) speaks of more general patterns as to where objectivity could not be guaranteed.

> Not all news is intended to be objective. There are forms of news reportage that traditionally have deviated from the 'objective model'. McQuail (1992: 189–91) identifies 'some older versions of news' such as the 'human interest, partisanship and the investigative' functions of news that are seen as legitimate parts of the practice of journalism, but each of which contradicts in some way what is expected of objective journalism.
>
> (Williams 2003: 126–7)

Further, for Fiske (cited in Williams 2003: 127), 'objective facts' always support one point of view, and this point of view is affected by the social, political and cultural context the journalist is operating in.

Noha Mellor in her study on *The Making of Arab News* sees that objectivity – if it is understood as presenting two opposing opinions – is beside the point, 'assuming that one of the two opinions is misleading or false, because then the media would be helping to promote this opinion' (Mellor 2005: 89). Mellor refers to Bekhait's 1998 study on Egyptian press news values. His study showed that objectivity ranked third on the list of principles journalists claimed to adhere to when reporting the news. Accuracy, on the other hand, 'was by far the most important factor for the majority of journalists, followed by honesty' (ibid.).

Some Arab scholars, like Hassan Tawalba (cited in Mellor 2005: 89) took their scepticism about objectivity to the extreme by stating that honesty should not be applied when 'dealing with the flow of information supplied by international (western) news agencies, which are supposed to be loyal to their western governments'. Thus, the claim of ultimate 'objectivity' is arguable and is bound by the cultural and social context journalists are operating in to produce news. These cultural and social aspects that influence or shape news reporting are mostly recognised in what Knightley (2000) calls 'the distinctive genre of war reporting', within which the work of the Lebanese journalists under investigation here falls.

However, the question that now arises (as far as this research is concerned) is what relationship exists between war reporting and propaganda. Oliver Boyd Barrett (in Allan and Zelizer 2004) recognises this relationship and claims that the genre of war reporting serves a propaganda purpose. However, he speaks of a 'genre' being exploited by the state and other propagandists 'in ways that cripple the capacity of media consumers to make useful sense of the world' (ibid: 25). Barrett's explanation lies within the negative connotation that was given to the term 'propaganda' following the First World War.

> Classic warfare is the epitome of a 'good story', high in tension and drama, with complex main plots and sub-plots played out within traditional binary oppositions of aggressor and victim, winner and loser ... War provides ritualistic challenge, testing, and evaluation, that call upon extraordinary resources and resourcefulness from media institutions, journalists, technicians, and other support workers. Their collective experiences feed the stuff of professional legend, confirming and renewing the narrative of what it means to be a 'journalist'.
>
> (ibid: 26)

Barrett makes a clear connection between propaganda and the news values of war reporting by stating that 'war reporting is generally one sided' (ibid: 29). Wars are covered through a reporter's lens. He sees the contextual aspect of war reporting as a good tool in the hands of propagandists.

> The media typically cover war from the point of view of the country in which they and their major owners and readers are based, reflecting the point of view of that country's government and its foreign policy elite.
>
> (ibid: 29)

In my research, I looked at objectivity in context and tried to re-think propaganda as a positive media tool that might be used by journalists in a crisis situation. That is the kind of propaganda this book is aiming to identify.

## Conclusion

This chapter has sought to answer how ethnography and the methodologies related to it can explore the social, cultural, religious and political contexts that journalists operate in, with a view to achieving the new understanding of propaganda mentioned above.

This chapter has also tried to establish how different cultural contexts might generate different understandings and implementations of the same set of news values. Journalistic norms of objectivity, neutrality and balance vary with the context. Different interpretations of news values and norms may produce different journalism in practice. It is essential to contextualise news values and norms if we are to identify actual examples of the suggested positive propaganda.

This chapter, along with Chapter Two, has examined the theoretical basis for analysing Lebanese journalists' performance during major escalations of conflict with the Israeli forces in south Lebanon.

Chapter Four further explores the issue of contextualisation, presenting the story of the Lebanese–Israeli conflict, but also of the Arab–Israeli conflict, a narrative that dominates the collective memory of most Arab populations and individuals, including the journalists under investigation in this study.

# 4

# OVERVIEW OF THE ARAB–ISRAELI CONFLICT

All your friends are false. All your enemies are real.

(Mexican proverb)

The Arab–Israeli problem evokes heated discussion about its exact nature, whether it is a clash of religions or races, or a territorial dispute involving historical claims to the land. Recent analysis tends to focus on the clash of nationalisms, which arose during the nineteenth and twentieth centuries

(Devore 1976: xxii).

J.C. Hurewitz wrote, in January 1949, that no area of the Middle East has had so much written about by so many, with so little concern for objective appraisal and analysis, as Palestine. Any attempt, said Hurewitz, to exhaustively analyse the books, pamphlets, official documents and articles of even the last dozen years would demand a volume in itself and the collective effort of many scholars, for no one can pretend to have read – let alone digested – all of this material (Hurewitz, quoted in Devore 1976: xxxiii).

This statement was only a warning, because the stream of literature on Palestine and the Arab–Israeli conflict has become an ever-increasing flood. Scholars in the field are 'tempted to consider building an ark to keep their heads above the deluge of paper' (Devore

1976: xxxiii). In his book *The Arab–Israeli Conflict*, Devore counted about 500,000 documents about this subject; we may assume that the number has at least doubled since then.

This chapter tries to give a short account of the Arab–Israeli conflict, its background and origins, where it started and how it developed. Within the wider frame of Arab–Israeli relations, the story of the Lebanese–Israeli conflict is offered later in this chapter. The reader will gather that this historical account is narrated from an Arab perspective, though I have used sources from all sides of the conflict. This perspective is intentional, because it is this account of the history that most Arab people, especially those living in Israel-Palestine and the countries around, have carried in their collective memory, generation after generation.

The historical account in this chapter covers the period up to the early 1990s, which is the period alluded to in the news reports studied in this book. It is this period and its historical connotations that are present in every media message put out by the Lebanese journalists covering the events under investigation in this study.

## Historical background

The conflict may be said to have lasted for at least a century. It began some years after an influx of Jews into Palestine in the 1880s. Then, and in the 1890s, the Jews were a tiny minority, numbering between 8,000 and 25,000 according to different counts, and relations with Arabs were reasonably cordial. Later, Jews arrived in larger numbers, and fears arose in Arab minds that something like a new crusade was beginning.

Arab–Jewish tensions grew steadily between the two world wars, but the presence of a third party, the British mandate government, had a dampening effect. It was not until Britain's withdrawal and Israel's declaration of independence in May 1948 that all hope of a peaceful solution collapsed. The expulsion of most of the Palestinian population in 1948–9, and the loss of their land and homes, created more bitterness than any of the five periods of struggle that followed: the 1956 Suez crisis, the Six-Day War of 1967, the October War of 1973, and the 1978 and 1982 invasions of Lebanon.

Human misery cannot adequately be conveyed in figures, and yet the statistics give some sense of the scale. The Palestinian death

Overview of the Arab–Israeli Conflict  57

toll from 1948 to 1993 was 261,000, as well as 186,000 wounded and 161,140 disabled. The civil wars in Lebanon – which resulted from complications in the Arab–Israeli conflict – claimed a further 90,000 lives, 115,000 wounded and 9,627 disabled, on top of 875,000 refugees (Heikal 1996: 7).

In 1994 there were 800,000 Palestinians in Gaza, 1 million in the West Bank, 2 million in Jordan and 400,000 in refugee camps in Lebanon, making a total of 4.2 million Palestinians living in lands close to their former homes. The Jewish part of Israel's population was about the same, including settlers in east Jerusalem, Gaza, the West Bank and the Golan Heights. In numerical terms there was an even balance between Israelis and Palestinians, but all the power was held by one side.

## Where it all started

> The Arab–Israeli conflict is a modern Gordian knot that continues to complicate recent history and current international politics. Regrettably, no modern Alexander... has appeared capable of solving the problem with a single decisive stroke. The vast complexities of the Arab-Israeli conflict are rooted in the history of Palestine, for centuries a critical area of cultural transition. Some commentators extend the issue almost back to Creation, although they rarely agree as to when even that event took place.
>
> (Devore 1976: xxii)

Part of the more recent 'vast complexities' can, perhaps predictably, be traced back to Europe. At the end of 1894 a French army captain, Alfred Dreyfus, was convicted (behind closed doors) of espionage for Germany, and sentenced to deportation for life to Devil's Island. The officer was publicly humiliated at the Military School: his sword was broken; he was stripped of his uniform; and taken away in chains. The mob present shouted, 'Death to the Jews'. The trial of Dreyfus on treason charges was the most controversial case of the day. It was eventually proved that Dreyfus had been a scapegoat, selected because he was Jewish (Heikal 1996: 19; Ovendale 1984: 1).

Although he too was Jewish, Theodor Herzl, the young Austro-Hungarian journalist who reported the trial, disliked Dreyfus, who was known for boasting about his family fortune. But Herzl became convinced that Dreyfus was innocent, and he was shaken by the hostility to Jews that was unleashed in France by the case. Six months later Herzl suggested 'a Jewish exodus' to barons Maurice de Hirsch of France and Nathaniel Rothschild of Britain. He told them that for nearly 2,000 years the Jews had been dispersed all over the world without a state of their own, and that if only the Jews had a political centre they could begin to solve the problem of anti-Semitism (Ovendale 1984).

The Dreyfus affair became the symbol of Jewish inequality in European society. It focused attention on anti-Semitism and it helped to give birth to the Zionist movement. Herzl is regarded as the founder of political Zionism. However, other writers before him had put forward the idea of a separate Jewish state:

> In 1833, Benjamin Disraeli, in his first novel, *Alroy*, outlined his scheme for a Jewish empire with the Jews ruling as a separate class. This scheme was moderated to the domination of empires and diplomacy by Jewish money in *Coningsby*, published in 1844. In *Tancred*, Disraeli explained history in terms of race, and saw the Jews as being a superior race. But in George Eliot's novel, *Daniel Deronda* (1876), one of the characters is there to show that the Jews still have a mission to fulfil: the repossession of Palestine.
>
> (Ovendale 1984: 3–4)

Political writers like Moses Hess, with *Rome and Jerusalem* (1862), and Leon Pinsker expressed similar ideas. Pinsker, a Jewish doctor from Odessa, argued in his book *Auto Emancipation* that anti-Semitism would persist wherever the Jews were a minority; thus, they needed a homeland of their own. When he was drafting *Der Judenstaat* ('The Jewish state'), Herzl was seemingly unaware of these earlier writings, though he was to some extent inspired by other colonisation schemes:

> Herzl's diaries show that in formulating his ideas he was influenced by the activities of Cecil John Rhodes, the great imperialist who bestowed his name on a country: in May 1895 Mashonaland and Matabeleland became Rhodesia

which was administrated by a chartered company, the British South Africa Company.

(ibid: 4)

Herzl had two possible regions in mind: Palestine and Argentina. Argentina was one of the most fertile countries – temperate, vast and sparsely populated – while Palestine was the Jews' unforgettable historic homeland, whose very name would be a good rallying point. In 1895 Argentina's population was almost 4 million, that of Palestine around 500,000.

His plan asked only that the Jews be granted sovereignty over territory adequate for their national requirements, and they would see to the rest. He was convinced the only solution to European anti-Semitism was the establishment of a Jewish national state. He persuaded himself, against compelling evidence to the contrary, that Palestine was a land without people, ideally suited to a people without land (Heikal 1996). Significantly, in his book Herzl did not mention how the local population was to be disposed of.

With the publication of *Der Judenstaat* Herzl became the ambassador of the emerging Zionist movement, and on 23 August 1897 he convened the first World Zionist Conference, bringing together Jewish representatives from many countries. Held in Basel, Switzerland, it is regarded by Jews as a landmark in the creation of the state of Israel. The World Zionist Organisation was created with the aim of establishing 'a home for the Jewish people in Palestine secured under public law' (Heikal 1996: 23).

After the Basel conference, the rabbis of Vienna decided to see for themselves what Herzl was talking about, and sent two representatives to Palestine. They found that he had over-simplified:

> 'The bride is beautiful, but she is married to another man.'
> It was a message Zionists did not wish to hear, and the inconvenient husband was never acknowledged.
>
> (ibid.)

Despite publicly presenting Palestine as a land without people, in 1895 Herzl noted in his dairies that something would have to be done about the Palestinian natives:

> We shall have to spirit the penniless population across the border by procuring employment for it in the transit

countries, while denying it any employment in any country. Both the process of expropriation and the removal of the poor must be carried out discreetly and circumspectly.

(Herzl, quoted in Said 1992: 13)

In his book *The Question of Palestine*, Edward Said wrote that, for much of its modern history, Palestine and its native people have been subject to denials of a very rigorous sort – in order to mitigate the presence of large numbers of natives on a desired land, the Zionists first convinced themselves that these natives did not exist, and then made it possible for them to exist only in the most rarefied forms:

> First denial, then blocking, shrinking, silencing, hemming in. This is an enormously complex policy, for it includes not only the policy of the Zionists toward the native Arabs, but also the policy of Israel toward its Arab colonies, and the character of the Israeli occupying forces on the West Bank and Gaza after 1967.
>
> (Said 1992: 17)

Yet a few at least of the Zionist immigrants were well aware that they were not coming into a land empty of civilised people. Asher Ginzberg, a Jewish writer who used the name of Ahad ha-Am, wrote after his first trip to Palestine in 1891:

> We are in the habit of thinking that all the Arabs are wild men of the desert and do not see or understand what goes on around them, but that is a great mistake. The Arabs, especially the town dwellers, see and understand what we are doing and what we want in Palestine, but they do not react and pretend not to notice, because at the present they do not see in what we are doing any threat to their own future... But if ever we develop in Palestine to such a degree as to encroach on the living space of the native population to any appreciable extent, they will not easily give up their place.
>
> (Ginzberg, quoted in Cooley 1973: 29)

Nonetheless, Ginzberg was an exception, and the denial of the existence of the Palestinian people as a nation was transmitted to future generations of Zionism.

Writing in the *New York Times Magazine* on 5 October 1986, the then Israeli Prime Minister Shimon Peres could still find it in himself to repeat the denial – despite the presence of nearly five million Palestinians – as if they and their land had been discovered by the incoming Zionists:

> The Land to which they came, while indeed the Holy Land, was desolate and uninviting; a land that had been laid waste, thirsty for water, filled with swamps and malaria, lacking in natural resources. And in the land itself there lived another people; a people who neglected the land, but who lived on it.
> (quoted in Said and Hitchens 2001: 5)

Said argued that Peres, the prime minister of Israel, had entirely transformed the people of Palestine into a mere tool of 'the Arab states' who incited them – as if to say that, on their own, the Palestinians would either have left or would not have resisted the incoming Zionist settlers:

> As ideological weapons, such notions had the effect early on of reducing reality in Palestine for Western audiences and policy-makers to a simple binary system [good and bad].
> (Said and Hitchens 2001: 5)

However, some Zionist leaders were not able to hide the pride they felt in wiping out the existence of the Palestinian Arabs. Moshe Dayan told *Ha-Aretz* on 4 April 1969:

> We came to this country, which was already populated by Arabs, and we are establishing a Hebrew, that is a Jewish state here. In considerable areas of the country [the total area was 6%] we bought the lands from the Arabs. Jewish villages were built in the place of Arab villages. You do not even know the names of these Arab villages, and I don't blame you, because these geography books no longer exist; not only do the books not exist, the Arab villages are not there either... There is no place built in this country that did not have a former Arab population.
> (Dayan, quoted in Said 1992: 14)

According to the most precise calculation yet made, about 780,000 Arab Palestinians were dispossessed and displaced in 1948 in order to facilitate what the Zionists called the 'reconstruction and rebuilding of Palestine' (Said 1992). These are the Palestinian refugees, who now number well over two million. We should also add to them the Palestinians held, since 1967, in the Occupied Territories – numbering 1.7 million – of whom half a million were part of the population of pre-1967 Israel. The 'transformation' of Palestine, which resulted in Israel, has been an extraordinarily expensive project – especially for the Arab Palestinians (Said 1992: 15).

## Arab awakening

At the end of the eighteenth century, Palestine had been in the hands of the Ottoman Empire for nearly 200 years; but the empire was weak, and Russia and Austria were nibbling at its extremities. It suited Britain to keep the Ottoman Empire intact as a means of restraining Russia, and as a way of protecting the best trade route to India (Heikal 1996).

The first threat to the Egyptian route came in 1798, when Napoleon occupied Egypt with the intention of bringing the Red Sea under French control. Hoping to close the secondary routes through Palestine too, he sought to populate the Holy Land with people who would be permanently in his debt. It was for this reason that Napoleon called on the Jews in the Diaspora to return to the holy land and rebuild the civilisation they had abandoned. 'Oh Israelites, come to your holy places,' his proclamation urged (ibid: 16). Nothing came of this because the Ottoman sultan, with the help of the British navy, sent a formidable army to oust the French, who withdrew in 1801. But Napoleon's proposal sowed an idea that was taken up by the British later in the nineteenth century.

> The aim was to solve two problems at once: to persuade the Jews to leave Europe, where they were unpopular, and establish them in Palestine where they could guard the contingency routes.
> (Heikal 1996: 16)

In June 1913, the first Arab National Congress was held in Paris. It was concerned with the potential chaos in the Arab provinces that seemed likely to result from the Turkish thwarting of Arab aspirations. The main item on the congress agenda was to establish decentralised governments in the Arab provinces. The Arabs in Palestine were conscious of this awakening. By 1891 some Arabs in Palestine were aware of another threat to their aspirations: the increasing influx of Jewish settlers. They started to demand an end to Jewish immigration and land purchase (Ovendale 1984: 10).

Because of the administrative structure of the Ottoman Empire, knowledge of the Zionist programme spread to Arabs outside Palestine. It is evident that the Arabs distinguished between the 'Ottoman' Jew and the 'foreign' Jew, considering only the former as deserving equal rights in a decentralised administration. They also knew the difference between 'Jew' and 'Zionist' (ibid: 10).

In the last two decades of the nineteenth century, urban Jewish immigration into Palestine increased rapidly. Jerusalem's Jewish population nearly doubled between 1881 (13,920) and 1891 (25,322). In Jaffa (Haifa in Arabic) and other cities, it grew at an even faster pace, alarming urban Palestinians and creating ill-will among them, according to Jewish sources of the period (Farsoun and Zacharia 1997: 58).

The first formally recorded act of Palestinian opposition and protest occurred in 1891. A telegram signed by a number of Palestinian notables, sent from Jerusalem to Istanbul, urged the Ottoman authorities to prohibit Russian Jews from entering Palestine and acquiring land. Opposition by native Palestinian Arabs to foreign immigration thus preceded the foundation of the organised Zionist movement.

> Jewish sources at the time observed that the declared aim of the Zionist Congress to establish a home in Palestine quickly affected relations between Palestinian Arabs and the Jewish immigrants.
> (Farsoun and Zacharia 1997: 58)

Between 1908 and 1914 nationalist opposition in Palestine to Zionism grew. There were fears that if the Jews conquered Palestine the territorial unity of the Arab world would be shattered and the Arab cause weakened. Unofficial opposition to Zionism began to express itself more spontaneously, directly and forcefully. In 1908, clashes between Palestinian Arabs and Zionist immigrant Jews occurred in Haifa (Jaffa), and peasants attacked Zionist Jewish settlers in the district of Tabariyya. From every city, including Haifa, signed statements were sent to the Ottoman authorities protesting at the sale of land to these settlers (Farsoun and Zacharia 1997).

By 1910, Palestinian newspapers and the public had raised a clamour over sales, by the rich merchant Emile Sursock of Beirut to the Jewish Colonisation Association (JCA), of land totalling 2,400 *dunum*[1] between Nazareth and Jenin. In 1913 the Sursocks sold another 2,000 *dunum* in the Marj Ibn Amer to the JCA, displacing hundreds if not thousands of peasant families:

> Many of the absentee Arab landowners belonging to large and wealthy Syrian and Lebanese families, such as the Daouks and Sursocks, sold their land to Jews, but surprisingly few Palestinian Arab families did, considering how heavily Arab farmers and tenants were in debt during the 1930s and 1940s.
>
> (Cooley 1973: 28)

By 1914, Arabs were aware that Zionism affected the wider Arab cause, not just local considerations in Palestine. Zionism was not responsible for the Arab awakening, but from an early stage it appeared as a threat (Ovendale 1984: 10–11).

Growing Arab consciousness and its politicisation in Pan-Arabism reinforced Palestinian identity. On the eve of the First World War, the Palestinian Arabs were on the verge of uniting as a nation. But Palestinian consciousness did not yet transform itself into an all-Palestinian, nationalist movement or develop an independent, centralised political organisation. The Palestinian Arabs were thus unable to act decisively on their own behalf, either against the Ottoman Turks before the First World War or against the British authorities during the mandate between the two world wars.

## British promises

The goal of the Zionist movement, as mentioned earlier, was to establish a Jewish state in Palestine, which consisted of present-day Israel, the West Bank, the Gaza Strip and Jordan.

> Israel was the result of many factors, of course, principally of the imperialist desire to divide and rule, allied with a Zionist program also determined to end anti-Semitic oppression. The various partitions that brought about the numerous

independent states of the Middle East left behind, if they did not altogether destroy, the notion of Arab unity that was a guiding idea in the area for the first half of the twentieth century.

(Said 2000: 226)

Palestine was one of several Arab territories ruled by the Ottoman Empire until its defeat in the First World War. At the end of that war, Britain gained control of Palestine and in 1922 the League of Nations granted Britain a mandate in Palestine. Throughout the war, Britain gave conflicting signals to Zionist Jews – who sought to establish, in Palestine, a nation-state for the Jewish people – and to Palestine Arabs, who likewise sought independence and self-government (Swedenburg in Hourani et al. 1993: 447).

To the Arabs, Britain promised 'to recognise and uphold the independence of the Arabs in all the regions lying within the frontiers proposed by the Sharif of Mecca'. This promise was given in exchange for Arab help in defeating the Ottoman Empire (Heikal 1996: 34–5, 'Hussein-MacMahon Correspondence', 1915).

To the Zionists, the British Foreign Secretary Lord Balfour promised to establish a 'national home for the Jews in Palestine' (Pappé 2008: 13).

Yet secretly, Britain had already agreed with its French ally that the two would divide up much of the Middle East and control it themselves, an agreement known later as the Sykes–Picot Agreement of 1916 (Cooley 1973: 31). Britain thus exacerbated the growing conflict between Zionists and Palestinian Arabs by its hypocrisy and inconsistency, when its deception of both groups became apparent.

## The Balfour Declaration

The British Foreign Secretary and later Prime Minister Arthur Balfour was a key figure in the founding of the state of Israel. Arabs never tire of repeating, with some historical justification, that many of the problems of the modern Middle East can be laid at the door of the British and their imperialist double-dealing. The most criminal act, according to the Arabs, was the so-called Balfour Declaration (Heikal 1996).

The declaration, which gave Britain's backing to the establishment of a national homeland in Palestine, had a curious origin. Chaim Weizmann was a leading émigré Zionist who found himself teaching chemistry at Manchester University during the First World War. By 1916, Britain was running out of natural acetone, which was needed to make ammunition for the Western Front.

Weizmann was put in touch with the Prime Minister David Lloyd George and was asked to find an artificial substitute, which he rapidly did, ending the nightmare prospect of Britain losing the war for a lack of high explosives. The declaration of the Foreign Secretary Lord Balfour that followed on 2 November 1917 was, at least in part, a reward for Weizmann's enterprise.

The trouble was that the British made overlapping commitments to the Arabs as a way of getting them to support the war against the Turks. When the Turks were defeated, Britain went back on its word to the Arabs and divided the region up between itself and France (Philo and Berry 2004).

Between the world wars it should be noted that, as far as the Jewish minority in Palestine was concerned, Zionism had very little to do with them. Despite the worldwide interest among Jews in the Balfour Declaration, it was given no publicity in Palestine, even among the Jewish community there:

> This fact was in keeping with the spirit, if not the letter, of Balfour's view that 'the present inhabitants' need not to be consulted—even though those present inhabitants also include Jews.
>
> (Said 1992: 19)

## The inter-war period

As the First World War ended, Britain and France moved to consolidate their control over Palestine, Syria, Lebanon and Iraq. In 1921, Winston Churchill suggested that 'Transjordan' (later called Jordan) be separated from the Palestine Mandate and ruled by Abdullah, the son of Britain's ally, Sharif Hussein.

One year earlier, Feisal, Sharif Hussein's other son, had been made King of Iraq in compensation for Britain's forcing him to relinquish the throne of Damascus, Syria. Feisal had assumed the Syrian throne and wrongly assumed that it was his due, given his and his family's support for the British against the Ottomans in the war. But, as Britain had already given up control of Syria to its French ally, Britain had to remove Feisal from Syria.

By 1922, Britain had direct or indirect control over Egypt, Palestine, Jordan and Iraq (as well as Kuwait and other Arab 'kingdoms' in the Persian Gulf). Additionally, France had created a new 'Lebanon' nation (with a slight Christian majority), carved out of greater Syria; it controlled both countries.

> But Palestine would not be governed easily. The conflicting goals of Zionism and Palestinian nationalism would not be reconciled. Britain flip-flopped for 25 years, first siding with Zionists then with Palestinians. The conflict only worsened as neither was satisfied in their national aspirations. World War II and the Holocaust only added more political and moral pressure to the situation. Still, the conflict was not to be resolved.
>
> (Ovendale 1984: 119)

Arab opposition to an Israeli state became evident after the Balfour Declaration of 1917. In the 1920s there were anti-Zionist riots in Palestine, which was then governed by Britain under a League of Nations mandate.

By 1947, unable to reconcile the mutually exclusive claims by two different groups to the same land, Britain – its empire crumbling worldwide – put the issue into the hands of the newly established United Nations. The UN recommended a partition of Palestine into two separate states: one Jewish and one Arab. The Palestinian leaders and other Arabs were, however, not willing to give up any more of their historic land to anyone:

> The Recommendation of the British government's 1937 Peel Commission—that Palestine be partitioned into separate Jewish and Arab states—was accepted by the Jewish community but rejected by the Arabs. The idea of partition remained latent until the scope of the Holocaust, and Britain's decision to withdraw from Palestine, prompted a vote in November 1947 by the UN General Assembly, successor to the League of Nations, to divide Palestine into two awkwardly demarcated states and internationalise Jerusalem.
>
> (Makovsky 1996: 2)

Palestinians saw the European leaders as being responsible for this problem. It was Europe that had created the Jewish refugee crisis – both through the Holocaust and (especially) afterwards. Palestinians and other Arabs (who between them then constituted 80 to 90 per cent of the population of Palestine; see Pappé 2008: 12–13) were determined not to be Europe's new victims. The Arabs of Palestine refused to give up their farms, and the land they lived in, to Jewish–European immigrants who would simply take over and become the new power in Arab lands at the very time when Arabs were struggling for independence from European colonial rule.

The Zionists, then led by David Ben-Gurion, accepted this partition plan, even though they had always dreamed of controlling the whole of western Palestine and Jerusalem. The Palestinian Arabs and the surrounding Arab states rejected the partition proposal. They felt Palestine was all theirs, that the European Jews were a foreign implant foisted upon them, and that they had the strength to drive them out. The British pulled out, leaving the Arabs and the Jewish immigrants to fight it out amongst themselves (Friedman 1998: 14).

Israel was established as a nation-state on 14 May 1948. For Zionist Jews, it was a day of deliverance, of independence, of freedom and hope. For Palestinians, it was a day of *nakbeh* or 'catastrophe', the day their own struggle for independence, freedom and hope was dashed. The battles that had been going on for years between the Zionists and the Palestinian Arabs erupted into a full-scale war between the new state of Israel and its Arab neighbours – Jordan, Egypt, Syria, Lebanon and Iraq.

Poignantly, the Jewish Israeli forces stood at about 35,000 men and women, many of whom had received training in the Second World War. The Combined Arab forces were about 40,000, most of whom were 'irregulars', with no formal military training:

> In the course of that war, the Zionists not only managed to hold all the areas assigned to them by the United Nations but to seize part of the land designated for the Palestinian state as well.
>
> (Friedman 1998: 15)

As a result of this war an estimated 600,000 to 700,000 Palestinian refugees fled from the massacres (Deir Yassin, Kibia, Kfar Qassem) that Haganah and Stren Zionist groups were committing against Palestinian Arabs to the Gaza Strip, Jordan, Syria and Lebanon (Makovsky 1996).[2]

Even after the defeat, Palestinian intellectuals expressed their convictions that Israel was a 'false nation and that they would keep fighting to get their land and rights back' (Durr, quoted in Cooley 1973: 78–9). Dr Ibrahim Durr, a Palestinian biochemist and writer, told John Cooley in the late 1960s that Israel is 'an artificial structure, a colony totally alien to the Middle East, especially as a manifestation of western interests and culture'. He found it 'lacking in the elements necessary for the survival as a state', after stating that Israel 'is a closed, racist, paramilitary society with an unchecked policy of expansion' (ibid.). Durr spoke of the loss of Palestine as a consequence of the Arab weakness at the time (ibid.).

However, in 2001 Edward Said offered another perspective on this continuous 'defeat':

> It is by no means an exaggeration to say that the establishment of Israel as a state in 1948 occurred partly because the Zionists acquired control of most territory of Palestine, and partly because they had already won the political battle for Palestine in the international world in which ideas, representations, rhetoric, and images were at issue.
>
> (Said and Hitchens 2001: 1)

## The Arab–Israeli wars

> [Noam Chomsky] sees the Palestine problem as 'a clash between total justice and total justice, since each side feels rightly that its national survival is the issue'. He calls for a revival of aspirations toward liberation socialist binationalism as the only realistic hope for peace.
>
> (Khalidi and Khaduri 1974: 4)

There have been a series of wars and territorial conflicts between Israel and various Arab states in the Middle East since the founding of the state of Israel in May 1948. These include the war of 1948–9 (discussed above), the 1956 Suez War between Israel and Egypt, the Six-Day (or June) War of 1967 in which Israel captured territory from Syria and Jordan, the October (or Yom Kippur) War of 1973, and the 1978 and 1982 Israeli invasions of Lebanon.

In the times between these wars, tension has remained high in the area, resulting in clashes and military operations taking place on both sides. However, following the 1973 war the main front – the area where these clashes and military operations were mostly concentrated – was within Lebanese territory. Further fronts were opened in 1987, when the Palestinians in the West Bank and Gaza Strip rose against the occupied army in a mass uprising that was later known as the First Palestinian *Intifada* (Arabic, literally 'shaking off').

In the coming section I briefly discuss these wars and try to show how the military and political situation in Lebanon became directly affected by the wider Arab–Israeli conflict.

## The Suez crisis, 1956

During the 1950s, nationalism spread among the Arab countries of the Middle East. President Gamal Abdel Nasser of Egypt and his followers sought to rid Arab lands of the influence of Western nations. On 26 July 1956, Nasser took control of the Suez Canal from its British and French owners. The canal connects the Mediterranean to the Red Sea and is a key shipping route between Europe and Asia.

Many Western countries protested at Nasser's action, and Britain, France and Israel secretly plotted to end Egypt's control of the canal. On 29 October, Israel attacked Egyptian forces on Egypt's Sinai Peninsula, which lies between Israel and the canal. Israel, with British and French help, occupied most of the peninsula. The UN called a ceasefire on 6 November 1956; by early 1957, Israel, under international pressure, returned the Sinai to Egypt. The canal reopened under Egyptian management in April of that year. After the Suez crisis, Arab guerrillas launched small-scale attacks inside Israel, and Israel responded with raids into Arab territory.

In 1964, the Arab League, inspired by the Egyptian president, Gamal Abdel Nasser, organised the Palestinian resistance groups under one umbrella, which became known as the Palestine Liberation Organisation or PLO (see Shlaim 2001: 230).

## The Six-Day (or June) War, 1967

> Since ... [the Suez crisis], Israel has expanded in size and in power. In 1967 it militarily acquired, and still holds, vast amounts of Arab land and people, including the entire mass of historical Palestine.
>
> (Said and Hitchens 2001: 2)

In May 1967, Nasser closed the Gulf of Aqaba to Israeli shipping, which was Israel's only access to the Red Sea. Avi Shlaim in his book *The Iron Wall* wrote that Nasser understood the psychological significance of this step. Shlaim added:

> [Nasser] knew that Israel's entire defence philosophy was based on imposing its will on its enemies, not on submitting to unilateral dictates by them. In closing the Straits of Tiran to Israeli shipping, he took a terrible gamble and lost.
>
> (Shlaim 2000: 237)

Shlaim believed that Nasser neither wanted nor planned to go to war with Israel. It was just one step to impress Arab public opinion in the face of Israeli threats to overthrow the regime in Damascus (ibid: 236).

By 5 June 1967, Egypt had signed defence agreements with Syria, Jordan and Iraq. These steps alarmed the Israelis. That day, they launched a surprise attack on Egypt. Syria, Jordan and Iraq joined Egypt in fighting Israel. Within hours, Israeli warplanes had destroyed almost all the Arab air forces. Israeli tanks then retook the Sinai Peninsula. Israel also gained control of the West Bank, the Gaza Strip and East Jerusalem. It had already taken West Jerusalem in the 1948 war. In the north, Israel took Syria's Golan Heights, an area bordering Israel. The fighting ended on 10 June. Israelis call this conflict the Six-Day War. Arabs call it the June War (Bregman 2000).

The war was followed by United Nations Security Council Resolution 242, which called for the 'withdrawal of Israeli armed forces from territories occupied in the recent conflict' (Philo and Berry 2004: 34). The resolution called for just settlement for the Palestinian refugee problem. Syria and the Palestinians opposed parts of the resolution on the grounds that it spoke of the Palestinians as a refugee problem without any mention of their right to self-determination and a national sovereign state (ibid; see also Seale 1989).

The 1967 war was a turning point in the Israeli–Palestinian conflict. Although it provided Israel with greater strategic depth and more defensible borders, it also made Israel responsible for the security and well-being of more than one million Palestinian inhabitants of the occupied territories and created another 200,000 refugees

(Makovsky 1996: 3). Moreover, by the end of 1969, 7,554 Arab houses had been razed and, by August 1971, another 16,212 houses had been demolished, according to the *Sunday Times* [London] of 19 June 1977 (Said 1992: 15).

After the 1967 war, the Palestinian Liberation Organisation (PLO) sought to become the representative of the Palestinians in world politics. It developed educational and social service organisations for Palestinians, mainly in the West Bank and Gaza Strip and in refugee camps in Lebanon and Jordan.

The PLO also began to take independent military action. In the late 1960s, PLO groups began to attack Israelis, both inside and outside Israel. Israel attacked Palestinian refugee camps in Jordan and Lebanon, where many guerrillas were based. The Israelis also assassinated a number of PLO leaders.

In 1969 Yassir Arafat, the head of the *Fatah* guerrilla group and movement ('conquest' in English) was elected chairman of the PLO's executive committee. Then, as now, the PLO was composed of a broad range of Palestinian guerrilla organisations representing many different political tendencies. The PLO was granted significant economic aid by the Arab states in order to carry on the battle with Israel. It soon took control of Palestinian refugee camps in Lebanon and Jordan, using them as bases of operation against targets in Israel and against Israeli targets abroad:

> In both Jordan and Lebanon the PLO assumed quasi-sovereign authority over certain regions bordering on Israel. Their raids on Israel brought massive Israeli retaliation, which created tensions between the Palestinians and part of the Lebanese community, and Palestinians and the Jordanian regime.
> 
> (Friedman 1998: 16)

## The October (or Yom Kippur) War, 1973

After the 1967 war, Egyptian and Israeli troops continued to attack each other across the western border of the Sinai Peninsula. Nasser died in 1970 as a result of a stroke, suffered while he was attempting to put down a 'civil war' in Jordan between PLO fighters and the Jordanian army of King Hussein, a war known as 'Black September' (explored later in this chapter).

In the early 1970s Egypt made numerous attempts to regain the occupied Sinai through diplomacy, but its peace overtures were rejected by Israel (Shlaim 2000). Anwar el-Sadat, who had succeeded Nasser, began plans to retake the Sinai Peninsula from Israel. He was joined by the new President of Syria Hafez al-Asad who sought to reclaim the Golan Heights. King Hussein declined to participate, fearing the loss of even more of his land should the Arab states not succeed against the powerful Israeli army (Bregman 2000).

On 6 October 1973, Egypt and Syria launched a massive assault on Israeli forces in the Sinai Peninsula and Golan Heights. The attack took Israel by surprise, in part because it came on Yom Kippur, the holiest day in Judaism (Rodinson 1985). At first, Egypt drove Israel's forces out of the western Sinai, and Syria pushed Israeli troops from the eastern Golan Heights. However, the United States gave Israel large amounts of military equipment and the Israeli army was able to regain most of what it originally occupied in 1967 (Philo and Berry 2004: 47). Israelis call this war the Yom Kippur War. Arabs call it the October War or the Ramadan War. The state of war between Egypt and Israel ended in 1979 with a peace treaty signed at Camp David.

## The Camp David Accords, 1978–9

In 1978, President Anwar el-Sadat of Egypt joined the Israeli prime minister, Menachem Begin, and the US president, Jimmy Carter, in signing the Camp David Accords. Under these agreements, Egypt recognised Israel's right to exist. In return, Israel agreed to give back to Egypt the part of Sinai it still occupied, having returned the far western part in 1975.

Sadat and Begin also agreed on the need for national independence for the Palestinians. In talks leading up to the accords, Egypt and Israel received promises of large amounts of US economic and military aid. In 1979, Egypt and Israel signed a treaty confirming their new 'peaceful relationship' (Rodinson 1985).

Most Arab leaders strongly opposed the Camp David Accords and the 1979 treaty. They believed that the unilateral separatist agreement of Camp David denied the legitimate rights of the Palestinians (Seale 1989). As a result, Egypt was expelled from the Arab League, an organisation of co-operation between Arab nations, in 1979. In 1981, an Egyptian religious group opposed to his policies assassinated Sadat.

## The First Intifada, 1987–91

In 1987, Palestinians in the West Bank and Gaza Strip began an uprising against Israel's military rule of those territories. The uprising became known as the *Intifada*, an Arabic term meaning 'uprising' or 'shaking off'. Demonstrations occurred throughout the occupied territories. Entire towns refused to pay taxes to Israel, and most Palestinians quit their jobs with Israeli employers (Friedman 1998). Most of the demonstrations were peaceful, but a few became violent.

The *Intifada* grabbed international attention and triggered criticism of Israel for its continuing control of the West Bank and Gaza Strip, and for its extensive use of force in trying to control the Palestinians. Many commentators said that somehow the Palestinian *Intifada* was influenced by the growing Lebanese resistance in south Lebanon against the Israeli occupation (Atwi 2000: 195–203).

## The Lebanese–Israeli conflict

Following an Israeli helicopter raid, which had burned 13 Lebanese civil airliners at Beirut International Airport on 28 December 1968, the Fedayeen (the military arm of the PLO) moved increasingly and openly into Lebanese bases. This brought into the open the entire issue of the Fedayeen presence in Lebanon (Cooley 1973: 104).

In the autumn of 1969, Lebanon had signed an agreement with the PLO in Cairo under President Nasser's auspices. This pact (called the Cairo Agreement) legitimised the Palestinians' right to operate from southern Lebanon (Fisk 2001: 74). Saeb Salam, the prime minister at the time, being an experienced politician heading a cabinet of 'young technocrats', promised to respect the Palestinians' 'freedom of action' from southern Lebanon, covered by the Cairo Agreement (ibid).

In May 1970, General Mordecai Gur, commander of Israel's northern military sector, sent an Israeli armoured brigade with air cover into the Arqoub. This is an area of Lebanese territory below the slopes of Mount Haramon, the partly wooded region of caves, defiles and hidden valleys where Israel claimed the Fedayeen had their main bases in Lebanon. During this operation the Israeli tank crews demolished Hebbariyeh, one of the Lebanese villages that had been heavily targeted by the Israelis. A few days later they withdrew, after failing to kill any significant numbers of assumed guerrillas (Cooley 1973: 87).

In September 1970, radical Palestinian guerrillas brought three hijacked airliners to Jordan and prevented the Jordanian army from getting near the planes or rescuing the passengers. Recognising he was on the verge of losing control over his whole kingdom, King Hussein decided to wipe out Arafat and the PLO by launching a full-scale offensive against the Palestinian refugee camps and districts in the Jordanian capital, Amman. The PLO responded by calling for Hussein's overthrow and vowing to wrest Jordan from his hands. The PLO lost, forcing Arafat to flee Amman disguised as an Arab woman (Friedman 1998: 16).

Arafat and the PLO immediately moved to Lebanon and set up their new base in the Palestinian refugee districts of Beirut and south Lebanon. It was at this point that the Lebanese conflict became fully intertwined with the Israeli–Palestinian conflict.

> Lebanon's delegation to the Thirty-Second General Assembly was headed by Mr. Fouad Boutros, the new Minister of Foreign Affairs, who met with President Jimmy Carter in New York on 5 October 1977, to emphasise, among other things, what he was to state in his speech before the Assembly:
>
> 'The war in Lebanon is, in most respects, the result of a prior injustice committed against a people driven out from its land and deprived of its country. Thus, injustice has itself provoked injustice and violence has engendered further violence in the host country of what befell Palestine.'
>
> (Tuieni 1979: 4)

In February 1972 the Israelis repeated their incursion of May 1970: for four days, they occupied Lebanon's Arqoub region while their soldiers blew up houses used by the guerrillas, killing about fifty of them with the aid of Skyhawk and Phantom fighter-bombers. When the Israeli forces withdrew, under the pressure of US disapproval and a unanimous UN Security Council resolution calling on them to withdraw and not repeat the attack, the Lebanese army was deployed in the Arqoub region for the first time since 1969 (Cooley 1973: 131).

After Arafat and his men had fled Jordan, they were welcomed by the Lebanese national socialist parties, mostly Muslims and Druze, who identified with their cause and thought they could have the PLO on their side in bringing pressure on the ruling Maronite Christians to share more political power (Fisk 2001).

Recognising this, the Maronite Christians wanted the PLO out, believing it was disrupting Lebanese life and, more importantly to them perhaps, that with its departure the Lebanese Muslims would be unable to press their demands for more power. The Muslims and left-wing political movements and parties (gathered in one body as the Lebanese National Movement or LNM) in turn opposed any crackdown on the PLO, which, in effect, had become their main support in bringing political changes to the way Lebanon was run, dominated by the Maronites (Friedman 1998: 17).

As a result of this political deadlock, the Lebanese Government and army became paralysed. The Christian Maronite groups turned to their own armies – the Phalangists and Tiger militias – to deal with the Palestinians. On 13 April 1975, some Phalangists ambushed and killed 27 Palestinian civilians riding in a bus through East Beirut. The next morning, Palestinian guerrillas backed by the LNM fought pitched battles in the streets of Beirut with the Phalangists and Tiger militias. Eventually, Christian elements of the Lebanese army sided with their tribe, Muslims did the same, and Lebanon soon found itself in a civil war that erupted on 13 April 1975 (see Friedman 1998; Fisk 2001; Picard 2002).

## The 14 March 1978 invasion

Israeli encounters with civilian villagers, the Lebanese left-wing factions and the Fedayeen continued. In March 1978, and in the absence of an effective government in Lebanon, Israel invaded south Lebanon, occupying almost 7 per cent of Lebanese territory in a campaign the Israelis called 'Operation Litani'.

The Lebanese suspected Israel might permanently occupy parts of south Lebanon and so secure control of new water resources. The projects Israel conducted on the Litani River later confirmed these Lebanese suspicions.

> There was ... a great symbolism in Israel's selection of the codename for its military operation. The Litani River, Southern Lebanon's principal lifeline, had always been coveted by Israel. Even before the inception of the Jewish State, when the borders between Lebanon and Palestine were being re-

> drawn by the British Mandate it was an essential economic component of the projected 'National Home'. When Israel was created by the 1947 UN resolution, which partitioned Palestine, a number of economic schemes were proposed for joint Israeli–Lebanese exploitation of the Litani waters.
>
> (Tuieni 1979: 5)

Even the most modest Lebanese attempts to divert minor rivers and springs in the same area had been blocked by 'Israeli incursions, shelling and the constant use of force, to keep open Israel's option on the Litani' (ibid.).

While the invasion was still under way, the United Nations Security Council approved Resolution 425, depriving Israel of the political dividends expected from Operation Litani's success. The resolution called on Israel to withdraw from Lebanon and established a United Nations Interim Force in Lebanon (UNIFIL). Lebanon announced that 1,168 people had been killed in the invasion.

Israel made no response to the UN Resolution, and its defence minister, Ezer Weizman, called for the establishment of a local militia in south Lebanon to collaborate with the Israeli army and maintain order in the area. The militia was formed and given the name the Southern Lebanon Army or SLA. Israel occupied south Lebanon up to the Litani River, with the exception of a 'pocket' around Tyre (Tuieni 1979: 467). It was first headed by a defected Lebanese army officer Saad Haddad and later by Antoine Lahed. The militia was nicknamed after Lahed and became known to the Lebanese as Lahed militia.

From March 1978 until June 1982, peace-keeping in Lebanon was undergoing a dramatic process, which made its ultimate success doubtful and the credibility of the international intervention highly questionable (ibid: 477).

## The 6 June 1982 invasion

> Incongruously enough, the incident that eventually brought war took place neither in Lebanon nor in Israel, but in London. On 3 June 1982, Palestinian gunmen of the Abu Nidal group shot the Israeli Ambassador to London, Shlomo Argov, and seriously injured him. There was no reason intrinsically why such an incident should turn into a *casus belli* and necessitate a massive Israeli invasion to wipe out

the PLO in Lebanon, especially given that Abu Nidal was a sworn enemy of the PLO and its leader Arafat, whom he often dubbed 'the Jewess' son', and had even sent his people to assassinate him.

(Bregman 2000: 158)

On 6 June 1982, the Israeli army launched a massive military operation against Lebanon, code-named the 'Peace for Galilee' operation, commanded by Ariel Sharon, the Israeli defence minister at the time and supported by the Phalangists.

> Sharon, like others in Likud, strongly believed that the destruction of the PLO in Lebanon would shatter Arafat's influence among the inhabitants of the West Bank. He said: 'Quiet on the West Bank requires the destruction of the PLO in Lebanon', and one of his colleagues, the then Foreign Minister Yitzhak Shamir, said: 'the defence of the West Bank starts in West Beirut'.
>
> (Bregman 2000: 155)

The Israeli army arrived at the gates of Beirut on 14 June 1982. The western part of the Lebanese capital was under siege for three months.

> Israeli aircraft dropped propaganda leaflets in a psychological warfare campaign to frighten the residents of West Beirut into leaving... [The Israeli army] bombarded PLO positions and residential areas of West Beirut by land, sea, and air for fourteen hours on August 1 in the most intense shelling of the besieged capital since the invasion commenced on June 6.
>
> (Tanter 1990: 149, 160)

On 21 August, Arafat and the PLO fighters evacuated West Beirut, leaving for Tunisia on board ships provided by the Americans, French and Italians. An American mediator, Philip Habib, succeeded in achieving an agreement between Arafat and the Israelis. The agreement stated that, if the PLO evacuated Beirut, the Israeli army would give assurances it would not enter West Beirut.

> The 1982 conflict was the first where Israel was not fighting the armed forces of another sovereign state. Lebanon has

been described as an 'involuntarily open society', since it had no effective government for seven years before the 1982 invasion.

(Mungham, quoted in Mercer et al. 1987: 263)

On 14 September 1982 the head of the Phalangists, Israel's prime ally, Bashir Jumayyil, was assassinated. Many Lebanese considered Jumayyil (also spelt Gemayel) a collaborator with the enemy:

> Israel had carefully cultivated Bashir Jumayyil for years, providing arms and training for his men and invaluable help abroad in his uphill struggle for international respectability. Israel had invaded Lebanon on June 6 [1982] for its own reasons, and without the Lebanese Forces' political support and rear-base facilities it is doubtful whether Prime Minister Menachem Begin and Defence Minister Ariel Sharon would have dared launch the operation.
>
> (Randal 1993: 3)

At 3:30 am on Wednesday 15 September, Jumayyil's military lieutenants met with Lieutenant General Rafael Eitan, Israeli Chief of Staff, and Major-General Amir Drori, in charge of Israel's Northern Command and in effective charge of the entire Lebanese operation. The Israelis were going to invade West Beirut – in defiance of promises to the United States, Lebanon, and the PLO made during the peaceful evacuation of more than 11,000 Palestinian guerrillas completed just two weeks earlier.

> Bashir's death simply left too many possibilities for error that could nullify Israel's sacrifices and benefits in the war to date. The Israelis had counted on Jumayyil to clean up West Beirut with its armed leftist militias and the two thousand PLO fighters, who, the Israelis had convinced themselves, on the basis of erroneous electronic eavesdropping, had been left behind.
>
> (Randal 1993: 13)

Hours later the Israeli army invaded West Beirut. On 16 September the Phalangists, under the supervision of the Israelis, committed a massacre in the Sabra and Shatila Palestinian refugee camps of almost 3,000 civilians, among them children and old people. On the same day, the first Lebanese resistance operation was conducted against the Israelis in Hamra Street in the middle of West Beirut. The Lebanese Communist Party, the Communist Labour organisation and the Lebanese National Social Party led the resistance operations at the time.

A month later, the aircraft that had been dropping leaflets trying to intimidate West Beirutis into leaving their city were now dropping leaflets asking the Beirutis not to shoot at Israeli soldiers because now the Israelis were leaving.

> Israel's previous military engagements were brief (four, six and eighteen days respectively in 1956, 1967 and 1973) and conclusive, but the 1982 conflict 'just kept rolling on' and has still in a sense to reach a conclusion. (Mungham, quoted in Mercer et al. 1987: 263)

## Some results of Israel's invasion

In 1984 Israel withdrew to what it later named its 'security zone' in south Lebanon, giving it total control over the Litani River and imposing a military administration run by the head of the SLA, a Lebanese officer (paid by the Israelis), Saad Haddad.

In the wake of 1982 Israeli invasion, Hezbollah, the Shiite Islamist Party of God, emerged. Resisting the occupation was one of the main reasons that brought several members and religious leaders of different Shiite political movements and groups together to form one party under the auspices of the Iranian revolution that had taken place in 1979. Hassan Nasrallah, the Secretary General of Hezbollah, told the party's paper *Al Ahd* on 21 November 1997, that 'had the enemy [Israel] not taken this step [the invasion], I do not know whether something called Hezbollah would have been born. I doubt it' (quoted in Saad-Ghorayeb 2002: 11).

A few months after the invasion, the Shiites of south Lebanon, who constitute the majority of the population there, became aware that the Israelis had come to stay and that they would not leave until they had achieved what they claimed to be their objective at the time, uprooting the PLO from south Lebanon (Jaber 1997: 15; Ranstorp 1997: 30). Poignantly, the Israelis initiated a plan, similar to that used in the West Bank, to administer the area through committees run by their proxy militia, the SLA (Jaber 1997: 15).

The Israeli army and its allies started pressuring figures in the local population to join the scheme, by taking their relatives as hostages into a camp they established in Ansar village near Sidon (ibid.). The camp, known as the Ansar concentration camp, because of its tents and barbed wire, was used to abduct and detain without trial those suspected of aiding and abetting members of the underground resistance movement that was sweeping the villages of south Lebanon (Jones 2002). What had started in 1982 as a small group of resistance fighters became a mass resistance movement, which led to the 1985 Israeli withdrawal from major cities and towns in south Lebanon.

In 1985, Hezbollah officially announced its existence and issued its mission statement. One of its main objectives was to resist the occupation until the Israelis withdrew from Lebanese territory. However, it was not until the late 1980s that the Hezbollah Islamic resistance gained the upper hand in fighting the Israelis.

By the early 1990s the Islamic resistance had become the only force with the logistic and military capabilities to fight the Israeli occupation in south Lebanon (for more information on the emergence, structure and objectives of Hezbollah, see Jaber 1997; Ranstorp 1997; Saad Ghorayeb 2002; Hamzeh 2004; Palmer Harik 2004; Qassem 2005).

Meanwhile, Israel was finding it difficult day after day to stop the resistance fighters from targeting its troops in the occupied zone of south Lebanon. The Islamic resistance, which had growing support and popularity among the local population, became Israel's number one target. Their war against the resistance fighters took various shapes and forms: commando operations, incursions and mini-invasions.

The 'Seven Days' Operation of July 1993 (code-named by the Israelis as 'Operation Accountability') and the 'Grapes of Wrath' Operation of April 1996 (studied in detail in Chapter Six) were two major attacks that Israel launched against Lebanese territory, targeting southern villages and cities outside the occupied zone and also the main power stations in the capital, Beirut.

These two operations, in 1993 and 1996, took place after Lebanon had survived its 15-year civil war and after all the Lebanese factions had agreed to put an end to the fighting and killing. They agreed on Lebanon's right and legitimacy to resist the Israeli occupation forces in south Lebanon until Israel implemented UN Resolution 425.[3] They also agreed that Lebanon was to be a united Arab state where Muslims and

Christians shared similar powers. They equally rejected all tendencies and attempts to divide Lebanon into miniature religious states (Al Abed 2001) and they declared Israel as a state enemy and those who established contact with the Israelis as traitors.

However, with this agreement, Israel lost the support of the right-wing Christian Phalangists who, along with the SLA proxy militia, were the main political supporters of Israel in Lebanon. The relationship between the Phalangists and Israel goes back to the early leaders of the Zionist movement (Eisenberg 1994).

This chapter has already sketched the development of Zionists' ideas on Palestine. Before we go further, it is appropriate to consider their view of Lebanon in order to complete the timeline up to the point left here.

## Lebanon in the Zionist mind

To make sense of Israel's incursions into Lebanon, we need to look now at the place Lebanon had in the early Zionist imagination, and how that interest originated and developed.

> Interest in the natural resources of the Galilee and a growing sense of possible political and economic opportunities among the Lebanese characterised the early period of Zionist attention to Lebanon.
> 
> (Eisenberg 1994: 38)

Encouraged by the vague border in the Galilee region, early Zionist strategists saw Lebanon, especially the southern portion, as an arena for potential Zionist settlement. Chaim Weizmann toured Lebanon in 1907. Two weeks later, he was back in Haifa, anxiously seeking support for several small industries he wanted to establish in Sidon.

> Saida [Sidon] is a good place in every respect. The raw material is available, there is a harbour, it is favourably situated, capable of development, and has a Jewish population.
> 
> (Weizmann, quoted in Eisenberg 1994: 39)

Thus, Weizmann had in mind the possibility of building Jewish settlements in southern Lebanon.

## Overview of the Arab–Israeli Conflict   83

The call for a Zionist policy of co-operation with the Lebanese Maronites came from a pro-Zionist journalist in Beirut. Writing directly to Weizmann, J.J. Caleb offered his unsolicited assessment of the Lebanese situation's relevance to the Zionist case. Caleb claimed they would be two minorities against the Muslims in the region. He maintained that, with Christian Lebanese assistance, the Zionists could splinter the Muslim–Christian bloc in Palestine. Besides, some Zionist leaders like Menachem Ussishkin claimed that part of biblical Palestine fell within Lebanon and Syria (Eisenberg 1994: 45).

Zionist activities in the first decades of the twentieth century found cause for encouragement in their encounters with the Maronites.

> On the surface, the Maronites and the Jews thought they had much in common: some Maronites saw themselves as modern-day Phoenicians bringing all the Phoenician Diaspora back to Lebanon, just as the Zionists were doing with the Jews; together they would restore the ancient Mediterranean.
> 
> (Freidman 1998: 135)

The past history of a Zionist–Maronite 'friendship' had emerged in 1860, during the Maronite–Druze civil war. The Druze had decidedly seized the upper lands and exchanges of killing took place between the Maronites and Druze. The Ottoman authorities refused to reply to the Maronites' call for rescue.

> In desperation, the Maronites cried out for help to the European nations. Two of the first European personalities to respond to their appeal were Sir Moses Montefiore, a wealthy Jewish communal leader in London, and Adolph Cremieux, a distinguished French Jewish statesman. Montefiore arranged for the Maronites' plight to receive prominent coverage in the London *Times* and set up a fund to assist the survivors, to which he gave generously of his own money. Cremieux proved instrumental in persuading the French to send troops to Lebanon to save the Christians. French intervention rescued the Christians and brought about the Maronite dominated Mutasarifyya.
> 
> (ibid: 51)

At the end of the First World War, when Britain and France carved up the Ottoman Empire's Middle Eastern possessions, France at one point had divided its League of Nations mandate into five separate states, including a Greater Lebanon run by the Christians. It added to the Christian Mount Lebanon region such predominantly Muslim areas as Tyre in the South, Tripoli in the North, and the fertile Bekaa in the East 'to make an economically viable state' (Randal 1993).

> In 1936, the Maronite Patriarch testified in favour of a Jewish state in Palestine before the Peel Commission, established to end the violence there. The following year, David Ben-Gurion, then chairman of the Jewish Agency,[4] told the Zionist World Workers Party meeting in Zurich that 'Lebanon is the natural ally of the Jews of the land of Israel ... the proximity of Lebanon will furnish a loyal ally for the Jewish state as soon as it is created'.
>
> (Randal 1993: 188)

It is documented that, after the Ottoman Empire's collapse in 1918, Zionists had tried unsuccessfully to persuade Britain to claim all of southern Lebanon up to the precious waters of the Litani River for Palestine, but France, as a mandate power over Lebanon and Syria, declined the request and announced the founding of 'the State of Great Lebanon' (Menargues 2006) in 1920 within its current borders. In what Israelis call the War of Independence, 'Israeli troops in 1948 occupied Lebanon up to the Litani River, withdrawing to the present border only in the following year' (Randal 1993: 189).

## Israel and Lebanon

In the mid-1950s, the then Israeli prime minister, Moshe Sharett, recognised his country's 'unfriendly' designs on Lebanon in a series of records in his personal diary (published in Hebrew in 1979, but only after Sharett's son faced establishment efforts to prevent its publication – as documented in Randal 1993).

> Long before the Palestinian guerrillas became a physical threat to Israel, Sharett recorded Israeli plans to destabilize, indeed dismember, Lebanon and install a puppet regime pliable to Israel's diktat. Various entries from the 1930s show Sharett discouraging Maronite extremist dreams of

enlisting Zionist help to undo the Greater Lebanon created in 1920. Sharett's February 27, 1954, entry deals with the then recently retired Prime Minister, David Ben-Gurion, Defence Minister Pinhas Lavon, and chief of Staff Moshe Dayan all of whom wanted to take advantage of a coup d'etat in Syria to invade that country. Ben-Gurion insisted that if Iraq invaded Syria, as seemed possible, 'this is the time to arouse Lebanon – that is to say the Maronites – to proclaim a Christian state. Sharett demurred: 'I said this is an empty dream'.

(Randal 1993: 189)

Sharett argued that 'not only were all Christians no longer a majority in Lebanon, but the Greek Orthodox minority wanted no part of a Maronite-dominated Christian state' (ibid: 191). On 16 May 1955, Sharett recorded:

> [For Moshe Dayan] all that is needed [is] to find an officer, even a captain. We should win his heart or buy him, to get him to agree to declare himself the saviour of the Maronite population. Then Israel would enter Lebanon, occupy the necessary territory and set up a Christian regime allied to Israel and everything would run just fine.

(ibid: 193)

What Sharett disclosed proved right in the light of what happened in Lebanon after 1975. Civil war enveloped the country. Israel did latch onto a renegade Christian army officer, Saad Haddad, who did its bidding in the southern border area.

Sharett revealed Ben-Gurion's beliefs:

> The state 'must invent dangers and, to do so, it must adopt the method of provocation-and-revenge...and above all—let us hope for a new war with the Arab countries—so that we may finally get rid of our troubles and acquire space,' Sharett's entry read, before noting, '(such a slip of the tongue—Ben Gurion himself said it would be worthwhile to pay an Arab a million pounds to start a war)'.

(ibid: 194)

At the same time, Ben-Gurion's 1948–9 diaries shed light on the extent of Israel's relationship with various Lebanese politicians in the late

1940s, as well as on Israeli contacts with a Phalangist envoy in the war's immediate aftermath.

> In 1946, the relationship with the Maronite community in Lebanon was formalised by an agreement between the Jewish Agency and the Maronite Church, but the agreement's limited value was reflected in the latter's insistence that the treaty be kept secret, and the ensuing controversy between Patriarch Arida and his emissary, Tawfiq Awwad, who both sought to disassociate themselves from it.
>
> (Rabinovich 1985: 104)

The Maronite Church did not want to put itself in a confrontation with the massive Arab sympathy and support for the Palestinians, even among Maronites themselves.

> Now the Palestinian refugees are pouring into Lebanon... One must also include the British consul general's observation that even Christians had begun to feel that the Palestinians were being wronged.
>
> (Eisenberg 1994: 97)

The Maronites mostly treated their contacts with Israel with secrecy until the early 1970s, when the PLO left Jordan for Beirut.

> Israel's involvement in the Lebanese civil war can be traced back – grotesque as it may seem – to a crucial meeting on the steps of the Magdalene Church in Paris. There, back in the early 1970s, an Israeli agent of the Mossad promised, albeit unofficially, to a Christian leader by the strange name of Mugabgab, that, if asked, Israel would assist the Christians in Lebanon. This led to a meeting in 1975 between Israel's Prime Minister Rabin and the Maronite Christian Leader Camille Chamoun, on board an Israeli destroyer in the Mediterranean, to discuss Israeli aid to the Maronites in Lebanon.
>
> (Bregman 2000: 149)

A year later, with the civil war in Lebanon raging and the Maronite forces under growing pressure and in serious military straits, a Maronite leader of the Al Kataeb Phalangist party, Joseph Abu Khalil, approached Mugabgab. Bregman (2000) recorded they set sail from Kaslik in Lebanon to the port of Haifa in Israel on 12 March 1976.

> Their ship was stopped at sea by an Israeli patrol boat, and after identifying themselves and explaining the purpose of their trip they were taken to Tel Aviv, where they met Israel's Defence Minister Shimon Peres. Peres asked Abu Khalil: 'why have you come to ask for weapons. We need ammunition'. Peres discussed the matter with Prime Minister Rabin, and they decided on a dramatic increase in material help to the Maronites in Lebanon.
> 
> (Bregman 2000: 149)

It is often alleged that Israel's principal motive in offering support to the Maronites in Lebanon was 'sympathy and compassion'. This, however, is not true; in providing supplies and some other assistance to the Maronites, Israel was serving what it saw as its own national interests. The Maronites were fighting the PLO and other traditional enemies of Israel (left-wing and Muslim parties) and, by assisting the Maronites, Israel was using a proxy to do its dirty work. Supporting the Maronites provided the Israelis, Mossad in particular, with a window to the Arab world, crucial for the purposes of gathering intelligence (ibid: 149).

> With political endorsement given, Israeli boats began sailing back and forth delivering arms to the Maronites. A boat would sail into Lebanese waters towing craft heaped with weapons and ammunition, and off the coast the craft would be released for the Maronites to tow away. Arming the Maronites was a major logistical operation and, although contacts with the Maronites in Lebanon were usually maintained by the Mossad, in this case the huge supply operation was supervised by the Israeli defence ministry. It is estimated that between 1975 and 1977 the Rabin government spent $150 million on arming the Maronites.
> 
> (ibid: 150)

In September 1976 the Phalangists officially announced the formation of their armed militia headed by Bashir Jumayyil (or Gemayel), the young son of Peir Jumayyil, the head of Al Kataeb, the main Phalangist party at the time. The militia was given the name of the 'Lebanese Forces'. Bashir established a good relationship with the Israelis.

> But perhaps most important were the development of Bashir Jumayyil's personality and leadership, the build-up of his party's and militia's power, and the dynamics of the relationship between him and his Israeli allies. By 1980, Bashir Jumayyil had developed, at least in some Israeli eyes, from the charming and volatile younger son of a veteran political leader into the mature head of the single most powerful political and military force in Lebanon, a real ally to Israel, and a man with the capacity to change the paradigms of both the Lebanese crisis and the Lebanese polity.
>
> (Rabinovich 1985: 108)

Bashir Jumayyil was the first to promise the Israelis that, with their help, he could 'reshape Lebanon and forge a peace treaty' (Friedman 1998: 138). Under the protection of Israeli tanks, Jumayyil was elected President of Lebanon in August 1982. The Israeli prime minister at the time, Menachem Begin, and defence minister, Ariel Sharon, met Bashir in Nahariyya and wanted Lebanon to sign a peace treaty with Israel quickly, no later than a month after Jumayyil's inauguration on September 23.

Jumayyil proposed instead a 'non-aggression pact'. He came to realise the dangers of a peace treaty with Israel – at least before an overall Middle East settlement was achieved (Randal 1993: 9).

> Begin cited [Saad] Haddad's case. Haddad knew how to take orders, 'knew what was best for both Israel and Lebanon; he was an example to be followed', he said. But even on that score there was confrontation. Bashir had wanted to put Haddad on trial for dereliction of duty and treasonable trafficking with Israel. Yet here was Begin insisting that Haddad serve as Defence Minister or army commander in Bashir's new government. Jumayyil and Begin ended up shouting at each other. Sharon said that when he held someone or something in his grasp, he did not give them up. Israel was in the driver's seat, he made clear, and Bashir had better do what was expected of him. Gemayel at one point held out both arms and said, 'put the handcuffs on!' Then he shouted, 'I am not your vassal!'
>
> (ibid: 10)

But for the Israelis he was. That was what irritated the Lebanese Forces; especially after the Israelis leaked news of what they had agreed would remain a secret conversation (ibid: 10).

After Bashir was assassinated, the relationship between the Maronites and the Israelis worsened.

> The Christians felt used by the Israelis...an outraged population, and a revivified opposition that were determined to get at the truth. Nor were they convinced that Israel was innocent of Jumayyil's assassination. Even in the Jumayyil family seat, the mountain village of Bikfaya, and even among key members of his clan, the episode at Nahariyya was cited as sufficient proof that the 'Israelis preferred a partitioned Lebanon to the prospect of a strong government under Bashir'.
>
> (Randal 1993: 21)

However, Bashir's brother Amin took power and was elected to the presidency – and what Bashir had not yielded was accepted by Amin. Lebanon signed a peace treaty with Israel on 17 May 1983. The treaty was not accepted by the left-wing and Muslim parties and a severe wave of fighting took place. The 17 May treaty was cancelled by the Lebanese Government on 5 March 1984. Cancellation was the condition that left-wing and Muslim parties, supported by Syria, had insisted on before Amin Jumayyil started negotiating how to end the civil war in Lebanon (Al Abed 2001: 146–7).

The civil war did not stop then. In the following years it was heavily fuelled. The Maronites ended up fighting each other – reflecting a time in Lebanon when almost every religious sector was fighting itself. Some 144,000 people died in the violence after 1975 and more than 184,000 were wounded, including 13,000 who were permanently handicapped, in a country of only about 3.5 million in 1990 (Blanford 2006: 41). About 90,000 families were displaced from their homes and at least 17,000 people simply vanished (ibid.).

It was not till 1990 that most of the Christian and Muslim leaders of Lebanon met in a reconciliation conference at Al Taif in Saudi Arabia and agreed to put an end to the civil war. This agreement was known later as the Al Taif Accord and the former Lebanese prime minister Rafic Hariri, who was assassinated in February 2005 by a car bomb, was the architect of this accord. (For more on the role Hariri played in bringing all Lebanese parties together to end the civil war, see Blanford 2006.)

Lebanon's official institutions thus regained their unity and power. The Lebanese Government declared its support for the Lebanese resistance against the Israeli occupation in south Lebanon. It also announced its support for the Palestinians' right to establish their sovereign state in Palestine and for the right of Palestinian refugees to return to their homeland (Al Abed 2001; Picard 2002). All Lebanese governments that took office after 1990 recognised the Islamic resistance armed struggle against the Israeli occupation as 'national resistance' (Palmer Harik 2004).

After 22 years of occupation, Israel made a unilateral withdrawal from south Lebanon in May 2000. On 24 July 2000, UNIFIL (the United Nations Interim Force in Lebanon) finally certified Israeli compliance with UN Security Council Resolution 425. However, there were a small number of issues still unresolved when the verification process came to a halt. Among those problems was Chebaa Farms, a small piece of land that Israel claimed to be Syrian land (related to UN Resolution 242), yet which Lebanon believes is Lebanese and that therefore needed to be liberated from Israeli occupation according to Resolution 425. The resistance declared the continuation of its military struggle until Israel withdrew from Chebaa Farms, released all Lebanese detainees from Israeli prisons and stopped violating Lebanese air space (O'Shea 2004).

Exchanging prisoners between Israel and Hezbollah was the main aim behind the resistance capturing two Israeli soldiers on the border between Israel and Lebanon on 12 July 2006 (*Assafir* 2006: Nasrallah's speech). On the same day Israel launched a disproportionate war against Lebanon, claiming that it wanted to destroy the resistance. Israel's war objectives were not met, and instead Lebanon's civil infrastructure was destroyed while Hezbollah and the Islamic resistance gained in popularity among the Lebanese and Arab population.[5]

# Conclusion

This chapter has sought to establish an historical account of the Arab–Israeli conflict and the Lebanese–Israeli conflict. It is a narration of how the history of these conflicts is seen in the eyes of many Arabs

Overview of the Arab–Israeli Conflict 91

and Lebanese. It was this historical account that would affect the way messages (reports and commentaries) were constructed and put forward by journalists from TL (Tele Liban) and Al Manar.

This chapter was divided in two: the first section introduced the Arab–Israeli conflict in general, explaining the background to the use of 'enemy state' rhetoric by the Lebanese journalists. The second section has been on Lebanon, its conflict with Israel, and how that has affected its stability and security, causing divisions between its religious communities. This section has indicated and explained the emphasis that has been put, by both TL and Al Manar journalists, on the need to achieve national unity. Uniting the nation, as chapters Six and Seven reveal, is what propaganda to the home front was aiming at, whether planned or not planned.

Before attending to the performance of TL and Al Manar journalists in covering the conflict with Israel, the next chapter tries to set the media scene in Lebanon. It explores the development and structure of the Lebanese broadcast media in general, and the TL and Al Manar television stations in particular.

# 5

## THE MEDIA IN LEBANON

Little has been written on the history and structure of television broadcasting in Lebanon. According to Dr Nabil Dajani of the American University of Beirut, most of the available literature on the topic is either outdated, too general or lacks precision (Dajani 2001).

However, Jean-Claude Boulos dedicated a whole book to the history of television in Lebanon, focusing mainly on Tele Liban and his long experience there as a broadcaster and later as chairman and general director of the company.[1] His book was written in French and translated into Arabic.[2] Thus, following extensive searches, it seems that Boulos's book is the only one devoted to the television industry in Lebanon. Other contributions are scattered in books on the Arab media or the Arab television industry in general.

This chapter aims to set the scene for an exploration of the Lebanese television milieu and tries to establish the position of Tele Liban and Al Manar TV in the development of this medium. This chapter's chronological account highlights the reasons behind the two stations' distinctive roles in the media war with Israel.

William Rugh states that Lebanon is a special case among Arab broadcasting systems, as it is among Arab print media systems. He asserts that

> Lebanese media institutions do not fit the model of the third world (public sector ownership, usually by a government agency) or of the West. Lebanese broadcasting has been at least partially owned and operated by the government.
> 
> (Rugh 2004: 195)

## La Compagnie Libanaise de Télévision (CLT)

The initiative to establish television in Lebanon came from two businessmen, Wissam Izzeddine and Alex Arida, who had little experience in television broadcasting. They envisaged their project in essentially business terms, 'giving little or no attention to its social implications and responsibilities' (Dajani 2001).

In October 1954, Izzeddine and Arida approached the government and proposed that they build a television station financed by the sale of advertising (Boulos 1995, Boyd 1993, Rugh 2004, Sakr 2001, Dajani 2001). After two years of negotiations they signed an agreement with the government on 9 April 1956 for the establishment of a station to operate two channels, 7 and 9 VHF, one for Arabic-language broadcasts and the other for foreign programmes (Dajani 2001).

At 6.30pm on 28 May 1959, the first television image was broadcast in Lebanon (Boulos 1995: 39). In Boyd's words, CLT thus became 'the first non-government operated, advertising-supported television station in the Arab World' (Boyd 1993: 73).[3] CLT operated from a building built especially on a hill in Talet Al Khayat in the western sector of Beirut (Boulos 1995: 31).

The agreement between CLT and the government consisted of 21 articles, addressing the terms under which CLT would operate, the most salient being that:

- The government does not give the company monopoly rights.
- Broadcasters should be under government scrutiny, and should not include programmes that threaten public security, morals or religious groups, or enhance the image of any political personality or party.
- Programmes should be restricted to education or entertainment, and advertising should not exceed 25 per cent of broadcast time.
- Television is to respect all laws and regulations relating to the rights of the press and of authors, and shall be subject to all laws and internal or international regulations dealing with wireless communications and broadcast institutions. It shall also exchange sound programmes with Lebanese radio[4] in the sphere of overall co-operation.
- The agreement, once approved officially, shall be in force for 15 years, at the end of which the government has the full

right to buy all facilities connected with the project, at prices specified by two experts, one representing the government and the other the company whose agreement has been ended (Boyd 1993: 72–3).

Also, Article 7 stated that 'government censorship on the TV network is guaranteed by Information Ministry employees' (Boulos 1995: 30). They were to pre-supervise all programmes and films prepared for broadcast. They had the authority to 'amend or delete any segment that contradicts the responsibilities that come from the existing conditions' (ibid.).

Further, the Lebanese Government had the authority to set editorial policy guidelines for news and special events coverage.[5] According to William Rugh, the government tended to exercise this right only 'as a veto power over sensitive issues in times of political crisis' (Rugh 2004: 196). The news was written and edited by television editors, using local reporters and international news services quite freely, and, in the spirit of the agreement, the news team were careful to 'avoid favouring one group or another, or criticizing a foreign power, so their political material tended to be much more bland than the press' (ibid.).

The bulk of their programming was non-political, and nearly three quarters of it was usually imported film or videotape. Foreign interests did not diminish over the years, either. The French supplied considerable material to CLT, and Channel 9 was dedicated to broadcasting mainly French programmes and news.[6] Thus, the channel's intended audience consisted of 'elite francophone people', as Jean-Claude defined them. In other words it targeted 'those who speak English and French and [therefore] appealed more to the advertisers' (Boulos 1995: 37). Channel 7, in turn, was completely dedicated to Arabic news and programmes and was defined as 'the popular channel' (ibid: 36).

After transmissions started, CLT established a separate company to handle its administration and advertising sales. This was known as Advision and 'had the American Time-Life organisation as a partner for a short period' (Boyd 1993: 73). Nevertheless, French interests in the station never diminished, but grew day after day.

The French supplied considerable material to CLT and their role in that station became so important that license agreements were negotiated directly between the French and Lebanese governments.

(Rugh 2004: 196)

## Compagnie de Télévision du Liban et du Proche (Tele-Orient)

In April 1959, another group of Lebanese businessmen approached the government with a request to set up a second television station, Compagnie de Télévision du Liban et du Proche (Tele-Orient). An agreement identical to the one granted to CLT was concluded in July 1959 (Dajani 2001).

The organisation, which agreed to the same conditions as CLT, was partly financed by the American Broadcasting Company (ABC). Later ABC sold its interest in the station to the British Thomson Organisation and the Rizk brothers, from a wealthy Lebanese family. Tele-Orient built its studios in Hazmieh, 15 km (24 ml) east of Beirut, and telecast one programme on two channels, 5 and 11 (Boyd 1993: 73). First transmissions began on 6 May 1962 (Boulos 1995: 113).

Despite efforts to increase revenue by producing programmes for export to the Arab world, financial problems plagued both CLT and Tele-Orient from the very beginning. Unable to compete successfully for both limited viewers and limited financial resources, the two organisations started to co-operate over advertising sales and sometimes even broadcast the same programme simultaneously. In 1968, Advision had become the sales agent for Tele-Orient as well as CLT, and in October 1972 Tele-Management was created to undertake all marketing and advertising sales for both television stations (Boyd 1993: 74).

Earlier, on 21 October 1967, CLT had modified its transmitters for French SECAM colour broadcasting, becoming the third television station in the world (after the Soviet Union and France) to introduce it. Meanwhile, Tele-Orient was preparing its transmitters to use the German PAL colour system (Rugh 2004: 196; Boulos 1995: 88).

Between 1972 and the outbreak of civil war in 1975, the television business seemed to stabilise. Both stations were returning a profit, and local production had increased because of the export market for

Lebanese taped television programmes. Both stations maintained a limited broadcasting schedule of only 6 hours a day (Boyd 1993; Boulos 1995).

In March 1976, the broadcast media became heavily involved in the disputes that were shortly to lead to civil war.[7] In the middle of the CLT evening Arabic newscast on 11 March 1976, a Lebanese army officer, Brigadier Aziz Al Ahdab, forced his way into the studios of Channel 7 and demanded airtime for 'Communiqué No. 1.'

> Owing to his status and his armed entourage, he was granted his wish. After televising the statement that proclaimed that he was the new ruler of Lebanon and stating that the president [Suleiman Franjieh] should resign, Al Ahdab moved to the Ministry of Information radio studios and broadcast what had been said on CTL. Thereupon he returned to CTL to supervise the French-language version of the communiqué on Channel 9. Employees of Tele-Orient, which had been transmitting the CTL Arabic program, immediately stopped transmissions after the statement was read. [Nonetheless,] Al Ahdab did not become an important force in the civil war, but he sparked a media war that had been avoided until that March evening.
> 
> (Boyd 1993: 76)

Hearing that these broadcasting facilities had been 'occupied' by Nationalist forces (mainly Muslims), supporters of the Maronite Christian president took control of Tele-Orient and the radio transmitters at Amsheet. Thus, each major warring group had a radio and a television outlet that could enthusiastically broadcast programming in support of its own side.

> Jacques Wakim occupied the screen in Al Hazmieh and was complimenting Franjieh's presidency while the presenters in Talet Al Khayat were praising the national movement's supporters.
> 
> (Boulos 1995: 126)

They were thus conflicting with each other, with contradictory news flashes and endless rounds of threats, insults, 'we shall overcome' speeches, patriotic songs and military marches being broadcast. Caught in the middle were the listeners and the viewers (Khoury, in

Boulos 1995: 76). It was not until a newly-elected president took power and the Arab peacekeeping force entered Lebanon in 1976 that the transmitters and studios were returned to their respective owners (ibid.).

It was on 23 September 1976 that Elias Sarkis became president. He was in deep need of a media outlet that would help promote his presidency and bring back peace and unity to the Lebanon after two years of civil war (Boulos 1995: 132). Radio Lebanon lost much of its audience after the establishment of the Phalangist radio station Voice of Lebanon in 1976. However, the government did not have the technical and financial capabilities to build its own television station (ibid.).

However, it happened that the two private television stations were facing very serious financial problems. They informed the government that they were threatened by bankruptcy and might stop operating. Both stations asked the government to consider an arrangement whereby the television system could be rebuilt (ibid.). A devastated economy, damaged transmitters and sections of the country without electricity for receivers had left both stations at a point where it was amazing that the stations were operating at all.

In late 1977, the two television organisations and their subsidiaries, Advision and Tele-Management, agreed to form a partnership with the Lebanese Government to create a single new national television station known as Tele Liban. The new organisation was half owned by the government, with the remaining half equally divided between the two private companies (Boyd 1993: 80).

## Tele Liban

On 7 July 1977, Legislative Decree No. 100 was published in the government's *Press Gazette* under the headline 'A licence was granted to establish a mixed company named Tele Liban, owned partly by the government and the private sector' (Boulos 1995: 133).

The company was formed 'to manage, organize and utilize the various television transmitting installations, and to undertake all commercial and television production tasks' (Dajani 2001). The new company was given a monopoly over television broadcasting in Lebanon until the year 2012. Tele Liban (TL) was to be managed by a board of twelve directors, six representing the Lebanese Government and six representing the two companies. The chairman of the board was to be appointed by the Lebanese Council of Ministers.

On 16 May 1977 a united news programme was broadcast from the studios in Hazmieh.

> John Khoury of Channel 5 [Hazmieh] began the prime time news bulletin on 16/5/77 by saying: 'I have good news for you'. The camera at that point zoomed out and two of Talet Al Khayat news presenters appeared at his side. Arafat Higazi of Channel 7 greeted the audience and said: 'A united news bulletin for a united country'.
>
> (Boulos 1995: 135)

Wissam Izeddine of CLT and Klaude Sawaya of Tele-Orient saw in Tele Liban's founding agreement two disastrous articles that could limit the company's development in the long run. Firstly, the appointment of TL's chairman by the government gave it the power to fire him or her merely for political reasons. Secondly, the appointment of a government commissioner on the TL board of directors was aimed in practice at reducing the board's freedom in decision making (Boulos 1995: 139).

While the formation of TL was obviously a sound step towards the creation of a national television system, several years of operation did not show any dramatic change from the two former privately-owned stations (Boyd 1993: 80), and the creation of TL did not improve public service. According to Dajani, the private sector in television now felt secure and free of the fear of losing its licence, since the government was now its partner (Dajani 2001). Lebanese officials were, on the other hand, content with their control of the overall management of this medium. They tended to focus on improving the physical aspects of broadcasting that had been wrecked by the war.

According to Boyd, William E. Osterhaus of Varitel Communications, San Francisco, California, spent several weeks in Beirut studying the Tele Liban operation, under a grant from the International Communication Agency (Boyd 1993). His October 1979 final report included 15 recommendations that could have provided a more solid basis for TL.

These included the suggestion that services such as Tele Liban 1, 2 and 3 be emphasised, rather than channels that were heavily identified with the previous ownership (7, 9, 5 and 11). Another recommendation suggested making one station site a transmission headquarters, the other production. Still another involved the elimination of the 'politically expedient but inefficient and disruptive practice' of switching weekly the origination of the main Arabic news programme between the former CTL and Tele-Orient studios (Osterhaus, 1979 in Boyd 1993: 81).

These recommendations were put aside and not taken into consideration, mainly because of the political and security instability Lebanon was witnessing. Israel had invaded parts of south Lebanon in March 1978 and declared them a 'security zone'. Israel's invasion deepened the division between Lebanese factions (see Chapter Four) and these divisions were reflected within TL operations.

## Tele Liban in the civil war

TL's situation became further complicated in July 1980. As a result of armed conflicts in east Beirut between two rival Christian factions – the Christian Phalangist Party and the National Liberal Party – Charles Rizk, the Tele Liban chairman, was kidnapped and held for several hours until he agreed to resign. He had refused to stop transmitting on one of the channels used by the Hazmieh (previously Tele-Orient) studio. The Phalange Party (Lebanese Forces) wanted to confiscate that channel to broadcast their own television programmes (Boyd 1993: 81).

On 6 June 1982 Israel invaded Lebanon, reaching Beirut. The second invasion widened the gap between those Lebanese who believed they were defending the country's independence by resisting the invaders and those who believed that Israeli forces could help them maintain their political supremacy over Lebanese soil (see Chapter Four). West Beirut was under siege for three months and during that time TL's news bulletin was broadcast from Hazmieh (Boulos 1995: 139).

On 6 February 1984 fierce fighting broke out again and the two channels produced two different news programmes. They were divided again in reality, if not on paper (ibid: 141). Each channel sided with the parties that dominated the area it was broadcast from.

TL's previously unified news staff was split and moved, primarily according to religious affiliation, so it was mainly Muslims who wrote the newscast from Channel 7 in West Beirut, while Christians generally wrote the simultaneous newscast from Channel 5 in Hazmieh. Audiences could easily tell the difference. Since both programmes were in Arabic, audiences could choose the news according to their political preference. With some irony, it could be said that the continuing bitter factional feuds in Lebanon helped maintain diversity in its media, but, as William Rugh suggested, this was 'at the price of even greater bias by individual broadcasting units' (Rugh 2004: 198).

As a result of the war, and following the realisation by warlords of the importance of broadcasting, other television channels began to emerge, representing the interests of the different warring factions (Fontan, in Sakr 2004: 167). The warring factions were encouraged by the deteriorating state of affairs in Lebanon and the further weakening of central government during the Amin Jumayyil presidency in the mid-1980s.

The Lebanese forces launched their own television station, known as the Lebanese Broadcasting Corporation, or LBC, which started broadcasting on 23 August 1985. The information minister at the time, Michael Samaha, took the company to court, because TL had a monopoly over the airwaves till 2012, but the civil war had weakened the judicial system in the country and the case never produced a judgment. LBC attracted many TL employees, and it was their expertise that started the new commercial company owned by the Lebanese forces (Boulos 1995: 141).

In the last 15 minutes of Amin Jumayyil's presidency in September 1988, Jumayyil signed a decree handing power to the leader of Lebanese army, General Michael Aoun. Acting Prime Minister Salim Al Hoss considered this step unconstitutional and announced himself the sole legal prime minister of Lebanon. The country's split was becoming deeper and so was the divide between the two Tele Liban channels. Hazmieh became the voice of General Aoun and the Talet Al Kahyat channel was now the voice of the Al Hoss government (ibid: 144).

## Tele Liban and the Taif Accord

The Taif Agreement, signed in 1989, supposedly marked the end of the civil war and presented a blueprint for national reconciliation (see Chapter Four). It recognised that the large number of unlicensed radio and television stations were a mixed blessing, as some of them did not comply with international rules and regulations governing the use of broadcast and reception equipment, channels and frequencies, and many lacked the techniques, methods and professional competences of modern media institutions.

The Taif Accord stated that the information media should be reorganised within the law and within the framework of responsible liberties that would serve moderate tendencies and the objective of ending the state of war. To address this, Audio-Visual Media Law No. 382 (discussed later in this chapter) came into existence five years later.

Meanwhile, General Michael Aoun refused to accept the Taif Accord and also refused to hand over the presidential palace to the newly-elected President Rene Mouad. By controlling the palace, he also controlled Tele Liban's Channels 5 and 11. On 22 November 1989, Rene Mouad, the first president to be elected after the reconciliation conference in Taif in Saudi Arabia (see Chapter Four), was assassinated and President Elias Hrawi was elected in his place. The Lebanese army was divided into those supporting Aoun and those supporting Hrawi.

On 31 January 1990 fighting erupted between the previous allies, Aoun and the Lebanese forces. To accompany their battles, Aoun (who opposed the Taif Accord) used Channels 5 and 11, and the Lebanese forces (who endorsed the Taif Accord) used LBC (Boulos 1995: 146). This lasted until 13 October 1990, when Aoun fled the presidential palace, first to the French Embassy in Beirut and then to France, after being attacked by Hrawi's army, backed by the Syrian army.

The information minister at the time, Edmond Rizk, met the directors of the Hazmieh channels and called upon them to accept the leadership of George Skaf, the TL chairman appointed by Hrawi and the Al Hoss government (ibid: 147). At that stage Tele Liban was reunified again and the need to reorganise the media scene in Lebanon had become a major talking point (ibid: 149).

As Jean-Claude Boulos (1995) pointed out, no audience in the early 1990s was as lucky as the audience in Lebanon. In Greater Beirut alone, the audiences could watch 17 channels, with their mix of different local and international programmes. Altogether, there were 54 television channels operating in Lebanon (1995: 151), though many of them served small geographic areas and operated from small flats with one transmitter.

Most important among these stations were LBC, which was the official organ of the Lebanese Forces, one of the major warring militias, and Al-Mashrek Television, which was established by Nationalist politicians opposed to the Maronite-Phalangist Party and the Lebanese Forces. Among the pirate stations at the time was New Television (NTV), which was established by the Lebanese Communist Party and later bought by an independent businessman.

Albert Mansour took over the Information Ministry from Rizk and started working on the new Audio-Visual Law. At the same time, he worked to bring TL back into one company. Most of Osterhaus' (1979) recommendations, mentioned earlier, were now implemented. The Talet Al Khayat building became TL's headquarters and the centre for news and current affairs programmes, while Hazmieh was allocated for other programming, such as entertainment and drama productions (Al Abed, interview with author, 2004).

## Tele Liban under Naim

Months before he became prime minister, Rafic Hariri bought TL's private-sector shares. In January 1993 Fouad Naim was appointed as TL chairman, and given the green light by the prime minister to improve TL transmission and production quality.

He immediately began to change TL from a shattered company into a first-rate television station. To achieve this, he unified the company logo and paid Saatchi & Saatchi (Lebanon division) to draw up a new look for the station. In the meantime, he introduced a new plan for the departments' structures. All news staff at Hazmieh were moved to Talet Al Khayat, while people working in drama production and entertainment programming at Talet Al Khayat were moved to Hazmieh (ibid.).

In 1994 the government took the decision to ban news and political programmes on all operating television stations in Lebanon except for TL. This decision came after some television channels participated in what the government sensed as provoking sectarian hatred, in the wake of Al Najat church explosion in Jounieh, 15 km (24 ml) north of Beirut, which killed 10 people at Sunday Mass.

In the same session, the government took the decision to buy all of TL's shares, so it would be completely owned by the government, and renewed Fouad Naim's chairmanship for another three years (Boulos

1995: 151). Naim was determined to turn TL into a public-service television station that would put the public interest ahead of that of the advertisers.

> When I was appointed as chairman I was totally convinced that TL had every chance to succeed. We had a rich shareholder, Rafic Hariri, who owned 50% of the company's shareholding. When Hariri became prime minister, I believed that TL had a better-than-ever chance to survive. Due to the hard efforts of both TL's new and old employees, in only three years TL became second in terms of viewer ratings in Lebanon and we were quickly heading towards the first position. Because TL belonged to none of the political parties or political figures in Lebanon, we were able to operate more freely, and without political constraints, though this led to the station closing down at a later stage. In fact none of the other political leaders cared because their own privately-funded television stations were operating and legally licensed.
> 
> (Naim, interview with author, 2004)

During 15 years of civil war, TL's journalists had been dragged into a state of being merely government employees, who came to work to sign in and then leave. More than 200 employees at the news department were employed to produce the half-hour news programme each day. According to Aref Al Abed, head of news during Naim's period, a new structure was introduced to produce four news programmes a day. The first one of the day was at 7.30am.

To make this early news programme run, journalists and technicians had to start their shifts by 4.00am, and so a decision was made to employ 'young enthusiastic journalists' to produce and present the morning news (Al Abed, interview with author, 2004). The news department was transformed in a short time into a 'veritable beehive', and TL's prime-time news soon gained second position in viewer ratings and was rapidly heading towards being number one (ibid.).

It can be argued that TL achieved this status through its response to the Israeli military operation[8] against Lebanon in April 1996, when it dedicated all airtime to live coverage of the events.

> TL achieved this prime position in television ratings during the April coverage. It happened that we had asked a statistics

company to conduct a study on TL viewership to identify our weaknesses and strengths at the time. The head of the company came back to us saying: 'You've gained the viewers' trust – even my wife and children wait for the breaking-news music of TL' to learn what was happening. Most of the people we interviewed said they switched to TL.

(Al Abed, interview with author, 2004)

Naim pointed out the fact that they had received 'very positive feedback from audiences all over Lebanon'. He stated that ratings went up to above 68 per cent of all audience viewing (Naim, interview with author, 2004). TL's superiority in covering the April events was also clearly documented in the Lebanese press (*Dalil Annahar*, 26 April 1996; *Al Sharek*, 27 April 1996; *L'Orient-Express*, issue of May 1996).

First we took the initiative before the other channels. We moved our transmission units to south Lebanon while others stayed in Beirut. What also characterised our coverage were the people who were working with us. They were more concerned with what was happening; they were active and more devoted. The quality of their production was much better than other journalists. TL's staff had less technical ability than the others, but the quality of our production was higher than our technical abilities. Competition was in the back of my mind all the time, though in events like this I did not think directly of the competition. All we thought about was: what was the best way to cover such a massive event? It appeared later that all the other channels were trying to follow what we did.

(Naim, interview with author, 2004)

Naim anticipated that TL would receive positive feedback from Lebanese audiences. He praised the performance of TL's journalists and employees, and the feedback their work received from the Lebanese public was not a surprise to him. Naim regarded television news as 'public service'. Casey and his colleagues (2002: 142) say that television news provides audiences with information about what apparently matters of worldly consequence and issues beyond audiences' immediate realm, and TL's news department was directed to do just that.

> It is my perception of the role of any media institution, to follow such a quick and effective response to events. We worked hard to move TL towards a public-service television model like that in some of the European countries. We achieved this goal to a large extent during our period. TL proved, more than at any other time, that it was a station that closely followed every aspect of Lebanese life. It had the ability to operate fast, take journalistic initiatives and be flexible. Later I felt sorry for what happened to TL. They did not allow it to grow bigger, to be more influential. Maybe we were scaring the competitive commercial channels.
>
> (Naim, interview with author, 2004)

Naim had asked the government for an increase in TL capital so the company would be able to keep moving forward, but the government took a decision in September 1996 to grant licences to five privately-owned television stations in accordance with Audio-Visual Law 382, ratified in 1994, and thus deprived TL of its monopoly over the airwaves without any compensation. The government accepted Naim's almost immediate resignation.

> They failed TL because there was no real understanding of what public-service television meant within the Lebanese political milieu. The excuse given at the time was 'What can a public-service broadcast station do that a commercial TV station cannot?' They were convinced that the state-run television was there to cover their activities. One minister said bluntly: 'Why have a state-run television if I can ask a commercial channel to cover my official and non-official activities? We don't need a public service broadcaster in Lebanon.' We used to tell them that television was not there just to make money. But these arguments were not understood in Lebanon.
>
> (Naim, interview with author, 2004)

Naim argued for freedom both from commercial interests and pressures and from state intervention. He was in favour of maintaining independence of expression. His understanding of public-service broadcasting thus matched that of the BBC. It is what Casey (2002: 185) and his colleagues see as 'a system that operates or is meant to operate in the public interest'. The public here is conceived as a 'national body of people' (ibid.).

However, in Lebanon the commercial television station was not seen an extension of public-service broadcasting, as in the UK (see ibid: 186), but as an alternative or replacement. Poignantly, with the lack of government financial support, TL was not able to compete with the commercial television stations. A few years later, the government took the decision to close down TL with the aim of 'restructuring' and 'streamlining' it. It was facing huge financial losses.

> Law 382/94 made Lebanon the first Arab state to authorise private radio and television stations to operate within its borders. This decision deprived the country's only non-confessional[9] station of a monopoly it had been promised would last until 2012. By licensing a total of six terrestrial stations, the law obliged Tele Liban to face five competitors in a country of just 4 million people [and] with a television advertising market that most people thought could support two or three stations at most.
>
> (Sakr 2001: 50)

The government decided initially to close for three months, but the closure lasted for several months after that. It was re-launched with 25 per cent of its old capacity-in terms of personnel, output and number of channels.

## Media Law 382

On 4 November 1994, the Lebanese Parliament adopted the Audio-Visual Law after four years of discussion. The law legalised channels already being broadcast illegally and introduced new ones, handing out licences on a confessional, political and geographic basis (ibid.).

As mentioned above, TL was deprived of its monopoly over the airwaves, with no compensation in return, although TL was exempted from the fees generally required from all other media outlets (*IIM*, issue 5, November 2002).

The law specified four categories for granting licences to privately-owned television and radio stations:

- Category One: Stations entitled to broadcast news and political programmes, among other programmes.

- Category Two: Stations permitted to transmit all programmes except news and political content.
- Category Three: Stations that broadcast coded signals, limited to subscribers.
- Category Four: Stations that broadcast via satellite and whose coverage extends beyond Lebanese territory. (ibid.)

The law required that stations apply for licences valid for 16 years, with categories One and Two paying higher licensing fees of LL 250 million[10] and an annual rent of LL 100 million (ibid). The licensing decision was made by the Council of Ministers, but a 10-member advisory body called the National Council of Audio-Visual Media was formed to review licensing applications and offer its opinion before submitting them to the council.

In terms of ownership, the law compels institutions to have nominal shares and prohibits any natural or legal person from owning more than 10 per cent of the company's equity (Boulos 1995: 308). Article 7 of Law 382 stated seven elements that the government could take into consideration when granting licences. Among these elements was the 'prohibition of transmitting any material that might encourage normalising the relationship with the Zionist enemy [meaning Israel]' (ibid: 308).

In February 1996 the government issued a complementary Decree No. 7997 based on Audio-Visual Law No. 382. The decree had been discussed previously and was enacted 15 months after it was passed.

> It was considered by many to be a restrictive law that banned stations from broadcasting news deemed to rouse sectarian or religious tensions, as seen in the eyes of the authorities, while others deemed it necessary considering the confessional and sectarian feuds in the country.
> (*IIM*, issue 5, November 2002)

Two years later, in accordance with Law 382, the cabinet decided on 17 September 1996 to legalise the most prominent of these television companies and grant them the special licence needed to broadcast news (Fontan, in Sakr 2004: 167). Four stations were legalised besides TL: the National Broadcasting Network (NBN), Future Television,

Murr Television (MTV) and the Lebanese Broadcasting Corporation International (LBC). The others were given a time limit of two months to liquidate their business.

According to Naomi Sakr, confessional thinking (based on sectarian loyalties and divisions) and the minimum number of constituencies that the government felt it needed to satisfy determined these decisions. Confessionalism[11] in broadcasting became institutionalised.

> Thus, besides Tele Liban, Maronite Christians were supposed to content themselves with LBC, Sunni Muslims with Future TV, Christian Orthodox with Murr TV and Shia Muslims with NBN.
> 
> (Sakr 2001: 51)

The sixth licence was eventually awarded to Al Manar TV, affiliated to Hezbollah, the Lebanese Shiite political group dedicated to resisting Israel's occupation of south Lebanon (ibid: 51). Al Manar was granted a licence as a 'resistance channel', which meant its licence would expire when the occupation ended. However, Al Manar was granted a full licence to operate as a national television station in 1997 after they were able to match the requirements mentioned in Law 382.

According to Naomi Sakr, this was only conceded after a political struggle in which Télé Lumière, an unlicensed Christian religious station, was allowed to continue broadcasting, 'supposedly to restore the delicate sectarian balance by providing a counterweight to Al Manar' (ibid.).

In 1999 the new government reconsidered the applications rejected by the previous government and consequently three more licences were granted. The stations receiving the new licences were ones that had opposed the former prime minister, Rafic Hariri. These were: New Television (NTV), in June, and the Independent Communication Channel International (ICNI) and United Television (UTV), in September. Both the latter channels had not resumed operations after they stopped transmissions in 1996 (Dajani 2001).

## Al Manar TV

Al Manar started its transmission on 4 June 1991 from a small apartment in the southern suburbs of Beirut. According to Al Manar's head of news, Hassan Fadlallah, they started transmitting six hours a day at most through a small transmitter that covered the southern suburbs of Beirut (Shames, *Assafir*, 24 December 2004).

The channel was brought to life by a group of enthusiastic young men (Krayem, *Assafir*, 28 December 2004), with the aim of spreading the resistance's message and accomplishments among the Lebanese public. As stated by both Krayem and Muhamad Haidar, chairman of Al Manar and member of Hezbollah's Political Bureau, they had started thinking of such a project as early as 1986.

> In the late eighties the Islamic resistance carried out operations that proved painful to Israeli positions in south Lebanon. The media coverage of these operations was weak, and the Israelis kept the killing of their soldiers in south Lebanon away from the Israeli and international media. They used to announce these killings after a day or two, saying that the soldiers had, for instance, died in a car accident. It was then that we decided that we needed our own publicity tool to uncover the Israeli lies. Thus, we started thinking of establishing our own television and radio stations.
> 
> (Haidar, interview with author, 2003)

Hassan Fadlallah revealed that the first resistance videotape was broadcast on Tele Liban's Channel 7 in 1986. However, as soon as Al Manar was launched, the tapes were sent to the newly established channel. From then on, Al Manar gained its reputation of being the 'resistance channel' (Shames, *Assafir*, 24 December 2004). Nevertheless, this reputation was confined to the small area its broadcasts then reached.

Between 1991 and 1996 Al Manar was developing its technical abilities and transmission powers. In September 1996 the government granted Al Manar a temporary licence as 'the resistance station'. The duration of the Al Manar licence was tied to the ending of the Israeli occupation. According to Krayem, that was an official admission by the government of the role Al Manar was playing and of the need for such a channel to portray resistance heroism and achievements until the liberation of the occupied territories in south Lebanon (Krayem, *Assafir*, 28 December 2004).

> There had to be a TV station that committed itself to bringing out images of the suffering of our people in the

occupied territories, the victims of Israeli arrogance, and that of those living in areas bordering the occupation who suffer its semi-daily aggressions, besides focusing on the resistance activity and establishing its role, hoping to formulate a resistant nation governed by justice and equality. Thus, Al Manar saw the light of day.

(Al Manar website, accessed 2 May 2000)

The Al Manar mission statement indicates the 'propagandistic nature' of the channel. It was founded on the basis of propagating resistance activities and displaying images of Israeli atrocities in south Lebanon. Thus Al Manar TV was established as the resistance's media tool in its fight with the Israeli army. Television is a popular media form that is constructed as an ordinary medium that fits with everyday life (Casey et al. 2002: 88). Al Manar, as its mission statement indicates, wanted the resistance struggle to be part of people's everyday lives.

Meanwhile, Al Manar worked on fulfilling the legal, structural, financial and technical demands needed to obtain a licence to operate as a privately owned commercial general television station. The Lebanese Media Group (LMG) was established, with shareholders from different Lebanese religious sects (both Muslim and Christian).[12] In July 1997, Al Manar and Radio Al Nour[13] were granted full licences under the name of LMG, but it was not legally registered until November 1998 (Krayem, *Assafir*, 28 December 2004).

After they were granted official full licences, Al Manar's offices were turned into several training workshops to equip the staff with the most developed techniques in media production. Many Al Manar journalists and technicians were sent on training courses in France, Syria, Iran and Egypt. Later the television station signed an agreement with the French Thomson Company to equip Al Manar with the latest technologies (ibid.).

By 1997 Al Manar's terrestrial channel was able to reach Lebanon in its entirety, as well as parts of occupied Palestine and Syria, and it broadcast 18 hours a day. It was preparing to launch a satellite channel, which came on air on 25 May 2000, the day south Lebanon was liberated (Haidar, interview with author, 2003).

By fielding an increasingly effective media team to videotape the general situation in the South and the daily attacks launched against the enemy, Hezbollah's television station, al-Manar, became the favoured source of information for those who wanted to closely follow events in the South. While other Lebanese broadcasters and foreign television journalists could only record Israeli/Hezbollah skirmishes from safe positions well behind the lines, Hezbollah cameramen, as noted above, often filmed right at the confrontation point.

(Harik, 2004, 133)

Since obtaining its licence from the government in 1997, the channel has increased its audience share to more than 15 per cent of the Lebanese people, from all groups of society. Krayem and other Lebanese officials stated that the channel has been declared the third most-watched television channel in Lebanon (Fontan, in Sakr 2004: 177–8):

> By welcoming speakers from all sectors of the Lebanese population onto its programmes, Al Manar has tried to identify itself as a television channel fostering inter-sectarian collaboration. Of importance when taking into account the television ratings for the whole of Lebanon is the predominance of Al Manar as a substitution channel, not constantly watched by non-Hezbollah viewers, but frequently consulted for specific programmes, especially the news.

(ibid: 178)

Al Manar succeeded in achieving this position by portraying a television message of inter-sectarian collaboration against a common Israeli enemy (ibid: 179).

## Conclusion

By the time TL's 'superiority' in responding to major events in south Lebanon was declining, Al Manar's star was rising. Al Manar continued the role TL had played, mainly during the April 1996 events, and on a daily basis.

The government in both cases used their media coverage as support for its political stance inside Lebanon and in the international arena. The government refused to abide by American and Israeli pressure to deprive the 'Islamic resistance' of its weapons and insisted that the resistance had the right to fight as long as the occupation continued. The April understanding that the government achieved with Israel – under the auspices of the United States, France and Syria, in April 1996 – stated clearly that the resistance had the right to conduct operations against the Israeli army in the occupied territories of south Lebanon.

This stance legitimised the resistance and its media at the national level. Accordingly, the government granted Al Manar a licence as a 'national resistance channel'. The 'Islamic resistance' gained, in the wake of the April 1996 aggressions and the first Qana massacre,[14] the nation's support. All sects and religious groups in Lebanon, and not just Shiite Muslims, showed solidarity with the resistance.

The next chapter, using an ethnographic approach, explores the events of April 1996 and how TL journalists covered those events. The aim is to identify the relationship between TL journalists' war reporting and propaganda principles and techniques. To achieve this, I investigate TL's news production processes and 'product'.

# 6

# TELE LIBAN COVERAGE, APRIL 1996: GRAPES OF UNITY FACING GRAPES OF WRATH

On 11 April 1996, Israel launched a massive military operation against Lebanon, code-named Grapes of Wrath,[1] claiming it was 'an open war' against Hezbollah's guerrilla fighters. However, its missiles targeted power stations, water supplies, bridges and civilian areas in Beirut and throughout the southern villages of Lebanon.

The operation lasted 16 days, yet Hezbollah remained intact. Israeli bombs and missiles killed and injured hundreds of civilians, among them children, women and elderly people.[2] The war displaced more than 400,000 people from their homes and damaged newly-reconstructed Lebanese infrastructure, mainly roads and power stations. In addition, the Israeli army destroyed houses in several villages, flattening them and burning fields of wheat and tobacco, depriving villagers of their main way of making a living (see *Assafir*, 11 to 26 April 1996, and Tele Liban news coverage 11 to 27 April 1996). During this operation Israel perpetrated five massacres, in Suhmur, Al Jmiajmeh, Mansouri, Nabatiyeh and Qana.

The Israeli army described its operations as 'surgical', whereas the Lebanese Government considered them as unacceptable aggression against its own sovereignty, and called on the international community to put pressure on Israel to stop its hostile attacks against Lebanon. Resistance leaders (mainly Hezbollah) declared the resistance would retaliate and would not stop its operations against Israel until Israeli forces withdrew from the occupied territories in south Lebanon (see *Assafir*, 11 to 26 April 1996, and Tele Liban news coverage, 11 to 27 April 1996). Lebanon at the time was still recovering from 15 years of civil war, which had destroyed its economy and divided both land and people (see Chapter Four). One of the public institutions that was then reunited and was trying to establish itself as a public-service media organisation was Tele Liban (TL) (see Chapter Five).

Part of south Lebanon and some nearby villages of the western Bekaa district were still occupied (known as 'the occupied zone' since the 1982 invasion – see Chapter Four), and news of Israeli attacks on Lebanese people and the resistance operations against Israeli troops was given priority on most television channels operating at the time. This news was prominent on TL, which was trying to establish itself as a public-service television station rather than just a government mouthpiece that put the authorities' voice ahead of the public's (Naim, interview with author, 2004).

This chapter presents part of this researcher's own story – an ethnographic account of TL's coverage during the Grapes of Wrath operation. To aid the structure and flow of the narrative, it consists of a self-reflexive narration and chronological analysis of 16 days of events and television coverage of major military incursions. The narration is based on 40 hours of TL prime-time news between 11 and 26 April 1996.

As suggested earlier, the methodology of this chapter is necessarily that of self-reflexive fieldwork, containing first-person narration. It presents the performance of TL journalists, including myself, during this period and examines it in relation to theories and norms introduced in Chapters Two and Three. It is a personal diary of the April 1996 events, produced by transcribing and translating prime-time television news archive and head-notes (memories brought up by watching the news coverage).[3] The narration is supported by interviews with most of the TL journalists and administrators who were directly involved in the April 1996 coverage. It is also aided by press archives. Drawing on the theoretical framework discussed in Chapters Two and Three, this chapter also aims to outline the news values and norms that characterised the work of Lebanese journalists in their coverage of events of April 1996 and to assess the impact of the historical, social and religious context on the way they operated.

Finally, this chapter tries to indicate or pinpoint features and performance related to the concepts and principles of propaganda presented in Chapter Two.

The story starts on 11 April 1996, when the first Israeli bomb hit a yard near Beirut international airport.

## Day one: Thursday 11 April 1996

On the first day of Operation Grapes of Wrath, Israel bombarded the southern suburbs of Beirut for the first time since 1982 and at the same time launched an aerial bombardment on several positions in south Lebanon. According to Fouad Naim, chairman of TL (1992–6), and Aref Al Abed, TL's head of news (1993–7), the scale of the bombardment and the 'intimidating statements' of Israeli officials – threatening to target the recently reconstructed infrastructure in Beirut and adjacent cities – meant that these attacks were not like previous ones. Al Abed believed it could be the beginning of an unlimited, wider operation:

> We were working and preparing our TV channel to be the best in the country. Taking that into consideration, I was asking myself whether we should just count on our correspondents in the south to shoot stories and send them with a driver to the headquarters in Beirut and risk the road trip delay or should we move a live transmission unit south and have live coverage. I consulted with the chairman, Fouad Naim, and we decided to transmit live from south Lebanon.
> (Al Abed, interview with author, 2004)

The decision was made, and preparations to establish an outside broadcast unit in south Lebanon were under way.

## Day two: Friday 12 April 1996

On that day Israeli aggression reached its peak in Suhmur,[4] where nine civilians were killed when Israeli jets bombed their house. Among the dead were women and children.

In addition, the Israeli army forced the inhabitants of 50 south Lebanon villages adjacent to the occupied zone (which Israel called the 'security zone') to leave their homes under threat of heavy bombardment. People were therefore fleeing their villages and heading towards the cities of Tyre and Sidon.[5] Israeli bombardment and air raids continued intensively and there was no sign the aggression would stop in the near future (*Assafir*, 13 April 1996).

> It seems Israel has taken the green light from the White House to proceed with its hostile attacks against Lebanon. The White House spokesman Michael McCary said Hezbollah is to be blamed for committing what he called 'some acts' that made it difficult to maintain peace and stability in south Lebanon and northern Israel. He added that the best solution is for Hezbollah to stop what he called 'provocative activities' against Israel... Prime Minister Rafic Hariri has repeated his statement that the solution to this vicious circle is for Israel to withdraw from south Lebanon.
> (TL news, 19:30, 12 April 1996)

The Lebanese army used TL prime-time news as a platform to circulate a coded message calling upon particular personnel to move to their positions. The message was first on the running order after the headlines; the news presenter read it out and then repeated it word for word. It read:

> In the wake of the attacks on the Lebanese army positions, the army's leadership is asking all military personnel that belong to 'K' units to join their military position immediately. I repeat...
> (TL news, 19:30, 12 April 1996)

This is practically what Merton (in Jackall 1995) refers to as a 'symbolic act'. Merton explains that 'propaganda of the deed proved persuasive among some who rejected propaganda of the word'. He states that 'listeners who revealed their profound distrust of the 'power of speech' were moved by the symbolic act' (Merton, in Jackall 1995: 263).

What the Lebanese army did was a symbolic act. The Lebanese army lacked communications resources (see Iskandar 2006: 59), and thus it used the media to call upon its troops to be on high alert and join their positions. This was also an act meant to tell the public that the Lebanese army was on the same side as the resistance movement. It was a statement indicating that the army takes Israel's intimidation and attacks as acts of aggression against Lebanon's sovereignty and national dignity, and that the army stands shoulder to shoulder with Hezbollah as a resistance movement in fighting the occupation.

## Day three: Saturday 13 April 1996

On the third day of the Israeli operation, an OB (Outside Broadcast) van with an anchor–producer (myself), a reporter (Nadine Majzoub), a cameraman (Mahmoud Jalloul), a director (Safi Al Aris) and two members of the technical team set off south to Sidon – *Saida* in Arabic, 48 km (30 ml) south of Beirut. It is the largest city in south Lebanon and known as the 'gateway city' to the south. Aref Al Abed described the first team who agreed to go to south Lebanon as suicidal. He said they all agreed to take the mission without question, even though they were aware of the dangers of heading south (interview with author, 2004).

According to Chairman Fouad Naim, the motives for such a decision were merely professional and the people who were chosen to carry out the coverage were also chosen for merely professional reasons.

> With an event like this, even if it had no patriotic aspects or national connotations to us as a company, I would still have taken the same decision to offer our audiences full and detailed coverage. If we were operating in a different country, and an event like this took place, I would have given it the same priority. If I was still the head of Agence France-Presse [AFP] in the region, as I used to be, and this happened in Lebanon or even in Israel, if the Lebanese invaded Israel and I was in Tel Aviv, I would have made the same decision. The bonus for us here was that we were part of this nation. The attacks were affecting us and our own people's lives.
> 
> (Naim, interview with author, 2004)

Naim was making reference here to the newsworthiness of such events, an aspect that matches the recency, immediacy and currency that Roscho (in Tumber 1999) said should be the criteria for assessing a news story for broadcasting or publication (see Chapter Three).

Our team was supposed to set up the technical equipment and then broadcast from the Sidon government compound. The TL chief editor at the time, Wasef Awada, explains that this site was chosen because of previous experience.

> In July 1993 Israel launched a military operation against Lebanon for seven days [and] on a smaller scale. We situated our live transmission in [this] compound in Sidon for safety reasons and we thought that those reasons were still valid. We could not have found a better location. In addition, the technical team was familiar with every aspect of the place, so setting up the live transmitters and connecting them to the outside broadcast van's control room would not take much time.
>
> (Awada, interview with author, 2004)

Thus, around four o'clock that afternoon, the latest developments of what we called the 'Israeli aggressive operation' against south Lebanon were covered live, minute by minute, from Sidon.

Among the stories that we broke from Sidon that afternoon was the Mansouri massacre. A missile hit an ambulance carrying families escaping the fire towards a safer place, a few metres (yards) away from a UN checkpoint near Mansouri, a coastal village. The massacre was accompanied by an Israeli announcement of their operation's code name.

> The third day of aggression, code-named by the 'Israeli computer' the Grapes of Wrath operation, exploded with hate and hit children and new-born babies inside ambulances. The occupation forces committed a massacre today when its air fighters attacked an ambulance. Six of the passengers were killed; among them were two children and a newborn baby. Eight of the ambulance passengers were injured. For more details, we go live to Zahera Harb in South Lebanon.
>
> (Al Ashi, TL news, 19:30, 13 April 1996)

Details of when, how and where were given, accompanied by images of the ambulance victims in Najem hospital's morgue, in the nearby city of Tyre, beside images of critically injured children lying in hospital moaning and crying. Names of the victims were announced too. However, one victim remained unknown:

> The body of a newborn baby was brought to hospital in Sidon. It is said to be one of the ambulance victims, but no one has been able to identify her full name yet, so she was registered as baby X.
> 
> (Harb, TL news, 19:30, 13 April 1996)

I remember that evening. I was full of fury, anger and sadness, but tried to be as calm as I could while presenting the story to Lebanese audiences. Being professional, at that point, meant that I should reveal all aspects of the Israeli attack on civilians and powerless villagers. Professional journalistic norms of objectivity and neutrality did not necessarily collide with my sympathetic reporting of the victims. Bringing factual images to my audiences and pin-pointing the scale of the Israeli aggression were clear objectives to me. I was clearly on the side of the victims, and it was not just that day's events that guided my position, but also a history of Israeli oppression and aggression against Lebanese and Palestinian people (presented in Chapter Four), some of which I had lived through before I became a journalist.

On that day, I realised I had two tasks to fulfil, as a journalist with access to information, sources and audiences: to report and inform, and to help. However, looking back at the coverage, a critic would say that our coverage was not impartial, and the truth we were seeking was 'positioned', because we made no attempt (did not even consider trying) to interview Israeli officials or spokespersons. However, as Lebanese journalists, we were operating within a certain political and legal context – Lebanese law prohibits contacts between Lebanese citizens and Israelis, including journalists. Thus, we were using sound bites and statements the Israelis had given to international news agencies. Besides, talking to the 'enemy' was not seen as a necessity; instead, it was seen as an act of treason and would be detrimental to the safety of Lebanon.

Thus, from 13 April 1996, Tele Liban became the voice of the southerners, both those who stayed and those who escaped and took refuge in other parts of the country. Our air time was open to refugees appealing for news of those whom they had left behind or who had moved on and whose whereabouts were unknown. Hospitals, civil defence centres, aid organisations, government officials, the Lebanese army leadership and resistance leaders were all treating TL as a nationwide communications channel.

One example is a communiqué issued by Hezbollah (the main resistance group) on the eve of 13 April 1996, after an earlier statement threatening the Israeli Government that the resistance was going to 'retaliate against its aggression, inside and outside Lebanon':

> Secretary General of Hezbollah Assayed Hassan Nasrallah has just declared a state of alert among Hezbollah militants and calls for the martyrdom regiment to join its positions immediately.
> 
> (AlAshi, TL news, 19:30, 13 April 1996)

This communiqué carried two messages: one for the Lebanese people, the audience, and one for the Israeli Government. It indicated that the Lebanese resistance would not stand still and watch the Israelis commit atrocities and that, if the Israelis decided to expand their occupation to other parts of south Lebanon, the resistance militants were ready to use their bodies as weapons to fight them. It aimed at assuring southerners that the resistance would not stand still in response to their suffering, but would also spread fear among the Israelis.

What distinguished this communiqué is that it was issued by what Hatem calls the 'leader symbol' (Hatem 1974: 81). Assayed[6] Hassan Nasrallah, the Secretary General of Hezbollah, was that symbolic leader whose high credibility carried weight not only among Lebanese, but also among some Israelis. Efrat Abraham, sister of an Israeli soldier captured by the resistance from inside the occupied territories, told *Maariv*, the Israeli daily, that for herself and her family Nasrallah was more credible than any of the Israeli leaders (translated from Hebrew in *Assafir*, 26 March 2001). Notably, during the April events, two leaders came to be symbolic: one was Nasrallah and the second was the prime minister at the time, Rafic Hariri, who led the political negotiations with world leaders to stop the Israeli assault, as this chapter will show.

Throughout the day we were guiding refugees where best to head, to public schools and other public buildings that were preparing to receive them, mainly in Sidon and Beirut. At the same time our correspondents in Tyre and Nabatiyeh were interviewing civilians who had decided to stay, despite the Israeli threats. Two reports from

Nabatiyeh and two from Tyre, each about three minutes, explained the 'strong will of those inhabitants who are committed to their land and would never submit it to the enemy' (TL news, 19:30, 13 April 1996). We ran sound bites from the villagers saying: 'Where shall we go? We are not going to leave our houses for the Israelis. We were born here and we will die here'. Such sound bites were repeated by villagers interviewed elsewhere for prime-time news.

We set up a small radio-monitoring unit in Sidon, to keep an ear on news from Israel's Arabic radio station and that of the Israeli collaborators – Lahed (see Chapter Four for information on who the collaborators were). Israel's Arabic radio and the Lahed station were putting out warning communiqués to the inhabitants of south Lebanon to evacuate their villages within a certain time, threatening that the Israeli army would raze their villages to the ground (Communiqué No. 4, Lahed Radio, 13 April 1996). We wanted to be aware of all these intimidations in order to draw people's attention to them in our coverage and be able to help them if they decided either to leave or to stay.

Looking back at what happened, I realise that Israel was using these communiqués to cause panic among the southern population to make them flee their villages, thus putting pressure on the resistance and the government to respond to Israeli demands to stop resistance operations in the occupied territories in south Lebanon. Accordingly, we were presenting the communiqués and then showing how people were not responding to Israeli pressures. We had news packages about how people were steadfast in their towns and villages, refusing to obey Israeli army orders.

> We established an open line between the newsroom in Beirut and our colleagues in Sidon, co-ordinating and exchanging information. The only thing we asked our colleague Zahera Harb to do in the first 24 hours of the coverage was to focus more on the people who decided to stay steadfast in their villages and towns rather than those who were leaving. We did not want to be accused by the Lebanese authorities of encouraging people to flee their villages. We did not want people to leave their land, but, at the same time, we felt responsible for informing residents about the Israeli warning statements.
>
> (Al Abed, interview with author, 2004)

Apart from this request, there was no editorial guidance on how and what to report from the field. It was up to the anchor–producer in Sidon to decide where to send camera crews. During the 16 days of military operations, the anchor–producers were guided by what was happening on the ground. The anchor–producer and the head of news used to conduct daily discussions over the phone about the running order of the prime-time news programme and how to distribute air time between the studio in Beirut and that in Sidon. All the anchor–producer who operated from Sidon and were interviewed for this study emphasised that there was no need of any editorial guidance on what and how to report. They were aware of what rhetoric to use. As mentioned earlier, they were operating with all the historical, political and legal aspects of the conflict with Israel in mind. For all of them Israel was 'the enemy' that was aiming to destroy their country.

Similarly, Fouad Naim (TL chairman) and Aref Al Abed (TL head of news) asserted that no Lebanese officials interfered in TL's decision to conduct live coverage from south Lebanon.

> Even though I had a good relationship with the prime minister, neither he nor any of his entourage interfered politically in what we broadcast and what we did not. As I said before, we were dealing with an enemy of the nation and the scale of events was enormous. The Lebanese politicians were busy looking into what Israel was doing and the scale of its operation.
> (Naim, interview with author, 2004)

One example of how certain events dictated air time priorities was the Mansouri village massacre near Tyre. Our first day of live coverage was marked by the horrifying images of the ambulance massacre mentioned earlier.

Reuters' reporter and camerawoman in south Lebanon, Najla Abou Jahjah, was filming the ambulance going by when an Israeli helicopter hit it with two missiles. A few seconds later, she filmed a father carrying two heavily bleeding children in his hands calling for help. Abou Jahjah managed to get to the hit vehicle where victims were still inside. The scene was dreadful, bodies of children, young girls and women were lying inside the smashed ambulance – some were still alive and moaning. Abou Jahjah focused her camera on a little girl full of dust and blood, calling her aunt in a low weak voice. The voice of the little girl was mixed with the sound of the ambulance windscreen wipers, still moving right and left on the dusty, broken windscreen.

Abou Jahjah's footage was broadcast unedited on TL from Sidon from 20:30 that evening, when Reuters decided to release it. She told TL six days later that she did not expect the missiles to hit the ambulance.

> The camera was rolling and I could see one of the girls opening her eyes. She looked at us and then lost consciousness. Another two girls were crying and moaning. I decided at that point to stop filming and went to call for help. I rushed to the nearby UN checkpoint and asked for help, but they were afraid to leave their position. It took them 15 minutes to join the father in trying to rescue his children.
>
> (Abou Jahjah, interview with author, 5/7, TL, 19 April 1996)

Abou Jahjah said that this filled her full of the anger of frustration at not being able to do anything. She tried to stay calm, but she couldn't; she was terrified, and anger was growing inside her towards the Israelis and towards the UN soldiers who did not rush to help with the rescue. Thus, her images came out as graphic close-ups of children's bodies.

Those images were a good tool for uniting the Lebanese people in hating the Israeli military machine that had caused this calamity. Goebbels states that propaganda to the home front needs to specify the targets of hatred (Doob 1995: 214). Abou Jahjah's images were a good tool in fulfilling this principle. The scenes of the massacre were too shocking for the anchor in TL studios in Beirut, Zaven Kouyoumdjian, who could not hold back his tears after showing the images and broke down in tears on air.

Israeli 'aggression', as it was called by all Lebanese media outlets, including TL, was escalating. The coverage from Sidon had to be extended to cover most of the 24 hours and, since Sidon did not have any hotels at the time, we had to sleep in Hammoud hospital near our transmission point. A bond was growing with local people. When we announced on air two days later that the TL team in Sidon was sleeping at Hammoud hospital, we had people from the neighbourhood coming to our transmission position and inviting us to sleep in their houses instead of the hospital.

Our coverage helped to achieve solidarity among the general public. Mervi Pantti and Jan Wieten describe how the media play an important role in managing emotions and repairing social life during tragedies. They state that the 'media can, for instance, actively contribute to turning a climate of anxiety and fear into one of restored morale and unification' (Pantti and Wieten 2005: 304). Our coverage helped to restore morale and unity. Something similar happened later with American news-magazine coverage of the events of September 11. Kitch has described in a study of American news magazines' reporting of September 11 how the lasting story of that day was not one of terror, death and destruction, but one of courage, redemption and patriotic pride (Kitch 2003: 222). Thus, coverage transformed the negative feeling of fear into the positive feeling of courage and patriotism.

## Day four: Sunday 14 April 1996

The next day, TL transformed itself from a channel that broadcast entertainment and news into a channel that broadcast only news, alongside social and political programmes that dealt with these serious events. The format of coverage was set: the airwaves were open for the anchor in Sidon[7] to feed the nation with any development taking place in the south, even if it was a small detail.

At the same time an anchor in Beirut would be ready, 24 hours a day, for any breaking news on the political, diplomatic and military fronts in other parts of the country. The airwaves were also open to refugees who wanted to send messages to their families or to ask for aid supplies. TL air time was also available, either through TL journalists or directly, for NGOs and government officials who wanted to guide the refugees on where to go and what to do.

On this second day of coverage, we felt that our responsibility towards our people was growing. The reasons were not just professional, but also national, as Nadine Majzoub explains:

> I tried to cover villages' bombardment as it was happening.
> I was always looking for the strong and expressive shots.

Personally, I did not use emotional words; shots, most of the time, were more expressive. And I always thought that telling what was really happening with a good shot (image) is better than using emotional and subjective words. I focused on one thing: a war was going on and the viewer had the right to see what was happening. Our main concern was to be accurate and communicate the true nature of the Israeli aggression.

(Nadine Majzoub, interview with author, 2004)

Nadine feels that what guided her performance was mere journalistic professionalism. However, in the words quoted she admits focusing on certain images that would reveal 'the real aggressiveness' of the Israeli army. She was not subjective with the language she used, but with the images she picked. Nevertheless, Nadine believes that what she has done did not collide with objectivity as a journalistic norm. She tends to relate objectivity to being factual, as other reporters and producers of the April events did.

One other thing that Nadine's words reveal is the difficulty of detaching yourself as a war reporter from the context (whether geographical, cultural, social or humanitarian) in which you are reporting. This relates to the concept of contextual objectivity, discussed in Chapter Three and illustrated later in this chapter. Similarly, the difficulty of detachment, especially when there are civilian victims, has been expressed by other war reporters like Kate Adie and Martin Bell, who questions the notion of objectivity in wartime. Adie says that, once you have to face the horrific realities of a conflict, 'any belief that the journalist can remain distant, remote, or unaffected by what is happening tends to go out the window in a hurry' (Adie 1998: 44).

The importance of images – as an effective tool to gain the solidarity of the rest of the nation with the people of south Lebanon – was recognised by all TL reporters and producers without any direct guidance. All the material gathered by our correspondents and reporters from their daily tours and visits to villages, towns and cities would end up in the Sidon governmental compound, where we established our centre of operation. We would run all footage live without editing, as soon as it arrived at the transmission centre in Sidon, and after that edit and package it into 3-minute reports for prime-time news. In the case of severe human casualties or brutal destruction, the images were run without editing, even on prime-time news – which might be extended from half an hour to two and sometimes three hours for this purpose. Lebanon's broadcast media at that time were still operating without any regulation, charters or codes (see Chapter Five on the media scene in Lebanon).

Showing graphic images of injured bodies was seen as natural and necessary to reveal the 'true nature' of the Israeli aggression – and during the 15 years of civil war, from 1975 to 1990, Lebanese broadcasting journalists had adopted the use of shattered bodies on the screen as normal. All journalists interviewed for this research believed that by broadcasting such graphic images they were communicating the 'real' situation on the ground to the Lebanese and wider Arab public. The 'reality' they were referring to was similar to what Durham and Singer referred to in their analysis of journalists' coverage of Hurricane Katrina. They stated that the reality that journalists report in the time of crisis is a 'shared interpretation of reality within the larger social context of the news environment' (Durham and Singer 2006: 6).

Soon after we started our live coverage we began receiving phone calls from besieged villagers, informing us of what was happening in their villages. We took their numbers and started calling them back, to clarify (or contrast with) news from Radio Israel (state-owned Arabic service) or Lahed Radio (owned by SLA and was transmitting from the occupied zone) on the situation in their villages. They became our citizen journalists. Some of these voluntary reporters, when they were not able to stay any longer in their village or town, passed our numbers on to other villagers and townsfolk who stayed behind. They would put them in touch with us before they left.

This way we were kept informed of what was happening to them and to the people who stayed in the village. We were able to identify the kind of aid they needed and the appeals they wanted to bring up on national television. One example of the appeals we broadcast ran as follows:

> We want to repeat the appeal by the people of Nabatiyeh[8] to the administration of the Power Company in the area. They want the power supply cut off from the high-voltage cables that feed the city. Israeli missiles cut the wires down and they

are lying on the streets. The streets are highly dangerous and the residents are not able to leave their houses.

(Harb, TL news, 19:30, 14 April 1996)

Some of those people had to leave their city later, to head for a safer place. They stopped and introduced themselves to us in Sidon before they continued their journey to their refuge destination.

Meanwhile, Israeli attacks on the fourth day of Operation Grapes of Wrath were escalated, as was the resistance retaliation – as the headlines of that day's prime-time news read:

> The Israeli aggression against Lebanon has exceeded the limits and recorded the largest amount of air raids on Lebanese soil since 1982.
>
> Israel has evacuated inhabitants from the area south of the Litani River, and more than 100,000 citizens have fled Tyre.
>
> Israeli aerial bombardment targets power stations in Beirut, the southern suburb of the city and the Bekaa valley in east Lebanon.
>
> The resistance records the largest missile attack on northern Israeli settlements in the history of the Arab–Israeli conflict.
>
> (Headlines, TL news, 19:30, 14 April 1996)

The Lebanese authorities were on high alert. The Lebanese High Relief Committee held open meetings, led by Deputy Prime Minister Michel Al Murr. The president of the republic, Elias Hrawi, had open meetings with cabinet ministers. House speaker Nabih Beri chaired a meeting of the parliamentary committees of defence and foreign affairs. Prime Minister Hariri started a diplomatic tour to Damascus, Cairo, Saudi Arabia, Morocco, Paris and London, calling for intervention by these governments to put pressure on Israel to stop its aggression. Hariri summarised for international media representatives Lebanon's position on what was happening:

> What Israel is doing will not lead to a solution, and, despite our own opinion of Hezbollah, Israel is occupying our land. Yet Hezbollah is leading the resistance, and what Israel wants from us is to fight the resistance on its behalf and that will

not happen. The solution lies in political negotiations that are based on Israeli withdrawal from the occupied zone in South Lebanon.

(Hariri, interview with CNN, TL news,
19:30, 14 April 1996)

The Minister of Information Farid Makari called on all local, Arabic and international media organisations to keep on reporting and revealing what he called 'the barbaric nature of the Israeli aggression against Lebanon'. He emphasised that reporting accurately and objectively what was happening could achieve this.

This position was portrayed in our coverage without receiving any political guidance from any of the government officials. All the journalists who were part of the coverage and interviewed for this research made such assertions, as did the key figures on the TL administration board in similar interviews. Their assertions coincide with my own memory of how we were running the coverage at the time. Israel was the enemy and Hezbollah fighters were resistance fighters. News priority was given to the casualties of Israeli aggression; and the resistance rockets shelling the northern Israeli settlements were presented as retaliation and revenge for the victims of Israeli aggression.

Lebanon, which had been torn apart during 15 years of civil war (see Chapter Four) was coming together for the first time and started to function as a unified civil society (Iskandar 2006: 73). Lebanon's Christian Maronite Cardinal, Mar Nasrallah Boutros Sfeir, called on all Lebanese to stick together in this crisis and 'help their brothers and sisters who are suffering in south Lebanon in every possible way' (Sfeir, TL news, 19:30, 14 April 1996). He asked the international community to help Lebanon survive the aggression. Churches were open throughout the country to receive the displaced. Similarly, Lebanese Muslim leaders made such appeals, and mosques were open to receive refugees, besides public schools and public universities. All of this was portrayed and reported on TL, thus making its screen 'linking the nation', which became one of the mottos of the coverage.

> Besieged families in the central sector are calling, through Tele Liban, on the government and all humanitarian

organisations to support them with food and water via the International Red Cross and UN troops. Many of the families are taking refuge inside the UNIFIL positions near their villages. Among these are 200 families taking refuge in the UN headquarters in Qana.

(Harb, TL news, 19:30, 14 April 1996)

Similarly to what was mentioned earlier, we started broadcasting interviews with refugees who regretted leaving their houses. For example:

> Anchor: Israeli bombs are chasing refugees from south Lebanon to Beirut and its southern suburbs.
>
> Refugee, surrounded by her crying children: 'I regret fleeing my village; I prefer dying there and not being homeless like this.'
>
> (TL news, 19:30, 14 April 1996)

We also broadcast news reports on villages and cities that the Israeli army had threatened would 'be bombed if not evacuated', highlighting the fact that people were refusing to leave their homes despite the Israeli threats.

## Day five: Monday 15 April 1996

On the fifth day of the attacks, Israeli threats and actions grew. They bombed the second largest power station in Lebanon, in a Christian neighbourhood dominated by militias who had supported Israel during the Lebanese civil war (see Chapter Four). Bsaleem station was the second power station Israel had bombed in less than 24 hours. This caused a power shortage all over Lebanon, and up to 8 hours of power cuts in Beirut and the Mount Lebanon area.

On that day we started broadcasting appeals and guidance for households on how to deal with the power shortage and asking them on behalf of the Ministry of Power 'to reduce their usage of electricity, because the damage is huge and it will take time and money to fix it' (TL news, 19:30, 15 April 1996). Images of the Bsaleem Power Station minutes after the attacks, with the fire still raging and dust filling the place, were broadcast unedited for about five minutes, during which time Israeli jets bombed again, killing and injuring firemen working on the scene.

This was accompanied by communiqués of Israeli threats that we also broadcast, but with the intention of challenging them or focusing on people or activities who did.

> The 'collaborators' radio station' [Lahed Radio] transmitted, a few moments ago, communiqué number nine issued by an Israeli military spokesman. The communiqué states the following: 'Bombing the southern suburbs of Beirut and Bsaleem power station is part of the new game rules Hezbollah has introduced. If Kiryat Shmona [a northern Israeli settlement on the southern borders of Lebanon] is not living in peace then Bier Al Abed, Haret Hreik and Bourg Al Barajneh [towns and districts in the southern suburbs of Beirut] will not live in peace, and if Kiryat Shmona is living in the dark then Beirut will live in the dark too'.
> (ibid.)

Thus the Israeli side of the story was not absent from our coverage. Their military and political statements were given air time, but were dealt with as claims or as 'hidden barbaric intentions'. We, as journalists, viewed Israel as an 'enemy state' and that position was clear in the rhetoric we used to present and analyse Israeli statements and communiqués. TL's introduction to the primetime news on 15 April 1996 was a clear example:

> Hours before the United Nations security council meets and before the arrival of French Foreign Minister Hervé de Charette in the region, Uri Lubrani disclosed in a press briefing the barbaric aspects of Israeli intentions against Lebanon:... 'We say that Hariri's tours are a waste of time because the solution is not in Cairo or Paris, but in Beirut'.
>
> Prime Minister Hariri announced from Paris that many forget to mention the occupation. 'They mention the Katyusha rockets[9] and Hezbollah, and they don't mention the occupation, which is the main reason behind what is happening now'.
> (Introduction, TL news, 19.30, 15 April 1996)

We were showing the impact of Katyusha rockets on northern Israeli settlements, but only after going through all the news of the 'Israeli aggression' and in not more than two minutes – sometimes in no more than 30 seconds. The resistance acts were always portrayed as retaliatory actions, acts of resistance, and Hezbollah (by name) was rarely mentioned as the perpetrator. Hezbollah was issuing its own communiqués on the rocket shelling and guerrilla operations against the Israeli army in south Lebanon, under the auspices of the 'Islamic resistance'. However, in our coverage we were using the word 'resistance' on its own, rather than the phrase 'Islamic resistance', giving the word a national patriotic sense, rather than confining it to a certain sectarian group.

We were applying a form of self-censorship in order to achieve a unified society in support of the resistance actions, which relates to Bartlett's definition of propaganda. He believed that propaganda is a 'process that aims... either wittingly or unwittingly, at producing whole nation groups in which all individuals think, act and feel alike' (Bartlett 1942: 14). Lebanon as a whole, in all its sectors and parties, was a target for Israel; this was expressed extensively in Lebanese officials' statements and activities, and was reported in our daily coverage. Christian districts were bombed by Israel, just as much as Muslim areas. Newly built power stations and highways were destroyed and the Lebanese had to live in the dark because of the Israeli aggression.

Press conferences and statements of Lebanese leaders were broadcast in full. Lebanon had faced sectarian and political divisions during its 15 years of civil war, including differences over the position to be taken towards Israel, as being a friend or an enemy state (see Chapter Four). We therefore gave air time to leaders of all different sections of society to express their position and opinions on the aggression, which mainly came in support of the resistance and in condemnation of Israel's aggression.

The top figures that were given prominence were the president of the republic, Elias Hrawi (Maronite); the House speaker, Nabih Beri (Shiite); the prime minister, Rafic Hariri (Sunni); the MP Walid Jumblat (Druze); Cardinal Mar Nasrallah Boutros Sfeir (Maronite) and the Secretary General of Hezbollah, Assayed Hassan Nasrallah. They were calling on all Lebanese to unite against the aggression and to show support for the people of south Lebanon, who were suffering the most. A unified civil society in Lebanon was in the making, and the Israeli attacks came to help reinforce and shape that process. The leaders emphasised joining all efforts to fight Lebanon's enemy – and they succeeded, as this chapter reveals below.

Statements and appeals were disseminated to influence people's opinions, emotions and attitudes, and this meets with NATO's definition of propaganda, as mentioned by both Wright and Tugwell:

> Any information, ideas, doctrines or special appeals disseminated to influence the opinion, emotions, attitudes, or behaviour of any specified group in order to benefit the sponsor either directly or indirectly.
> (Wright 1991: 73; Tugwell 1987: 409)

On this fifth day of attacks, the House speaker, Nabih Beri, visited the southern city of Tyre,[10] challenging the Israeli threats to bomb the city if it was not evacuated. As a leader of the Shiites, who form the majority of the population of southern Lebanon, he called on all citizens who had left their houses and fled to Beirut to return to the south. Beri told CNN (the only other television channel transmitting live from Tyre):

> Shimon Peres said that if he was asked to choose between war and peace he would have chosen peace. From here we say to him, thank you for the peace you have shown us, which only reflects your criminal intentions and attitudes.
> (Beri to CNN, re-broadcast in
> TL news, 19:30, 15 April 1996)

A detailed report on Beri's visit to Tyre was broadcast in TL prime-time news:

Beri visited the UN Headquarters in Tyre and made a phone call to the force commander of the United Nations Interim Force in Lebanon (UNIFIL), Major-General Stanisław Wozniak.

[Footage of Beri talking on the phone with Major-General Stanisław Wozniak]:

'Tell the Israelis we got their message, they won't be able to destroy us and we will remain here with our people supporting their steadfastness. They are not targeting Hezbollah, as they claim; they are bombing civilians and destroying their homes and villages.'
(Beri, TL news, 19:30, 15 April 1996)

A report on how people were surviving life in Tyre, and how much were they attached to their land, followed the report on Beri's visit. The message was for the people to stand fast in their city. It was a counter-message to that distributed by the Israelis. Goebbels' propaganda principle 19 states that 'propaganda cannot immediately affect strong counter-tendencies: instead it must offer some form of action or diversion, or both' (Doob 1995: 214). The Lebanese authorities' message was aiming at making steadfastness the form of action or the diversion from feelings of despair and defeat that the Israelis were trying to enforce through their communiqués.

However, that did not cancel out the fact that those who decided to stay in nearby villages were under Israeli scrutiny, suffering from food and water shortages and lacking the simplest needs for survival. Thus, the report on the opposition of Tyre was followed by images of a UN convoy carrying food supplies to besieged villagers near Tyre. This convoy was hit by Israeli shelling in an attempt to prevent the convoy from reaching its target. 'UNIFIL sources have told TL that the convoy will try getting to those villages tomorrow, after making a new round of negotiations with the Israeli' (Harb, TL news, 19:30, 15 April 1996). The images carried the voices of the UN soldiers swearing at the Israelis (but without actually naming them) for bombing near the convoy vehicles and causing such panic among the team involved. The images were shot by one of the TL cameramen who was accompanying the convoy.

Soon after, this story was followed by appeals from hospitals in the area to supply them with medical and humanitarian aid for families who had taken refuge in hospitals, and appeals to help set up additional morgue places.

> Najem hospital in Tyre is calling through Tele Liban on the Ministry of Health to supply the hospital with extra fridges for the morgue. It cannot take more martyrs.[11] Otherwise, they need ambulances to come and take the bodies of the ambulance massacre martyrs to hospitals in Beirut. Also, the hospital has shortages of medicine and blood supply.
>
> (ibid.)

Meanwhile, Prime Minister Hariri met the French President, Jacques Chirac, in Paris and held a press conference with the French and foreign media there. Hariri spoke in English, French and Arabic; his press conference, which lasted about an hour and a half, was broadcast fully with subtitles at the end of the 15 April 1996 news bulletin. The press conference re-emphasised what he called 'the ground rules of the Lebanese position', gave full support to the resistance and raised question marks about the Israeli intentions behind the operation.

> Israel occupies our land and there is a resistance to this occupation. If we agree or we don't agree with the resistance's political line or history or relationships,[12] that has nothing to do with the fact that our land is occupied. It is the occupation that created the resistance. What should we do, deprive the resistance of its weapons to make the occupation easier for the Israelis! This is impossible. It is not just us that say that: everyone in Lebanon rejects that. No Prime Minister of Lebanon will agree to deprive the resistance of its weapons as long as Israel is occupying our land. Israel is reinforcing Hezbollah by maintaining the occupation.
> 
> (Hariri, TL news, 19:30, 15 April 1996)

'We are the victims, and we have the right to resist the occupation' – that was Lebanon's message to the world. The footage – of destruction and shattered bodies of innocent people – broadcast on television added value and credibility to the message. Nationally, victimising the nation and emphasising the right to fight oppression was a unifying feature.

The chairman of TL, Fouad Naim, denied having followed government guidance to feature victims in TL's coverage. He said they were newsworthy stories and that the government might have actually benefited from TL's coverage to put its argument forward (Naim, interview with author, 2004). Naim, like others among my colleagues who asserted an absence of direct guidance on what to report and what not to, dismissed the concept of any 'managed', 'planned' or 'systematic' attempts to manipulate ideas and attitudes – attempts that most propaganda scholars assert should exist to meet the definition of propaganda (see Chapter Two).

However, performances like this can still be related to propaganda. Thomson points out that it is unwise to insist on the words 'deliberate' or 'systematic' in any definition of propaganda (Thomson 1999: 1). He states that too many great movements of mass persuasion have begun and continued without any master plan (ibid: 3).

## Day six: Tuesday 16 April 1996

On the sixth day the crisis was still not resolved, but international political initiatives to try to put an end to the military escalation in south Lebanon started to float to the surface. France sent its foreign minister to the region to try negotiating a ceasefire and the United States presented an end-to-violence initiative, but Lebanon found it hard to accept. The American initiative consisted of seven points, one of which stated that Hezbollah should abstain from any activity at the border of the occupied zone or inside it, which meant putting an end to resistance operations against Israeli forces in the occupied territories of south Lebanon. Now humanitarian aid started arriving in Lebanon, from both Arabic and Western countries.

On the fourth day of live coverage, Zaven Kouyoumdjian took over from me as anchor–producer in Sidon. I joined the UNIFIL (United Nations Interim Forces in Lebanon) team, which was trying to take in food and supplies to the besieged villages, along with a cameraman and an assistant.

Phone lines were cut off in the Tyre and Nabatiyeh areas, so Zaven Kouyoumdjian lost contact with the besieged families and with TL correspondents. He was able to establish connection half an hour into the news bulletin, and appeals started flowing on air from the villagers and hospitals. Tele Liban announced that day that its airwaves would be available to any citizen who wanted to send messages to their families in Beirut or in the south at any time.

By doing this we were bringing people together and communicating to the whole nation the suffering of those who had fled and those who remained steadfast in their villages and towns. Sympathy brings unity. We were being sensational, in the professional sense of that term. However, by examining it retrospectively in relation to propaganda principles and tools, we were simply using emotions, one of propaganda's key elements (see Chapter Two) to achieve sympathy and unity, but without any structured or prepared plan.

By that Tuesday, refugees were getting aid supplies from all parts of Lebanon and abroad, and from international aid agencies. The High Relief Committee[13] and the Lebanese army were establishing aid centres where volunteers could go to help package aid units for the refugees and then distribute them. Reports on the refugees' conditions in Sidon, Beirut and Mount Lebanon were included in the news bulletin. There was also a report on the condition of the power stations that had been hit by the Israelis and another report on the consequences of the electricity shortage for the everyday life of the Lebanese people. France announced that day that it would help in repairing the power stations.

Prime-time news ended with an interview with Prime Minister Hariri at the end of his visit to Saudi Arabia, commenting on the American initiative for a ceasefire. He announced that he had been introduced to it by the US ambassador in Saudi Arabia and would discuss it with the president of the republic and the House speaker on his arrival in Beirut. However, in the interview, Hariri doubted it would be possible to accept some of American initiative points, especially that of asking Hezbollah, regarded by Lebanese as a resistance force, to stop all its military operations inside and on the borders of the occupied zone in south Lebanon.

## Day seven: Wednesday 17 April 1996

The President of Lebanon Elias Hrawi (a Maronite Christian) headed a ministerial meeting in the presidential palace, which discussed developments in south Lebanon and the US and French initiatives for a ceasefire. The ministerial meeting concluded with a recommendation to start broadcasting the news of the 'aggression' via satellite.

> It was agreed during today's meeting to establish an operations centre under the supervision of the Ministry of Information for the satellite transmission that will be devoted to broadcasting what is happening in South Lebanon. This transmission aims at exposing the brutality of the Israeli aggression against Lebanon.
> 
> (TL news, 19.30, 16 April 1996)

A crew from Tele Liban accompanied the Lebanese prime minister on his tour to the so-called 'world capitals of decision' and supplied the prime-time news with daily packages reporting the outcome of each visit. On that day a long report was broadcast covering his meeting with John Major, the British prime minister at the time, and included a press conference he held in London with the British media.

> British journalist: Are you optimistic towards achieving a political solution?
>
> Hariri: Yes, I am. Nobody can continue bombarding civilians and killing children and women indefinitely. That is what the Israelis are doing now and not achieving anything. Yesterday Hezbollah launched a Katyusha after 7 days of bombardment and Hezbollah is still intact. What does this mean? It means a military solution cannot solve the problem ...
> (Hariri, London, TL news, 17 April 1996)

Hariri meant to use the phrase 'Hezbollah fighters' when talking to international audiences about the resistance's military operations in south Lebanon. He identified Hezbollah fighters as 'resistance fighters' when communicating with Lebanese and Arab audiences. National and regional audiences recognise Hezbollah as a resistance movement, while many in the Western media label Hezbollah as a 'terrorist group', supported by the fact that it is listed on the United States list of terrorist organisations (see Harik 2004).

In all his statements to the Western media, Hariri was presenting Hezbollah's activities in south Lebanon as part of the legitimate fight to resist the occupation. He was detaching the government from being able to pressure the resistance to stop its activities, but at the same time he did not criticise those activities. He was insistently bringing all foreign journalists' questions on Hezbollah back to the government's initial argument: that, if Israel withdrew from south Lebanon, the problem would be solved.

In accordance with this, a national conference was held in Ashrafieh (in a predominantly Christian area) attended by representatives from all religious sectors and all parties (and thus the whole spectrum in Lebanon). They all condemned the Israeli aggression, declaring their full support for the resistance and emphasising the people's unity in backing the refugees in what they needed. Hezbollah was represented at this conference and was addressed as the foundation of the resistance.

That day, it was announced officially that the number of people displaced from south Lebanon now exceeded 400,000. Tele Liban declared the establishment of an emergency team, from among its employees and other volunteers, to receive appeals and phone calls from refugees regarding their conditions. The team – as announced by its leader at TL, Samar Shalak, on the evening of 17 April 1996 – was also to conduct field inspections. They were called the 'Tele Liban emergency team' and, three days after its launch, this was given a special one-hour spot ahead of the prime-time news.

On that day a TL crew was able to enter two besieged villages with one of the UN convoys. The convoy was bringing in food, milk, water and medical supplies. I was the reporter who accompanied the convoy from TL and, to my surprise, the besieged families in Bute Al Siyyad in the central sector recognised me and were concerned about my safety more than theirs. One little detail that made me realise how much those people were connected with the small screen was when they noticed that I had not had time to change my clothes for three days. They thought of this as being an act of solidarity with them and expressed their appreciation to me.

In Zbqeen, the other village, conditions were even worse. The residents gathered inside a UN position on the outskirts of the village. They asked if we would record their messages to their families, who had fled the village earlier for other parts of the country. We recorded more than 20 messages, and promised to broadcast them as soon as we got to our OB van. That day, the villagers also asked the UN officer in charge of the convoy to take two old men with the convoy, so they would be able to join their peers in Tyre to go on *Hajj*.[14]

The wife of one of the two elderly men came to me and asked me to take care of her husband, Abu Abbas, 'for he is old'. She started crying, and I cried with her and hugged her, and this was shown on television. When we all arrived safely in Tyre, I addressed Um Abbas, the wife, live on air, telling her that Abu Abbas had arrived safely in Tyre and that he was on his way to Beirut to go on *Hajj*. The footage of me hugging Um Abbas and crying was later used in a promotion for TL's live coverage from the south, with the slogan 'TL: compassion'.

After seven days of coverage this promotion was broadcast. In effect it said: we are not detached from people's suffering and we are on the people's side. We sympathise with them and try our best to be of help to them.

We were not neutral. Our audiences did not expect us to be neutral, but expected us to be 'objective' and highlight the aggressions. This was a clear case of the 'contextual objectivity' discussed in Chapter Three. According to Iskandar and El-Nawawy, such contextualisation reveals 'a situational position, a way by which collectivism among participants within the same "context"—whether cultural, religious, political, or economic—is realized and engaged' (Iskandar and El-Nawawy 2004: 320). They state that 'it is precisely this contextualization that aggravates and complicates the pursuit of "objective" coverage within the news media setting' (ibid.). They believe that

> Contextualization further confuses attempts at even-handedness and efforts to cover all sides of a story. Particularly in times of war, it is the context within which a reporter operates that makes communication with the 'enemy' unacceptable.
>
> (ibid.)

Iskandar and Nawawi's notion of 'contextual objectivity' explains the absence of any attempt by Lebanese journalists, including myself, to communicate with any Israeli official or spokesperson.

During the period of the Israeli attacks, Tele Liban became a transmission centre for some of the prominent international media organisations. To mark this, Nesrine Sadek put together a report on the facilities TL was offering foreign reporters:

> Tele Liban, and mainly the Telet Al Khayat building, has been transformed into a centre for international news agencies and TV stations to feed their home centres with their reports on the aggression. They are sending their information through the TL satellite station in Jourat Al Balout [north of Beirut]. Reporters and journalists from Reuters, APTN and EBU are feeding images to almost all European channels, to the BBC in London, TV5 in Paris and ABC in America. They all transmit from Tele Liban, which is offering them the equipment and technical facilities to send their reports and inform the world about what is happening here.
>
> (Sadek, TL news, 19:30, 17 April 1996)

In addition, CNN and its correspondent in Beirut, Brent Sadler, were given permission and technical support to operate a link-up directly from Tyre through the TL satellite station in Jourat Al Balout to CNN's headquarters in Atlanta.

## Day eight: Thursday 18 April 1996

One headline dominated the news coverage on 18 April: 'A day of massacres from Nabatiyeh to Qana'. Around two o'clock that day I was at Najem hospital in Tyre, investigating the ambulance massacre for the weekly current affairs show, *Khamseh ala Sabaah* ('Five over Seven'), that I was co-producing and co-presenting with Zaven Kouyoumdjian.

While I was interviewing the director and owner of the hospital, Dr Najem, a nurse interrupted the interview to tell us they had received an appeal for help from the UN headquarters in Qana. Israel had bombarded the compound and the human casualties were massive. Minutes later, injured people started arriving at Najem hospital, the nearest to the compound. The bloody scene at the hospital was horrendous; I was not even able to keep up with counting the injured.

I called the news room in Beirut and the news team in Sidon and fed them the story, emphasising the fact that something horrific had happened in Qana and that the bloody scenes in Najem hospital indicated a massacre. We called on all medical units and ambulances to head to Qana to help in the rescue. My cameraman was filming the wounded and the dead, lying in the hospital corridors, non-stop. Blood was everywhere. Within a few minutes another TL cameraman arrived at the scene. I asked one camera crew to take the tape to the transmission unit in Sidon and head with the second camera crew to Qana. In less than 15 minutes the rushed footage taken at Najem hospital was running on air just as it was shot, with no editing.

> Maybe our presence there partly assisted in spreading those appeals. We were asking every ambulance in the area to head to Qana and help with the rescue mission.
> (Harb, TL news, 19:30, 18 April 1996)

When we arrived in Qana, the scene was clearly drastic. The moment the villagers saw us, they started shouting at the camera, waving their hands in every direction, asking us to film and to tell the world what Israel had done to innocent people. They guided us to one of the containers where the villagers were sheltering, but the UN soldiers refused to let us in; within moments, the civil defence rescuers were pushing us into the container, challenging the UN soldiers. There we stood in the middle of the shattered bodies of women, children and old people. By then we heard only the voices of the rescuers asking us to film, to record the images and transmit them to the world.

When we left the container, foreign and local reporters were all over the place and most of them were crying along with their cameramen. Some of the UN soldiers were weeping too. When we approached them, they had one word to say: 'massacre'. The UN soldiers' reaction towards what happened was emphasised in my piece to camera; there was no exaggeration in what we showed and told you. It was a massacre and those soldiers – who were viewed as 'neutral' – were evidence of that.

> I just want to end up by saying, no one will forget the tears of a UN soldier who was crying today over the body of a child whom he was playing football with minutes before the attack took place ... It is a horrific massacre: those are the words of the UN soldiers serving in Qana.
> 
> (Harb, TL news, 19:30, 18 April 1996)

An hour after the mass killing took place, shocking images of the massacre were running uncut on air from Sidon. The tape we filmed in Qana was broadcast on TL without any editing. Through TL, and only shortly after the massacre, the pictures of Qana were distributed to all Associated Press Television (APTV) subscribers around the world. According to Ahmad Hindawi, APTV's operations manager at the time and the regional manager of APTV Middle East later, no one knew the scale of the massacre in Qana. When TL broadcast the images of the casualties in Najem hospital, he thought that the images were worth sending to the AP newsroom in London:

> I was at the TL centre in Telet Al Khayat [in Beirut] standing by the set linked to the satellite station in Jourat Al Balout [north of Beirut], preparing to send TL's exclusive footage from Najem hospital to the London bureau, when TL broadcast the images of the massacre from Qana. I got TL's permission and plugged their live footage to the set connected straight to our bureau in London. The whole newsroom in London was in shock, I was told.
> 
> (Hindawi, interview with author, 2004)

The whole nation was in shock and we, as journalists, were at that point a crucial part of the nation. We did not need to do much or say much to express the cruelty of the aggressive attack that hit Qana. The Qana massacre added to the growing feeling among all Lebanese that the nation was under unjustified attack by a huge military force, which was already occupying 10 per cent of Lebanon (see *Assafir*, 19 April 1996).

What made the national feeling grow more bitter was that Qana had been preceded on that day by another massacre. Early that morning an Israeli jet had fired three to four rockets on a three-storey building in the southern city of Nabatiyeh, killing 11 members of the same family. Among them was a four-day-old baby called Nour. Images of a rescuer carrying Nour's dead body, after recovering it from underneath the rubble, crowned the images of the Qana victims.

> Nour Al Abed – a new name added to the ongoing tragedy south Lebanon is suffering since the intensive hostile attacks started eight days ago.
>
> [Background sound of people shouting, asking the rescuer who was showing Nour's body to the camera to wrap the body and take it away from the camera]. Nour was born on the fourth day of the aggression, but she didn't know how her tragedy would end. [An image of a civil defence rescuer carrying Nour between his arms and driving her to hospital is run on screen with no comment.]
>
> (Kouyoumdjian, TL news, 19:30, 18 April 1996)

Stories and memories of previous massacres committed by the Israeli army in Palestine, Egypt and Lebanon were brought up in our coverage. These related what had happened in Qana and Nabatiyeh to previous Israeli practices towards Arab civilians since the establishment of Israel in 1948 (see Chapter Four). Thus, TL's prime-time news on the eve of the massacre was full of historical connotations:

> Israeli bombs have spread since sunrise over the fragile bodies of children and newborn babies and the weak bodies of the elderly, tearing them into pieces, cropping 106 lives and more than 200 injuries. In response to the tragic footage of the massacres, Israeli Prime Minister Shimon Peres was not able to justify what happened except by asking, apparently surprised: 'Why were there civilians in Nabatiyeh?' However, he was not able to explain the barbaric bombardment of the

UN headquarters in Qana, which resulted in a massacre that goes beyond what happened in the Deir Yassin massacre and that of Baher Al Bakar and Al Haram Al Ibrahimy.[15] Peres called his cabinet for an emergency meeting this evening to evaluate the situation after the massacres. Tele Liban reporters and cameramen were among the first to arrive in Qana. Their memory and cameras recorded a day that would never be forgotten in the history of humankind. Tele Liban ran exclusively the first footage of the massacre on air, which enabled international TV channels to feed these images from Tele Liban to the world. In all cases the images do not need any commentary. We go straight to South Lebanon with Tele Liban's team, Zaven [Kouyoumdjian] and Zahera [Harb] ...

(Awada, TL news, 19:30, 18 April 1996)

I was the reporter who covered the massacre, and Zaven Kouyoumdjian was the anchor–producer of the day in Sidon; we were thus the team that broke the story to the nation. We both used sentimental words. He was asking me about the children of Qana, about the eyewitnesses and the UN soldiers who broke down in tears. I was talking about those whom I called 'those who suffered survival, those who lost most of their family members and wished they were among the dead'. The images of the massacres were repeated over and over again, and stories of the survivors and the situation of the injured were revealed minute by minute.

While the prime-time news programme was running, a helicopter flew over Sidon, but no one was able to identify whom it belonged to until Hammoud hospital called and told us that it was a UN helicopter transferring an injured child from Qana to the hospital. He was unconscious. They were not able to find out his name, so they called him 'Baby Helicopter'. Zaven [Kouyoumdjian] adopted the name and called on those who had missing children in Qana to come to Hammoud hospital to check if 'Baby Helicopter' was their child (Kouyoumdjian, TL news, 19:30, 18 April 1996). We were both expressing our bare feelings and wanted to communicate these to whoever was watching. We were emotionally involved and we wanted them to be involved too.

> Lebanese were dying and I was covering it. It is very normal and human to be affected by such horrific scenes. I was

> involved. Using emotional words or sentences was part of the 24-hour live coverage 'show'... I think the whole coverage was a very emotional moment in post-war Lebanon... I was under fire. Lebanon was being attacked. I was Lebanese, reporting to a Lebanese audience on a Lebanese channel. It was very clear to me. In such moments, it is not a question of objectivity and neutrality. It is what you feel and what the nation feels. I was angry at what Israel was doing – and I showed this through my work.
>
> (Kouyoumdjian, interview with author, 2004)

Zaven's questioning the need for objectivity on those occasions when a journalist is eye-witness to acts of injustice or war crimes matches what Kate Adie and Martin Bell, veteran BBC war reporters, expressed in their autobiographies (see Chapter Three).

David Mannion, Editor-in-chief of ITV, equally questioned the ability of reporters on the ground to be balanced and detached during their coverage of the later Israeli–Lebanese war in July 2006. Mannion told *Broadcast* magazine on 4 August 2006 that he tells his reporters to strive to be accurate, fair and honest. Mannion added:

> As for balance, it's my belief that it would be quite impossible to ask an individual reporter covering one incident on one day in one war to be always balanced. Imagine this. A reporter is standing in the middle of a hospital ward. Children, some with arms and legs blown away, others blinded by shrapnel, are screaming in fear and agony. It is tough, but it is still necessary in my view to be fair and honest, but it is not reasonable and/or necessary in my view to ask him or her to be balanced. It is even ok to be angry.
>
> (Mannion, *Broadcast*, 4 August 2006)

If being balanced was a dilemma for foreign reporters covering a war far away from home, imagine what it would be like for a journalist like the TL reporters (including myself) who were reporting a war taking place in their own land and affecting their own people.

The Qana massacre came to be a means to demonise the enemy and to provoke hatred against its perpetrators. We were provoking patriotism among our audiences, implementing unconsciously one of the propaganda techniques discussed in Chapter Two: 'shaping audience perceptions' (see Jackall 1995; Jowett and O'Donnell 1999).

This relates to one of Goebbels' principles of propaganda, which states that it must 'facilitate the displacement of aggression by specifying the targets of the hatred' (Doob 1995: 214). Additionally however, what was happening falls within what Jowett classifies as 'white propaganda', where 'the source of information is correct and the information in the message is accurate' (Jowett and O'Donnell 1999: 15).

Our unit in Sidon became the centre of communication between hospitals and rescuers, civil defence rescuers and their headquarters, and between Lebanese officials on the one hand, and hospitals and civil defence organisations in south Lebanon on the other.

All Lebanese officials who headed south that day, and the days after, paid TL's live studio in Sidon a visit and made statements on how were they going to answer the humanitarian appeals we were receiving from southerners, hospitals and civil defence organisations. Qana dominated the news – 106 civilians died there and more than 200 were injured, including four UN soldiers – and footage from Qana dominated the screens of all local television stations. They all had reporters in there at different times. Nevertheless, TL had the privilege of operating live from the south while the others had to drive back to Beirut with their material. However, after Israeli warships cut off the coast road between Beirut and Sidon, their mission became more difficult.

Lebanese television stations from different political and religious backgrounds were unified in the language they used in talking about the massacres. Anyone who died in the massacres was called a 'martyr' and what Israel did was described as hostile, aggressive and a war crime against humanity. Even within TL itself, employees who classed themselves as right wing and journalists who used to believe Israel was their friend during the years of the civil war adopted the same language in condemning Israel for what it was doing at the time (see Chapter Five for information on the divisions among TL employees and journalists during the civil war in Lebanon).

> The Qana massacre shocked and moved them. The images had their effect on them, as it did with the whole nation. The tragedy made them stop being argumentative about how their colleagues in the south are covering the attacks. Qana made them adopt their colleagues' line of coverage.
>
> (Awada, interview with author, 2004)

TL Chairman Fouad Naim, the head of news, Aref Al Abed, and the ten reporters and anchor–producers who operated from south Lebanon all assured their people that they were not exaggerating or inventing stories in their coverage. For Naim it was 'the propaganda of the truth'.

> We were not hiding anything. On some other occasions we emphasised and highlighted the aggressive nature of the attacks because it was happening on our land and affecting our own people. But with Qana what the Israelis were doing did not need exaggeration. I believe what we did was reflect the reality of the attack. We were showing the images of destruction and massacres as they were. In covering the Qana massacre, I believe we were completely objective; we did not need to decorate the coverage with any national slogan or metaphor, because the images were speaking for themselves.
> (Naim, interview with the author, 2004)

So there was a crafting of messages for a purpose – a kind of information war, but the aim here was to communicate what was demonstrably the 'truth' of the Israeli aggression.

As mentioned before, Naim and Al Abed denied any interference from the government, the prime minister or his communication adviser in editorial decisions. TL journalists interviewed for this research assured us of this and revealed that no one was telling them what to say or what not to say. The only guidance they were receiving was how to prioritise events. All were guided by their cultural, social and political backgrounds, in addition to their professional expertise (Kandeel-Yaghi, interview with author, 2004).

> We felt under attack. It was a war targeting our families, relatives and friends. We were feeling the urge to defend them. Being a citizen of this country meant that we as journalists and the people of south Lebanon were in one battle, the battle of defending our nation. One thing was clear to us: you could not be neutral in your feelings towards your nation.
> (Kamouneh, interview with author, 2004)

Patriotism and nationalistic attitudes ran high among all Lebanese journalists in the wake of the Qana massacre. Diana Moukaled of

Future TV (owned by late Prime Minister Rafic Hariri), who was among the first to get to Qana, revealed that when she returned to Beirut, she was completely devastated by what she had seen, such that she almost collapsed. The prime minister's media and political adviser at the time, Nouhad Al Mashnouk, came to Future TV and calmed her down.

> He said: 'Today we won the war. We did not lose it. Those who died gave us victory. We will not let it go' and that was what happened. Lebanon took advantage of the massacre politically on all three levels: locally, regionally and internationally.
>
> (Moukaled, interview with author, 2004)

Moukaled, like the TL reporters, spoke of the relationship that connected her to the people of south Lebanon. She said that she knew what to say and what terminology to use, without being guided. She grew up knowing the tragedies the Israeli occupation was imposing on the people of south Lebanon. This 'living tragedy' as she called it, was what had guided her through her work. However, Moukaled pointed out that on the fourth day of the aggression the prime minister's media and political adviser attended their editorial meeting and instructed them to focus in their coverage on those who decided to stay in their homes and who had thus refused to submit to Israeli threats. Notably, though, such meetings with the media adviser did not take place at TL during the days of the Israeli operation. Discussions and consultations were only with the head of news and the chief editor.

However, what Diana said reminded me of the request by the head of TL news, Aref Al Abed, at the beginning of our live coverage. He asked me to focus on the people who stayed in their villages and towns, rather than those who were leaving. He believed that we should not be encouraging people to leave their places, which meant that they were both trying to disseminate the same message.[16] They were both encouraging journalists to craft the same message, a message of steadfastness. However, both Al Mashnouk in an informal chat and Al Abed in an interview asserted that there was no deliberate or contrived plan for crafting certain messages. For both of them it was 'the logical thing to do in such circumstances'. Looking at it from a theoretical perspective, they both fitted the role of propagandists on that specific occasion. They were both encouraging journalists not to spread panic among the population of south Lebanon, which would be the case if they focused on showing people fleeing their homes.

On the evening after the Qana massacre, most government ministers gathered at the presidential palace in Baabda and discussed with President Hrawi what should be done in political and humanitarian response to Israel's open war against Lebanese civilians and infrastructure. That meeting was covered live on TL from the presidential palace.

Full coverage was also given to House speaker Nabih Beri's[17] press conference in Baabda. Beri, like others, related these massacres to previous Israeli massacres and made comparisons between what had happened in 1982 and what was happening now. His speech was patriotic, calling indirectly on all citizens to support each other and stand against the occupier. He aimed at raising the spirits of those who had stayed in south Lebanon and warned those in other parts of Lebanon that Israeli aggression would not be limited to south Lebanon alone.

> [Talking head]...We want the members of the [United Nations] Security Council to watch closely the brutality of these massacres. I've just spoken to the foreign minister and to the president asking them to appeal for a United Nations assembly meeting urgently and to put one item on its agenda: the Israeli massacres committed against Lebanese civilians... Israel should be unmasked in front of the whole world.
> (Beri, TL news, 19:30, 18 April 1996)

Again, Beri's appeal revealed elements of propaganda. By asking to hold back the UN security meeting on Israel aggression for another 24 hours – so the UN Security Council members could watch the images from Qana – he was counting on their emotional response to such images. Those pictures were the tool the Lebanese government was aiming at using to bring to the UN Security Council the 'truth' about what was happening in south Lebanon, and thus they would force it to stop its aggression. The images were treated as evidence of Israeli 'brutality'.

The Lebanese foreign minister at the time, Fares Bouize, was more specific in relating what happened in Qana and Nabatiyeh to historical aspects of the Arab–Israeli conflict. Talking after his meeting with President Hrawi and House speaker Beri in Baabda, he said

> [Close-up frame, talking head] What happened today I think will enter the history of international terrorism. And we want to tell Peres: congratulations! You have taken the banner from the Ergon and Stern Zionist groups with your brutality...
> (Bouize, TL news, 19:30, 18 April 1996)

Similarly, the statement by Walid Jumblat, the Druze leader, head of the Socialist Progressive Party and a government minister, after meeting President Hrawi, came to summarise all the patriotic atmosphere that other statements had expressed. He said: 'We are in a real war situation, full of blood and fire, and there is no nearby solution and we are not begging for anyone's sympathy' (Jumblat, TL news, 19:30, 18 April 1996).

Israeli reaction to the casualties in Qana was not ignored in the coverage, but it was dealt with suspiciously.

> The Israeli cabinet is meeting urgently tonight to evaluate the situation after the massacre its troops committed against Lebanese civilians today. Ehud Barak, Israeli foreign minister, confirmed the meeting. Barak said the bombing of Qana was a mistake, he claimed that he feels sorry for the civilian victims and as usual he blamed the resistance for what happened.
>
> The Israeli environment minister, Yossi Sarid, said even if Hezbollah is causing harm to our citizens that does not mean we allow ourselves to go and bomb civilians the way we did today. Sarid hoped the current government would learn from what happened with the Likud in 1982.
> (Awada, TL news, 19:30, 18 April 1996)

This story was followed immediately by a news story stating that the Islamic resistance had retaliated in response to the massacres and bombed northern Israeli settlements.

> The Islamic resistance retaliated and bombed the Israeli colonies in Northern Israel with 10 sets of Katyushas. The Israeli army announced that one man was injured in the

shelling. Timor Goksel, UN spokesman in south Lebanon, revealed that 500 Katyusha rockets have been fired since the beginning of the aggression till now on the Northern Israeli settlements.

(Awada, TL news, 19:30, 18 April 1996)

On the evening after the Qana massacre, the Lebanese information minister at the time, Farid Makari, revealed that the cabinet would discuss at its meeting the next day the possibility of transmitting Tele Liban news on satellite 'so the rest of the world can watch what is happening here' (Makari, TL news, 19:30, 18 April 1996). At that point our target audience expanded from viewers in Lebanon to viewers in the whole Arab world and the Diaspora.

A national conference was held in Ashrafieh (a Christian district in east Beirut), and every political and religious sector in Lebanon was represented.

[Deputy House speaker, Elie Ferezli, head of the conference, talking to camera]: 'Israel has always tried to circulate the idea that Lebanon is not a unified body and the Lebanese are separated into different religious sectors and parties. This meeting today aims at telling Israel that we are united against your aggression and would always be united.'

(Ferezli speaking to Kamouneh,
TL news, 19:30, 18 April 1996)

Kamouneh's report was followed by a story from Agence France-Presse (AFP) to justify what had been said about the solidarity of all Lebanese sectors against Israeli aggression.

AFP had a report today titled 'the Christian area[18] in Lebanon that hurried to show solidarity with and support for the resistance'. The report said: 'The Christian area in Lebanon started a charity campaign to support the displaced people of south Lebanon, and that people are rushing from all over Lebanon to offer help and aid.'

(AFP report, TL news, 19:30, 18 April 1996)

The news programme on that day had many supporting messages from different political and religious sectors in the Lebanese society. The programme ended with a live interview with the health minister,

Marwan Hamade, who stopped in Sidon on his way to inspect the situation in the hospitals in south Lebanon. Hamade emphasised what most Lebanese politicians and leaders were emphasising, the relationship between these massacres and the long list of Israeli massacres committed against Arabs since the establishment of Israel.

> Israeli massacres today are episodes in the long history of Israeli massacres, starting with Deir Yassin to the massacres they committed during the 1982 invasion [Sabra and Shatila] to what happened today. I hope that, some day, Israeli leaders will be prosecuted as war criminals in the world tribunal, as happened to the war criminals in Bosnia.
> (Hamade, TL news, 19:30, 18 April 1996)

Zionist militias attacked Deir Yassin village in April 1948 and killed what was left of its inhabitants (see Chapter Four). For Arabs, Deir Yassin had since become the symbol of the 'Zionist brutality and lack of mercy' (ibid.). By drawing parallels between the Qana massacre and Deir Yassin, Hamade brought to the surface all the negative perceptions of Israel that the Lebanese and Arabs carry in their collective memory. The psychological elements of significant symbols had been identified by Ellul (1965/1975) and Lasswell (cited in Thomson 1999) as the most favourable elements of propaganda (see Chapter Two). However, propaganda here was not targeting the enemy. It targeted the Lebanese and Arab audiences, aiming at achieving national solidarity, as well as regional, political and financial support.

The Lebanese ambassador to Washington at the time, Tabbara, revealed that during the first seven days of the Israeli offensive on Lebanon the American administration did not want to interfere or pressure Israel to stop its assault on Lebanon. Nevertheless, the US administration's position changed after footage of the Qana Massacre dominated the screens of most international television stations. According to Tabbara, the images of Qana made them want to act quickly to negotiate a ceasefire (interview with author, 1999).

## Day nine: Friday 19 April 1996

This was the first day after Qana. The countdown to end the military operation started. Days were then numbered as after or before the Qana massacre.

The Qana aftermath programme was dominated by the images and sound bites of survivors, the injured and families of the dead. New images from Qana were revealed and old images were repeated. Horrific, graphic and detailed images of the massacre were played repeatedly.

The opening scene after the headlines was of a burned child swathed in bandages, lying in one of Sidon's hospitals, telling the camera what happened to him and his family.

> The boy: I was sitting beside my mother and father. I woke up here and I do not know where they are now.
>
> The reporter: Why did not you hide?
>
> The boy: I could not hide.
>
> (TL news, 19:30, 19 April 1996)

Later in the programme we revealed the boy's identity and the fact that his father, mother and one sister had died in the massacre; the boy was left with one sister, who was also suffering from bad injuries. The programme's opening sequence continued with the camera moving to another eight-year-old boy lying in bed, describing in his words what happened and how he survived the massacre.

Then the camera moved to a woman sitting beside her child's bed in hospital. She was full of tears, trying to tell us how she found herself surrounded by bodies:

> [Weeping voice] We were just sitting when the missiles started falling around our heads. I didn't know what was happening, but when the bombardment stopped I looked around me and everyone was martyred, except us.
>
> (ibid.)

All anchors and reporters were wearing black in token of bereavement. The introduction (which in the Lebanese news culture tends to carry the same character as a newspaper opinion editorial) considered the opening sequence as testimonies to the survivors and aimed to emphasise the brutal nature of the attack on Qana, after the UN Security Council had failed to meet Lebanon's calls to condemn Israel.

> These are testimonies from those who survived the massacre in Qana, who took refuge with the United Nation forces, but

the enemy's burning bombs chased them even under their international shelter. These testimonies are hard proof of what happened in Qana, but the UN Security Council was not even able to come up with a verbal condemnation of this massacre. All they did is to call for a ceasefire – that is still far away from implementation.

(Al Ashi, TL news, 19:30, 19 April 1996)

The programme focused on the international condemnation of the massacre and highlighted Pope John Paul II's condemnation, which was preceded by the head of the Lebanese church, Nasrallah Sfeir, calling on all Lebanese Christians and Muslims to stand behind their fellow brothers and sisters in south Lebanon. The live coverage from south Lebanon continued, and details of the situation in villages and cities permeated the programme – which was extended to three hours, instead of the half an hour it took in normal situations. On that day we started co-ordinating voluntary work, not just to help the displaced and those who stayed in their villages, but also to give comfort to the martyrs' families and organise search teams to reunite families scattered between different hospitals.

The story that overshadowed the whole programme was that of Muhammad Deeb, whom we identified earlier as 'Baby Helicopter'. In her report on massacre survivors, Nadine Majzoub visited Hammoud hospital and met four-year-old Muhammad. Until that day neither of Muhammad's parents had shown up, and all Muhammad was able to say after he regained consciousness was his first name.

> His name, until this morning, was 'Baby Helicopter' and the reason is that a helicopter had brought him to Hammoud hospital from Qana the day before. All he knows is that his name is Muhammad. He asks for his mother all the time and does not know that his life will not be as comfortable as it was. [Images of a child connected to serum pipes showing that his leg was mutilated from the knee down. His face looks beautiful, bearing only one minor injury that does not affect its innocence. Nadine approaches him with the microphone:]
>
> N: What is your name?
> M: Hammoudi [diminutive for Muhammad].
> N: How old are you?
> M: Four.

N: Where were you?
M: Up there ... [meaning Qana village].
N: Why are you sad?
[He does not answer and tries to remove the pipes and starts moaning.]
N: What's wrong?
M: I want to drink Seven Up.
N: You want Seven Up?
M: Yes.
N: If we bring you Seven Up, will you talk to us?
M: I want my mother [starts crying] ... I want my mother.
(Majzoub, TL news, 19:30, 19 April 1996)

Nadine believed that Muhammad talking to the camera would reveal the 'reality' of Israeli army aggression. Thus, offering him Seven Up to talk did not raise any ethical concerns for her. In fact, talking to injured people in their hospital beds, showing graphic images of dead bodies, was seen by most journalists as a normal procedure to reflect the tragedies of the war. Hence, for almost 20 minutes, the tragedies of the survivors were highlighted through their own voices. It was emotionally moving, to the point that the anchor, Souad Al Ashi, was in tears when she appeared again on air from Beirut after this transmission from Sidon.

The government met and announced that Monday 22 April would be a day of national mourning. The cabinet agreed to a proposal by the information minister, Farid Makari, to allow Lebanese channels to broadcast news via satellite and called upon the establishment of a committee, headed by Makari, to supervise the transmission.

Naser Kandeel, deputy chair of the National Media Council in Lebanon and a member of this committee at the time, explained that the committee had a non-partisan role to organise the output that TV channels would be sending to a dedicated channel, established for the purpose of spreading Lebanon's voice to the outside world (Kandeel, interview with author, 2004).

It was the coverage of the Qana massacre and the reaction of solidarity that it generated on the national level that brought to the government's attention the importance of using the media as a tool for disseminating its message to audiences in the Arab world and abroad. Kandeel then agreed that television coverage had become an important tool of the war.

In the wake of the Qana and Nabatiyeh massacres, the whole nation adopted the slogan 'a nation at war'. As part of this, studies were suspended in all schools till the end of the attacks, people opened their houses for the displaced, and voluntary workers from all over Lebanon joined teams from the health and social ministries and NGOs to help the victims. The Lebanese were, for the first time since 1975 (see Chapter Four), united around one cause: fighting the Israeli attacks. TL was the channel that helped the Lebanese express that unity, and it was not expressed only in Lebanon, because we had reports and images of solidarity demonstrations taking place in Washington, Bonn, Istanbul, Oslo and Paris, organised by the Lebanese and Arab communities in those countries. TL started broadcasting messages and statements of support from Lebanese and Arab communities around the globe.

Even though none of this was organised or orchestrated by one body or party, it all translated into a great input in the information war. Transmitting the images of these demonstrations and broadcasting the messages and statements made these movements seem contagious, with ever more people stepping up to show solidarity and support. It was unplanned but a clear implementation of 'the band wagon', a propaganda device introduced and theorised by Jackall (1995: 222). It is a device that makes us all follow the crowd and do the same. The theme is: 'Everybody's doing it' (ibid.).

## Day ten: Saturday 20 April 1996

This was the second day after Qana. International political initiatives to put an end to the escalation increased. Foreign ministers of the United States, France, Italy and Iran arrived in Damascus.

> On the 10th day, the enemy's warships separated South Lebanon from other parts of the country, to put more pressure on Lebanon...
> (Headlines, TL news, 20 April 1996)

While political discussions were taking place in different world capitals, Israel kept its military operation going.

We had a team sent to Qana to file a report on the situation in the village two days after the massacre.

> Qana is empty. Its inhabitants left it, hoping to come back soon, but it is still empty. The echo and heavy silence is filling the space in Qana as if it is grieving for those who lost their lives two days ago in the massacre. The village is still a target of Israeli bombs, though a few people decided to stay – despite the dangers. Words, it seems, cannot express what is in their hearts. [Sound bite of an old lady, addressing the TL team with tears]: 'God protect you from any harm. God protect you from any grief.'
> 
> (Majzoub, TL news, 19:30, 20 April 1996)

Images of the massacre were repeated for the third day and along with them reports on the conditions of the injured and those who survived. Attention was given to the solidarity movement that was sweeping Lebanon.

> This afternoon hundreds of students from different religious sectors and political factions gathered in the Martyrs' Square in downtown Beirut and protested against the international inability to stop the Israeli aggression against Lebanese civilians. The demonstrators carried pictures of the children who died in Qana. Political parties and social and cultural movements and committees all over Lebanon have called for another sit-in tomorrow in front of the National Museum under the slogan 'Grapes of Unity in the face of Grapes of Wrath'.
> 
> (Ousi, TL news, 19:30, 20 April 1996)

On that day a delegate from the Association of Banks in Lebanon visited Prime Minister Hariri and donated one and a half million dollars to the High Relief Committee to help in aiding the refugees and the displaced people of south Lebanon.

On the international level, the Lebanese situation was on the agenda of the G7 Summit in Moscow after it had been introduced by President Jacques Chirac of France. This step was referred to as the 'internationalisation of the Lebanese crisis'. According to TL's prime news of the day, the American president, Bill Clinton, who was attending the summit, did not welcome this step, but did not veto it either (ibid.). Prime Minister Rafic Hariri used his personal relations with the world leaders to seek their support for the Lebanese cause. Iskandar explained the importance of Hariri's relations:

> Hariri secured [French President Jacques] Chirac's undiluted help in responding to the tragedy, convinced [British prime minister at the time] John Major of the enormity of the butchery, persuaded [the then Russian president] Boris Yeltsin to champion the Lebanese cause and to chastise Israel at least verbally, and passed a convincing message to the German chancellor. In the United States, Hariri depended on the support of Prince Bandar Bin Sultan, the Saudi ambassador who had developed close ties with President Clinton, as he had with George Bush Sr. Clinton was fearful of the loss of his Middle East peace initiative and therefore instructed his Secretary of State, Warren Christopher, to do everything possible to address the impact of the Qana Slaughter.
> 
> (Iskandar 2006: 80)

## Day eleven: Sunday 21 April 1996

On the eleventh day of the aggression, Israel suggested an immediate truce, but Lebanon was sceptical. The editorial introduction to TL's prime-time news read:

> On the 11th day of the aggression the aggressors called for an immediate truce after the world was stirred with the news of the massacres they had committed in Lebanon. The enemy's government announced the truce would be a step forward to achieve a long-standing ceasefire agreement. AFP reported, according to an Israeli governmental source, that [Israeli prime minister at the time] Shimon Peres asked American Foreign Minister Warren Christopher to carry an offer for immediate truce to the Syrians and the Lebanese and that the ceasefire could start this evening.
> 
> (Salemeh, TL news introduction, 19:30, 21 April 1996)

Despite the 'truce offer', Israel continued its shelling and kept the coastal highway that connects south Lebanon to other parts of the country closed by fire. However, it was the news of Muhammad Deeb's death that marked the news programme of that day. Raja Kamouneh, the anchor–producer in Sidon, and Nadine Majzoub, the reporter who interviewed Muhammad when he arrived at hospital, broke the story emotionally to the nation. They transformed the death of Muhammad Deeb into a very personal and emotive incident:

> Muhammad Deeb or Baby Helicopter, as we knew him, died yesterday at the age of four after being critically injured during the Qana massacre. The massacre that killed children, women and old people, killed with them humanity's conscience. We met him in Hammoud hospital and felt that childhood must defeat the brutality and hostility of the occupier, even if this brutality had cut out parts of his fragile body [shot of Muhammad's mutilated leg], but it seems that God has answered Muhammad's calls and made him rest beside his mother, whom he asked for several times during our interview with him. He also asked for Seven Up. [Repetition of the interview with him when he was calling for his mother and asking for the drink.] Muhammad was moved from the care unit to the recovery suite after his situation was recorded as stable, but late last night his heart stopped after being affected by a clot. [Sound bite by Dr Ghassan Hammoud, the head of the hospital, explaining the reasons behind Muhammad's death.] [Shocking images of Muhammad in the morgue; after we've seen him talking and moving his hands and playing with his hair, we see him lying in the morgue.]
>
> (Kamouneh and Majzoub, TL news, 19:30, 21 April 1996)

Because Muhammad was considered the last martyr of the Qana massacre, Nadine's interview with him, two days before he died, became greatly newsworthy. According to Majzoub (interview with author, 2004), most television channels in Lebanon wanted to broadcast the only interview recorded with him.

> At the beginning, the interview by itself was sentimental, because of the interviewee's age and condition and the words he was using. His death later was a shock to me. I felt deeply sad. It was not intentional to use sentimental words. I did not think at all of influencing the audience. By the end of the day, this war was against all Lebanese parties and people. I wrote this story for no one in particular and for everyone,

nationally and internationally. Knowing the capability of Tele Liban at that time, I wanted the voice of Muhammad to reach out to the world. My words came from the bottom of my heart.

(Majzoub, interview with author, 2004)

Nadine, as with other TL reporters, questioned the term 'objectivity' in such circumstances. She was crafting a message of influence, and emotions were her guide. Nadine's uncertainty, as a journalist covering war in her own country, about the meaning of 'objectivity' and 'neutrality' in such circumstances has been a common feature among all TL reporters who covered the April 1996 events. Many scholars recognise the difficulty of achieving ultimate objectivity in certain circumstances. Among them is Williams, who speaks of a time when the media were supposed to be partial, such as during a time of war when not supporting their own country's war efforts would seem 'inappropriate' (Williams 2003: 126).

Tele Liban's journalists and camera crews were portrayed as an example of the will to defeat all obstacles that the 'enemy' was forcing on the Lebanese. Thus, the story of how the TL crew managed to cross one of the rivers that runs between Sidon and other villages in Iqlim Al Kharoub (in the foothills of the Chouf Mountains, south-east of Beirut), without the need to go via the coast road, became a news item.

> We drove through Iqlim Al Kharoub and when we arrived at Alman we had to cross the Awali River [north of Sidon]. We used a big stump to get to an old bridge that was in use before the opening of the coastal highway. The wooden bridge was forgotten after that, but the villagers in Alman led us to it, and here we are in Sidon after a trip of 4 hours, which usually takes half an hour.
> 
> (Kamouneh, TL news, 19:30, 21 April 1996)

On that day, the Lebanese army started the process of installing a metal bridge over the river, reconnecting the south to other parts of the country away from the eyes of the Israeli warships.

## Day twelve: Monday 22 April 1996

On the twelfth day of the aggression, TL's prime-time news introduction said what most Lebanese realised that day: 'It sounded clear that the news about an immediate truce that Israel leaked last night was only a mirage' (TL news, 22 April 1996). While Lebanon was in mourning, Israel escalated its attack and kept the southern region cut off from the rest of the country by targeting anything that moved on the coastal highway.

> Mourning covered Lebanon from South to North, grieving for the victims of the Israeli Massacres. [Pictures of road closure. They took out the headlines jingle.]
> (Headlines, TL news, 19:30, 22 April 1996)

On 22 April 1996 the TL prime-time news programme was broadcast via satellite. A new channel was introduced, called 'News of Lebanon', using a frequency owned by Prime Minister Hariri on the Arab satellite ARABSAT.

> The channel was operating 18 hours a day with a news programme running every hour, on the hour. Six TV channels that had been granted licences earlier that month were asked to participate in supplying news programmes to the channel, in addition to another nine channels that were running without licences. However, the main supplier of news to the channel was Tele Liban.
> (Kandeel, interview with author, 2004)

Kandeel revealed that a meeting with the heads of these television channels took place before the channel went on air. The discussions centred on four main aspects: the need to emphasise that we were subject to an aggressive attack; the need to highlight the resisting will of the people who had decided to stay in their villages to confront the Israeli threats; the need to emphasise national unity; and the need to stress that Arab and other international public opinion could make a difference in this crisis (ibid.).

These were the key messages the government wanted television stations to address in their news coverage. This was the first meeting that a government official had organised with representatives of Lebanese television stations to present them with guidelines. However, these guidelines were crafted along the same lines that TL journalists and administrators had adopted since the first day of the aggression.

On the same day, President Elias Hrawi left Beirut for the United Nations to deliver Lebanon's speech at the General Assembly meeting. Hrawi carried with him a videotape, compiled by TL's news department, on the human and material losses Lebanon suffered during the continuous Israeli attack on its soil (Al Abed, interview with author, 2004). President Hrawi referred to this while talking to the journalists who accompanied him on the plane to New York:

> I'm not going with a complaint, but carrying the voice of Lebanon. What are those children's faults? Why have we to pay for other people's politics? [referring to the Israeli elections that were due to take place in July 1996]
>
> Because of the mourning situation [full of tears] I refused to have an official farewell at the airport. My faith in my country is stronger than anything else. I'm with those who are grieving today, with those ringing the church bells and those praying in mosques.
>
> (Hrawi, TL news, 19:30, 22 April 1996)

President Hrawi's speech and his clearly genuine tears on the plane could be considered or related to the 'plain folks' propaganda device suggested by Jackall (1995) in Chapter Two, where the leader will present himself as one of the public, sharing their feelings, fears hopes and anxieties.

Meanwhile, news stories on the Qana massacre's survivors were presented. For the first time we heard the story of Saadalh Balhas, who had lost more than 20 members of his family in the massacre. Another story marked this programme: that of Israa Al Lakees, a four-year-old child who had gone into a coma after being critically injured by an Israeli raid on her home in the southern suburbs of Beirut. TL's Chief Editor, Wasef Awada, filed the story on Israa's condition, and came to celebrate her recovery from the coma.

> Yesterday Muhammad Deeb, the four-year-old boy, closed his eyes after he had appeared full of life, moving and talking, despite the critical injuries he had received in the Qana massacre. Today, Israa Al Lakees, another four-year-old, opened her eyes after she fell unconscious for a whole week because of her injuries caused by the Israeli air raid on Mreijeh [a district in the southern suburb of Beirut].

> Israa had almost entered the toll of martyrs after being in a coma for a week, but divine intervention kept death away from this innocent child. She opened her eyes today in the intensive care unit in Heart of Jesus Hospital. Israa Al Lakees compensated us for the hot tears we shed on Muhammad Deeb yesterday. Thank you, God. [Images of Muhammad in bed in the morgue, then images of Israa in hospital moving her eyes.]
>
> (Awada, TL news, 19:30, 22 April 1996)

## Day thirteen: Tuesday 23 April 1996

Negotiations around the American and French political initiatives to achieve a ceasefire continued in Damascus, Beirut and Tel Aviv. However, the news showed uncertainty on whether Secretary of State Warren Christopher was heading to Beirut to finalise the ceasefire or not.

The focus in TL's introduction that day was on drawing the map of meetings that had taken place in the three capitals. However, the first item on the running order remained the situation in south Lebanon. A report on the latest attacks on the southern villages and the coastal road was presented, then the story of a graveyard that was being prepared to host the martyrs of Qana.

> [Background ambience of bulldozers in action]: The graveyard is just metres away from where the massacre took place. The UN's headquarters overlooks the space in which 106 martyrs are going to rest. The bulldozers work whenever the shelling stops and the chosen land should be ready in two days... Families and relatives of the victims agreed on the collective funeral and graveyard, and the burial ceremony awaits the end of the Israeli aggression. Meanwhile, the bodies of the martyrs are lying in special fridges in Al Wastani area in Sidon.
>
> (Harb, TL news, 19:30, 23 April 1996)

The story of Muhammad Deeb continued, and we were able to interview his father. We found him sitting beside his niece in a hospital in Tyre. He had lost his wife, four sons, his sister and her three children, and the only other member of his family still alive was his niece.

> I was looking in hospitals for my wife and sons till I was told that my wife and three sons Ali, Kasem and Sadek were dead. Then I started looking for my son Muhammad. People told me they'd heard on Tele Liban that there is a child in Hammoud hospital called Muhammad. I headed to the hospital and found my son. I hugged him and Muhammad asked for Seven Up. When I saw him I felt like hope has returned to my life, but on the second day there were complications and they took Muhammad to the intensive care unit, then they came and told me he'd died. He had asked me for a Seven Up and I brought him one. [Repetition of Muhammad's interview]
> 
> (Deeb, TL news, 19:30, 23 April 1996)

Through our detailed coverage we were able to guide many people to their families or lost ones and we were assisted, as mentioned before, by hospital administrators, NGOs and civil defence crews.

## Day fourteen: Wednesday 24 April 1996

Predictions that had dominated the previous days' news materialised. The US secretary of state, Warren Christopher, came to Chtaura (east of Lebanon) and met with House speaker Nabih Beri and Prime Minister Rafic Hariri to finalise an understanding to end the attacks. Implementation of a ceasefire was to be expected in 48 hours.

Israel meanwhile accelerated its aggression against Lebanon, 'neglecting all the efforts made to achieve a ceasefire' (Introductory headlines, TL news, 19:30, 24 April 1996) and launched an aerial bombardment against the villages of south Lebanon, accompanied by heavy mortar shelling.

> The raids today targeted the river crossings and public roads that link villages together and those linking the villages to the main cities.
> 
> We will be back to you with the details of the military escalation during the bulletin.
> 
> (Harb, ibid.)

A summary of the attacks, village by village, was presented. On that day we called on people to stop risking their lives by trying to drive on the coastal road. We were asking them to start using the temporary bridge installed by the Lebanese army over Al Awali River, an area the warships' guns could not reach. Besides the reports on the shelling, we ran reports on people who had resisted Israeli threats and stayed in their homes in the villages and cities of south Lebanon. The meetings between Lebanese President Hrawi and American President Clinton were covered in detail and given priority.

> [Talking head at press conference] The only way to end Lebanon's problems is to achieve a comprehensive peace in the region and no one is working on that. We are sorry for the death of the civilians. We will offer President Hrawi emergency aid supplies to help restore some of the destruction caused by this cycle of violence. The ceasefire should have been achieved yesterday or the week before.
>
> (Clinton, TL news, 19:30, 24 April 1996)

Clinton's address to the Lebanese journalists accompanying the Lebanese president was repeated twice in the news programme.

Next, another story was introduced from Washington. A demonstration had taken place outside the White House while the meeting between the two presidents was in progress. The demonstrators were calling for American intervention to stop the Israeli aggression against Lebanon.

> Lebanese immigrants came today to Washington, from Detroit and many other American cities. Among them is Mrs Bitar. She lost her two sons, Hadi aged eight and Abed Almouhsen aged nine, in the Qana massacre. They had both been spending their vacation with their grandmother in Qana. She did not say a word. All she did was carry her sons' pictures on a poster that said: 'Israel killed my two sons'. Another demonstration is expected today outside the Israeli embassy in Washington.
>
> (Salemeh, TL news, 19:30, 24 April 1996)

The Lebanese army was issuing a daily detailed summary of the attacks and we were presenting it as quoting the Lebanese army. However, our own coverage of the attacks came first. We were using the army's communiqué to sum up the attacks of the day.

As mentioned before, the army was in a defensive position, shooting when they were shot at. They did not have the artillery to attack, and thus their units in the south took the responsibility of supporting the villagers and inhabitants who had decided to stay. The soldiers all resolutely stayed at their posts among the villagers, encouraging them and giving them confidence that they would be protected if Israel decided to invade, and performing at the same time a humanitarian role by supplying food and water to the besieged people.

From the eleventh day of the aggression (Sunday 21 April), we started running reports on these army units. Every day we tried to visit a different unit and file a report on their activities. By doing this we were trying to emphasise two matters: firstly, that people should not be questioning the army's role at that time and, secondly, we were telling people around those army positions that they could come and seek help from those units if they needed it. TL journalists were functioning as conduits between the inhabitants and the army units that were embedded in the community and we were supporting both of them.

## Day fifteen: Thursday 25 April 1996

Despite the political attempts to end the military operations, Israel continued its bombardment. Again, they were targeting bridges and public roads (Yaghi, TL news, 19:30, 25 April 1996).

More stories on Qana victims and survivors kept coming, and we kept reporting them. Every news programme after the Qana massacre carried a story or two about the victims and the survivors. One of those stories was the story of Mariam and her brother Ibrahim. Highlighting their condition in a previous report led to facilitating their trip to France for expertise not available at that time in Beirut.

> [Voiceover:] Mariam Ismaeel, aged 12, and Ibrahim Ismaeel, aged 8, think their mother, father and sister are in one of Beirut's hospitals. They don't know that they all died in the massacre. Mariam and Ismaeel both lie in hospital in Sidon, next to each other, where we met them.
>
> [Mariam talking to the camera; her face was severely damaged by fire in Qana:]
>
> I want to tell my parents if they are watching me that I'm fine here in the hospital and so is my brother and all we want is to hear from them, and to know that they are ok.
>
> [The camera moves to Ibrahim:]

> I want to tell my mother and father that I am fine and I want to go and see them in Beirut.
>
> [Voiceover:] Mariam and Ibrahim were transferred to Jiatawi hospital in Beirut and from there they will be taken to France for hospitalisation because of their critical injuries.
>
> (Harb, ibid.)

## Day sixteen: Friday 26 April 1996

The ceasefire was announced from Beirut and Tel Aviv, and was to start at four o'clock the next morning.

> An understanding has been achieved and announced by Prime Minister Hariri, with Foreign Minister De Charette at his side in Beirut, and Shimon Peres, with [Warren] Christopher at his side in occupied Jerusalem. Prime Minister Hariri announced that this understanding closed the door against any chance of a repetition of what happened and it is going to lead to long-term stability and protection for civilians. Hariri assured his listeners that the resistance exists within the framework and principles that serve national interests and approaches. However, Prime Minister Hariri stated that a just and permanent solution will only come when Israel leaves our land and withdraws from South Lebanon.
>
> (Awada, TL news, 19:30, 26 April 1996)

The understanding not only protected civilians on both sides, but gave legitimacy to military resistance to fight the occupation in south Lebanon. For the first time in the history of the Lebanese–Israeli conflict, through the auspices of the United States, Israel admitted the Lebanese right to fight the occupation in south Lebanon. Lebanon considered this a political victory and it was clearly portrayed as such in the TL news.

House speaker Nabih Beri used the news media to call on all displaced people to organise their return home from six o'clock on the second morning. We started broadcasting the places where Lebanese army and public-service buses would be waiting the next morning to carry people south to their homes and villages. We had to run that several times during our programme.

## Reflections and conclusion

The memories encapsulated in this chapter brought many tears to my eyes, as if the stories were taking place now and not more than ten years ago. My memories of the emotional distress and frustration I felt in witnessing the killing of innocent children reminded me of how those emotions changed into anger. For 16 days I tried to be the victims' voice to the world, or, as I felt at that time, to whoever was watching. I realised that objectivity as a journalistic norm, especially when covering wars, could hardly be an absolute measure of conduct.

The way we, the Tele Liban journalists, interpreted objectivity identifies completely with the way we were reporting, even though we were emotionally involved with what was happening. Our 'objectivity' fell within the cultural, national and social context we were operating in.

What the narrative, the story of this chapter, suggests is that journalists cannot detach themselves when covering a war launched on their country. Thus patriotism and nationalism marked Lebanese journalists' work during those 16 days of coverage. They identified themselves as members of the nation; they sympathised with their fellow citizens and were emotionally involved.

I still remember my cameraman trying to lead the way for me with his camera to get into one of the targeted containers in Qana. The container was full of shattered bodies of innocent men, women and children. The UN soldiers were trying to keep people away. He was shouting in despair: 'Let me go in! These are my people.' They were indeed 'our people' and that made all the difference for me and my colleagues.

Partisanship in TL journalists' commentaries became clearer in the wake of the Qana massacre. However, when interviewed later they dismissed the word 'propaganda' because they too think of it as a negative practice. Only the chairman of TL, Fouad Naim, answered the question of whether our coverage was propaganda by saying: 'If anyone accuses us that we were conducting propaganda, then yes: we were. It was propaganda of the truth'.

Looking at it retrospectively and from a distance, it was surely a 'positioned truth', a 'truth' told through the eyes of one side of the conflict, but none of us saw it as such at that moment. It was our version of the 'truth', which then – because it was believed in so fervently and so nationalistically, because it was lived and embodied in our daily encounters with shattered, innocent bodies – comes to seem to be an 'objective truth'.

We were all driven by our experiences as Lebanese citizens over the course of a lifetime, by our sense of the wrong being done to our country. We were driven by the need to report and highlight the scale of the Israeli offensive and to communicate the suffering of the people of south Lebanon to the rest of the Lebanese public. Our coverage also aimed at achieving national unity against the Israeli aggression. So what the Lebanese journalists are arguing here, and what they did then, come to seem to be not propaganda (in its negative form) but 'truth' – as Naim said – and a form of what I have argued earlier in this book to be a context-specific form of liberation propaganda.

However, as the detailed presentation of the events and the coverage shows, many aspects of propaganda techniques were evident in this coverage. The propaganda conducted here was mainly propaganda 'to the home front' – the term that Goebbels used to differentiate two kinds of propaganda: one that targets the home front and one aimed at the enemy (see Chapter Two). Although the 'propaganda' we conducted does not match with most of Goebbels' 19 principles, it nevertheless corresponds with at least two of them: firstly 'to diminish the impact of frustration at home' and secondly to 'specify the target of hatred', in this case the Israeli aggression (see Goebbels' principles in Doob 1995: 214).

Further, the devices of name-calling and glittering generalities – identified by the Institute for Propaganda Analysis, mentioned in Chapter Two – were also applicable in our coverage. We (the journalists who covered the events) used terms like 'aggressor army', 'the enemy forces', 'a state thirst for blood' and a 'blood-loving government'. We used rhetoric like 'the Grapes of Wrath operation exploded with hate'. We were appealing to people's emotions of love, brotherhood, honour and freedom. We were also appealing to people's political and historical heritage, which is in fact quite similar to what Al Manar journalists were doing and which is illustrated in Chapter Seven.

None of the Lebanese journalists covering the April events was operating in accordance with previously structured plans drawn up by a propagandist. However, the work that I and other Lebanese journalists were doing was absolutely 'intentional'. Our training, our experience as Lebanese citizens over the course of the Arab–Israeli conflict, our sense of the harm and damage caused to our country, all made it possible for us to be totally sure and focused about what had to be done and could be done.

Applying illustratively some of Jowett and O'Donnell's divisions of propaganda analysis, discussed in Chapter Two, to the TL journalists' performance during the April 1996 events, we observe the following:

1. There was no orchestrated or managed campaign. Journalists were acting upon their own beliefs and ideas. Israel was an enemy state that was occupying their land and was launching an attack on their civilian people. Their ideology was simply generated from the history of the Arab–Israeli conflict and the Lebanese–Israeli part in this. They did not agree that they were applying or implementing the Lebanese Government's political and humanitarian messages in their coverage. However, looking through the chronological narration of that coverage, we can see that TL coverage was in many ways reflecting the government's messages and particularly those put forward by Prime Minister Rafic Hariri. The purpose was to unify the people against one enemy, Israel, and stay defiant, which, as will be illustrated in Chapter Seven, was a common denominator with Al Manar journalists as well.
2. The media campaign took place amid a war that was launched on Lebanon's civil population and infrastructure by a foreign country, Israel, which occupied 10 per cent of Lebanese territory. The Israeli military operation was associated with the long history of the Arab–Israeli conflict. It took place while Lebanon was trying to get back on its feet as a unified civil society after 15 years of civil war, which included two Israeli invasions of its land. Thus, the shared ideas and ideals, the shared experiences, the shared threat, the interpersonal relationships, all produced a very consistent and common approach, which became very deliberate in terms of personal commitment. So the way we reported was intentional, though the media campaign was not managed or planned.
3. No propagandist, as identified in Chapter Two, could be branded here. There was no person or group of people who had put into action a clear and structured plan to conduct a propaganda campaign.

4. The media campaign targeted Lebanese audiences in the first place. After broadcasting began on satellite, the target audience widened to cover Arabs and Lebanese in the Arab world and in the Diaspora. The images then became a propaganda tool beyond the home front. This campaign was not targeting the enemy (which, as discussed in Chapter Seven, was the case with the Al Manar campaign) but the wider Arab and international audience, non-domestic audiences, seeking support, help and solidarity. These images and stories became powerful tools in propagating the idea of Lebanese victimhood, which can readily be argued to have led in the July 2006 war to Israeli military attacks on the transmission centres of several Lebanese television stations, including Tele Liban. The attacks destroyed Al Manar TV's headquarters in the southern suburbs of Beirut in an attempt to silence its images and messages (more about the role of Al Manar will be presented in Chapter Seven). These attacks were new and different aspects of the media war between Lebanon and Israel, which opens the way for new research questions.

5. As the narration of events shows, Lebanese and Arab audiences responded to TL messages for help, unity and solidarity in clear and demonstrable ways. The late prominent journalist and writer Samir Kasir[19] described the performance of TL during April 1996 as highly professional. He said (in an article in a French magazine) that TL as a public-service television station had ousted all competition in its wide and accurate coverage. Kasir praised what he called the 'calmness and professionalism' of my performance specifically, which in his words 'projected the voice of an emblematic figure of the coverage of TL' (Kasir, *L'Orient Express*, May 1996).

The media campaign conducted by TL journalists during the events of April 1996 has many features that match propaganda principles, devices and definitions illustrated in this chapter and discussed in Chapter Two. Nonetheless, it also differs in several respects.

Our coverage was factual. We did not fabricate news; we did not deceive our audience. The footage of guiltless victims killed by Israeli bombardments and air raids spoke for itself. We all believed (even years after the events, when I raised the question) that we were 'objective' in our reporting. However, as discussed earlier, ultimate objectivity was actually unachievable. Journalists are affected by the historical, cultural, social and political context they operate within. Thus, the objectivity that all journalists interviewed for this research claimed was contextual. Journalists reporting war when their country or nation is under threat can hardly achieve any other kind of objectivity than precisely this.

The Lebanese journalists (of both TL and Al Manar, as will be demonstrated in the next chapter) believed they were serving their people's cause by highlighting and exposing the Israeli aggression. I was personally affected by the scale of the Israeli brutality in killing civilians and destroying homes, and felt compelled to report this Israeli brutality to my audiences. In most of my coverage I remember that the only people who were on my mind were those poor and powerless villagers whom I had met during our regular attempts to break the siege Israel had imposed on them. I wanted to help these villagers, and images and words were my only tools.

However, looking back at my performance in a retrospective and reflexive way, I realise that my reporting was affected by the horror I had lived through and witnessed at the time. As a journalist I went 'native', in the anthropological and ethnographic sense (see Chapter Three), and, as anthropologists have come to understand, objectivity and distance are impossible in such a context, where the only truth is one that is positioned or contextual. Impartiality in such circumstances is more than difficult to maintain. But these complexities, as I have argued earlier in elaborating a meaning for the term 'liberation propaganda', are exactly what were involved in what the TL journalists were doing in this context.

## Summary

In this chapter I have tried to outline the news values and norms that characterised the work of Lebanese journalists in their coverage of the April 1996 events and the impact of the historical, political, social and cultural contexts on the ways in which they operated. I have tried to indicate features and performance related to propaganda notions and principles.

This chapter demonstrates that Lebanese journalists were applying some of the propaganda tools and techniques I have outlined earlier in this book, without realising that many aspects of their performance matched some propaganda norms. However, it nevertheless also clearly demonstrates that they were propagating the cause of their people by avoiding deception, lies and the fabrication of news. Their aim was to help Lebanon achieve its sovereignty and freedom by ending the Israeli occupation of its southern territories.

The April 1996 Israeli military operations against Lebanon gave prominence to the Islamic resistance in south Lebanon and its operations against Israeli forces in the occupied territories. Almost without exception, the whole of Lebanon was united around the right of resistance. The role the media played in uniting the people of Lebanon against the one enemy paved the way for Al Manar TV, which is affiliated to Hezbollah, to announce itself as Resistance TV and start a media campaign to highlight the rightness of the resistance and demonise the abilities of the Israeli army.

What started as an un-planned and un-structured media campaign with TL became a planned and structured media campaign with Al Manar. Driven by the same aim (that is, liberation) as the TL journalists, Al Manar's campaign expanded the target audience to cover the enemy's soldiers and some sections of the enemy's society, in particular, the soldiers' mothers. Chapter Seven therefore looks into the performance of Al Manar TV during certain notable military incidents in the period between 1997 and 2000, the year that Israel withdrew from most of the land they had occupied in south Lebanon, except for seven farms that border both Syria and Israel.

# 7

# LIBERATION MEDIA: HEZBOLLAH AND AL MANAR, 1997–2000

> We are less qualified in one respect: the propaganda. They are trying to hit our weak points and we have to hit back.
> (General Kobi Maroum, commanding officer of Israel's Golani Regiment serving in south Lebanon, *Yediot Ahronot*, 5 January 1998)

Israel's Grapes of Wrath operation in April 1996 against Lebanon served to give new status to Hezbollah's Islamic resistance. Despite the great destruction the operation inflicted on Lebanon and despite all the talk of ending Hezbollah's Katyusha short-range rocket attacks against northern Israel, the number of rockets raining down on Galilee appeared to increase during the military operation.

The Hezbollah military apparatus was intact and, as Hala Jaber in her book *Hezbollah* indicates, the group's popularity became unquestionable.

> The guerrillas whom Israel was set on destroying at the start of the campaign had suffered few casualties and their popularity had risen. For the first time since the group had come into being, Lebanese of all religions, sects and classes rallied around the Party of God's Islamic resistance in an

unprecedented show of support and solidarity. Even Israel's old-time allies of 1982, the Christian Maronites, managed to put aside their political differences and supported the resistance.

(Jaber 1997: 196)

After the events of April 1996, Lebanese society as a whole showed a tendency to defend those who chose to resist. Hassan Ez-Addine, head of Hezbollah's media relations (2001–4) and former press officer, believed that Lebanese television stations – notably Tele Liban (TL) – were able to present the real, 'aggressive' image of the Israeli attacks against Lebanon:

> They were able to reflect the fact that Lebanon was the victim and that Israel is the aggressor. The Israelis attacked every village, town and city in south Lebanon. They destroyed the country's infrastructure. They killed innocent people and the Lebanese stations were able to show that in detail, minute after minute. This resulted in the wave of support the refugees received all over Lebanon, and the amount of support the resistance received morally and financially from all sectors of Lebanese society. The message the media was able to deliver – along with their resolute position in support of the resistance and images of the steadfastness of the resistance fighters – helped in achieving the victorious April Understanding that made the enemy itself recognise our right to fight their soldiers to liberate our land.

(Ez-Addine, interview with author, 2004)

Hezbollah's new, popular political status produced a new media strategy and performance. This chapter explores Hezbollah's media plan, its structure and units, and the role that Al Manar TV,[1] affiliated to Hezbollah, played in implementing this media plan. To illustrate this, I analyse Al Manar's journalists' performance during certain military incidents and encounters between the resistance and the Israeli army in south Lebanon. What started with TL as un-structured and un-organised media campaign aiming to defy the enemy by uniting the nation around its government and resistance fighters was translated by Al Manar into an organised, strategic plan to use the media systematically as one of the tools to achieve liberation.

# Liberation Media: Hezbollah and Al Manar, 1997–2000

This chapter consists of a chronological narration and analysis of Al Manar's coverage of ten major military incidents, mainly in south Lebanon, between 1997 and 2000, the liberation year.[2] The narration is based on 20 hours of Al Manar's news coverage.

Unlike the previous chapter, this chapter does not use the first-person voice, because I did not work with or for Al Manar TV, though I shared common cultural and national aspirations and principles, and had connections with them. As my methodology suggests, any account such as this (one that tells a story, though not with the same reflexivity here as in Chapter Six) is carried along by the major events that were reported – and, in this case, developed by Hezbollah's personnel through Al Manar. The events are looked at chronologically, rather than thematically, in line with the pattern established in the previous chapter.

As mentioned in Chapter Three, I am studying Lebanese journalists' performance and conduct as a 'complete participant'. Having connections with Al Manar journalists and being given access to their archive helped in building the ethnographic story of their coverage. This narration is aided by interviews conducted with these journalists and with the administrators who were directly involved in the coverage studied here. It is also aided by interviews with Hezbollah's media personnel. Press archives from Israeli, Lebanese and pan-Arab papers are used to highlight or support the story told. These news cuttings were collected from Lebanese newspaper archives and from two documentation centres in Beirut: the Arabic Centre for Information and the Consultative Centre for Studies and Documentation.

Importantly, the performance of Al Manar journalists in the 1997 to 2000 period is presented and examined in relation to propaganda principles and techniques, along with journalism's norms of objectivity, neutrality, accuracy and impartiality, introduced in Chapters Two and Three. The narration was produced by transcribing and translating the television news archive and interviews. Field-notes were derived from journalists' own memories of the events under investigation. This chapter follows the same process of narrativising data and carrying out analysis, as applied in Chapter Six.

Thus, it draws on the theoretical framework discussed earlier – and is particularly centred around the norms and values of journalism, and their implementation in time of war. It aims to outline the news values and norms that characterised the work of Al Manar journalists in their coverage of major encounters between the resistance and Israeli troops between 1997 and 2000, and the impact of the historical social, cultural and religious context on the way they operated.

It therefore also seeks to pinpoint features and performance related to the concepts and principles of propaganda as presented in Chapter Two. Specifically, this chapter identifies similarities and parallels between Al Manar journalists' performance and that of Tele Liban journalists in their coverage of the April 1996 events discussed in Chapter Six. This chapter is divided into two sections: Hezbollah's media plan and the Al Manar TV coverage.

## Hezbollah's media strategy

According to Professor Muhammad Mohsen,[3] an expert on propaganda and public opinion at the Lebanese University, Hezbollah had had a clear and organised media plan since the early 1990s, but this plan was reinforced after the events of April 1996.[4]

> In 1996 Hezbollah realised the importance of a professional and organised media performance and also recognized the importance of building on the people's consensus around the resistance. I believe that the 1996 war was a turning point in Hezbollah's media performance and conduct. They became more organised and precise in the content and style of the messages.
> (Mohsen, interview with author, 2004)

Mohsen pointed out that there was a clear change in Hezbollah's media policies in the wake of the events of 1996, because they had new audiences that they needed to address – beyond their natural constituency, their party members and close supporters. Thus they had to consider the shift in character of their audiences. They institutionalised their media operation as units and centres (discussed below). They opened up to receive some 1,200 foreign reporters in their offices during the 1996 events alone (Mohsen 1998). They granted interviews with Hezbollah's political figures, and dedicated English- and French-speaking personnel to explain Hezbollah's (and Lebanon's) position in the Arab–Israeli conflict.

# Liberation Media: Hezbollah and Al Manar, 1997–2000  177

As a result, Mohsen says that Hezbollah's media performance had developed dramatically since 1982, the year the idea of forming a party first arose (for more on how Hezbollah came to exist, see Saad Ghorayeb 2002, Qassem 2005 and Jaber 1997). According to Mohsen, Hezbollah's media management reached its climax in the year 2000. That was the year Hezbollah fighters were able to celebrate the defeat of the Israeli army in south Lebanon and the withdrawal of Israeli troops from the territory that Israel had occupied for 22 years (Mohsen 1998).

Hezbollah came into existence in 1982, following Israel's invasion of Lebanon. However, its existence was not made official until 1985, when Israeli occupation troops retreated into south Lebanon and established what they called their 'security zone', which constituted 10 per cent of Lebanese territory (see Saad Ghorayeb 2002, Qassem 2005, Hafez 2001, Jaber 1997 and Jaber 1999).

## How the strategy developed

Mohsen (interview with author, 2004) considered that Hezbollah's media strategy went through four main phases:

1. In the preparatory period from 1982 to 1986, Hezbollah distributed its messages through flyers, leaflets, banners, signs, wall pictures, and political and religious festivals. These were the tools for what Mohsen calls the 'populist media'. Mohsen related these tools to those used by the communists in their build-up to the October revolution in 1917 (for more on the role of media in the Bolshevik revolution, see Thomson 1999).
2. The period between 1986 and 1990 was used to get Hezbollah 'in the picture', whether it was reported positively or negatively, to publicise Hezbollah and its role in fighting the Israeli occupation.
3. At the end of the 1980s, cameramen started joining the resistance fighters during combat. Filming of operations became a regular feature from 1990 onwards, reaching its climax in 1993, when cameramen were killed during combat (see below for discussion of the role of the resistance cameramen as part of the Military Media Unit).
4. The events of April 1996 and the governmental and public support the Islamic resistance gained – support enhanced by TL journalists'

coverage of events (see Chapter Six) – made that year a turning point. Those events were the catalyst for Hezbollah's new, more organised and precise media strategy, which Mohsen asserts clearly helped in achieving liberation in 2000.

The April Understanding[5] gave international legitimacy to the 'Islamic resistance' (Hezbollah's military wing) in fighting Israeli forces in the occupied territories in south Lebanon, and this led Hezbollah's leadership and its media personnel to think of new media strategies. This strategy aimed at targeting new audiences in and beyond Lebanon, not just the Muslim Shiite community in Lebanon and other Hezbollah supporters.

According to Muhamad Haidar, the head of Al Manar TV and a member of the Hezbollah Political Bureau, and Mouafaq Al Jammal, Hezbollah's press officer between 1996 and 2000, they now targeted five groups: the resistance fighters and their families, the Lebanese community at large in all its religious sectors and parties,[6] the wider Arab world, the Israelis (soldiers, their mothers and the military and political elite) and the international community (Al Jammal and Haidar, interviews with author, 2000, 2004).

Hassan Ez-Addine considered the years between 1997 and 2000 to be the climax of Hezbollah's media campaign. They were the years that 'preceded the liberation' and witnessed the 'countdown to victory', marked by the Israeli withdrawal from south Lebanon (Ez-Addine, interview with author, 2004). This came after a unilateral decision by Ehud Barak, the Israeli prime minister at the time, to withdraw without any prior conditions.

## Arab and Israeli 'truth' and propaganda

One of the experts who worked on drawing up and finalising these new strategies and plans (who asked, for his own security, to remain anonymous) revealed that a group of experts in political propaganda and psychological warfare was appointed to draw up Hezbollah's new media strategy. Among other things, they outlined the organisational structure of the media war with Israel.

The expert added (interview with author, 2003) that these media plans took into consideration media policies and propaganda techniques developed and tried in previous wars, such as Grenada and Vietnam. For instance, they decided that it was important to give alternative access to information to local and foreign journalists. Hezbollah viewed its position as being like that of the Vietcong or the revolutionary government of Grenada that the United States wanted to overthrow. (For more information on war and the media in Vietnam and Grenada, see Hudson and Stanier 1999 and Knightley 2000).

So what had been – in the performance of Tele Liban journalists in April 1996 (discussed in Chapter Six) – reactive, largely unplanned and not deliberately structured with any propagandistic intent, became a clearly outlined, planned and structured system of media operations by Hezbollah's media people, and consequently by Al Manar. This development meets two of the main criteria that Taylor identifies in defining his understanding of propaganda: the connection between 'truth' and propaganda, and revealing the truth and gaining credibility (Taylor 2003: 5–6).

Importantly, for Mouafak Al Jammal, credibility was at the core of these media policies and strategies, for they were basically trying to counter Israeli propaganda.

> We faced the necessity of confronting Israeli propaganda – that was full of lies and hatred against all Arabs, and especially against us [Hezbollah and the resistance]. We were aiming to try and persuade media organisations worldwide to change the term 'terrorists' to 'fighters seeking to liberate their own occupied land', to replace the word 'gangs' by 'resistance groups', to change the phrase 'terrorist attacks' to 'resistance operations'.
>
> (interview with author 2000)

The Hezbollah team were equally aware of the connection between 'truth' and propaganda, and how, according to Goebbels, propaganda has nothing necessarily in common with truth and objectivity (Thomson 1999: 4).

Hezbollah's media personnel were convinced that the real motives and causes behind their struggle were distorted by the Israeli public relations machine and that they therefore had to disseminate their side of the story. They needed to tell the 'truth about their struggle', said the anonymous expert. The words 'truth' and 'credibility' were emphasised when talking about the resistance's military operations in south Lebanon, particularly in reporting the military losses Israel was suffering in the occupied territories. Importantly, they considered deception a flaw that would affect their cause negatively.

Nayef Krayem, chairman of Al Manar and the Hezbollah-affiliated radio station Al Nour (1997–2001) and former head of Hezbollah's Central Media Unit (1996–7), who was identified as the man behind the development of this political propaganda, told the *Daily Telegraph* in April 2000:

> For 40 years the Arab media were useless. But we have learned from the failures of the past and the success of the Israelis in this field. Of course, the Israelis are stronger than us worldwide, but in this conflict there is no doubt we have the upper hand.
>
> (Krayem in Philips, *Daily Telegraph*, 12 April 2000)

Krayem was referring to what Rugh categorises as the 'mobilising' and 'loyalist' media systems in the Arab world. The first is characterised by the almost total subordination of the mass media to the political system and state regimes, and the second consists of privately owned media organisations that are loyal to the state regime (Rugh 2004).

These media systems tend to exaggerate the strength of the state, and one of the examples that Krayem related was that of the Egyptian broadcaster Ahmad Said, of Swat Al Arab,[7] during the 1967 war with Israel. Ahmad Said kept telling his Arab listeners that the Arabs were winning the war – while the residents of Jerusalem were watching Israeli tanks taking up position near their homes.

This version became known as the Ahmad Said war. To many Arabs, the defeat came as a shock; indeed, many commentators believed that the Arabs lost the 1967 war not just because of military inability, but because of Ahmad Said's misleading information and exaggeration (see Khoury 1995). The late head of the Journalists' Syndicate in Lebanon, Riyad Taha, wrote a book – *Al Iaalam wal Maaraka* ('The media and the battle') – about the Arab media's failure to present the Arab side of the story to the international community and the way the Zionist movement had succeeded in putting its argument forward. He argued that world leaders viewed the Arab–Israeli conflict through the prism of Israeli eyes (Taha 1973).

Supporting this, Edward Said, in Gauri Viswanathan's book *Power, Politics and Culture* (2004), speaks of how Israel's version of the history of its conflict with the Palestinians and the Arabs is the one widely circulated in the West. Said also asserts the need to emphasise the facts and realities which support the Arab and Palestinian cause of liberation and independence. In the same way, Greg Philo and Mike Berry in their book, *Bad News from Israel* (2004), speak of the effectiveness of the Israeli PR machine in building contacts with journalists, and passing information and views to journalists on issues related to the Palestinian-Israeli conflict.

Hezbollah's media people were aware of the strengths and weaknesses of the messages Israel tended to circulate to the international community and they started drawing up plans and strategies on how to counter it. Krayem wrote that Hezbollah media's main aim was to counter Israel's 'false' messages – which aimed at demonising the resistance fighters' motives and abilities, and claiming themselves as the army that could not be defeated (Krayem 1998: 49).

Countering Israeli messages was also practised by TL journalists during the coverage of the April 1996 events (see Chapter Six). However, Hezbollah media people and consequently Al Manar journalists took it to a more strategic level and applied organised counter-propaganda policies. These policies, as in the TL journalists' case, fall within the framework of defensive as opposed to offensive, and integrative rather than subversive, forms of propaganda, as discussed in Chapter Two. The kind of liberation propaganda this book is arguing for involves aspects of the kinds of defensive, integrative counter-propaganda that both the TL journalists and the Hezbollah media people, including the Al Manar journalists, were applying.

However, in contrast to the TL journalists' unstructured coverage, Hezbollah's media strategies and policies were practised through particular devices, units and practices, and what follows is a summary of these.

## Al Manar's Political Propaganda Unit

At the end of 1997, Al Manar brought together all media production related to the resistance in a new unit, calling it in Arabic 'Qsem Al Diaayah Al Siyasiah', which translates literally as the 'Political Propaganda Unit'.

Hussein Hmayed, head of the unit at the time, explained that after the 1996 events they felt the need to organise and develop their performance in promoting the conduct of the resistance. 'In the administrative structure we were part of the programming and promotion department' (Hmayed, interview with author, 2003). This unit was only responsible for producing patriotic video-clips and flashes that praised the resistance fighters and sought to demoralise Israeli soldiers and Israeli military institutions. Some of these were broadcast in Arabic, some in Hebrew, and in some cases translated into both languages.

The unit lasted till the liberation and then it became part of a new department called the Resistance Department.

## The Military Media Unit

Most Hezbollah media personnel interviewed for this research talked about the 'media traps' they planted on several occasions for the Israelis. One of these took place in 1994 when the resistance attacked an Israeli position called Debshe, in occupied south Lebanon. They raised the flag there after destroying the position.

The resistance distributed a press release about the operation without showing any pictures, and the Israeli army denied the operation, saying that none of their soldiers had been killed and that nothing had changed in Debshe. The Hezbollah media people, at that point, released the videotape of the operation, which showed dead soldiers and how the fighters had climbed the hill and planted their flag (Al Jammal, interview with author, 2000). The Israeli press then attacked the Israeli Army for lying, using such phrases as 'Hezbollah media humiliated the military institution' (*Assafir*, 21 September 1996, n.p.).

This directly led to the idea of having a cameraman as a fixed member of every operation that took place, thus becoming part of the team. Copies of films became routinely distributed to local television stations, as well as the offices of international and Arab media organisations and news agencies in Lebanon. An embargo on the timing of the release of such film, however, remained in the hands of Hezbollah's media people.

The use of such a cameraman had started in the late 1980s, though this was not particularly professional until after 1996, when trained personnel came to accompany the groups. These had the ability to film day or night with equipment that was able to catch detail from a great distance. As the head of the Military Media Unit, Haj Maitham, said, it became a priority for the fighters to keep the camera safe and keep the tapes with them (interview with author, 2004).

> Before 1996 there was no specialised unit responsible for filming operations. We used to depend on volunteers and not professional, trained and equipped personnel. In 1996 an organised formation was introduced that was given hi-tech equipment and a specific space. [Also,] the problems the unit faced were studied and solutions were sought. For example, at the beginning, we did not have a person dedicated to looking after how this unit was operating, but after 1996 a small section was introduced within the resistance to take care professionally of this issue.
>
> (ibid.)

The film shot by Military Media Unit cameramen would first be broadcast on Al Manar, and then distributed to local and international news agencies and television stations in Lebanon. One of the aims of showing these films, besides documenting Israeli losses, was to tell young Lebanese, 'If these guys can do it, you can do it too' (Krayem, interview with author, 2000).

Tel Zalmnobites, of the Israeli magazine *Bmsehneih*, wrote a report about the effectiveness of the filming of the resistance's operations, headed: 'A film directed by Hassan Nasrallah' (Secretary General of Hezbollah). The report revealed how the footage of Debshe (see above) had left its imprint, since '[an Israeli] soldier has been always told that the Israeli army never leaves its position and the Israeli army could not be defeated' (*Bmsehneih*, 21 September 1996, n.p.).

> So successful has the Hezbollah campaign been that the Israelis are about to withdraw from Lebanon – a practically unheard of example of the most powerful army in the Middle East retreating before Arab guns. Israeli losses in Southern Lebanon are not enormous – about 25 killed a year – but the fact that Hezbollah cameramen have caught the moment when Israeli mothers' sons are killed has had a

fatal effect on public opinion, making it impossible for the [Israeli] army to continue.

(Philips, *Daily Telegraph*, 12 April 2000, n.p.)

Similarly, the Israeli daily *Yediot Ahronot*, in an article in April 1997, discussed the power of 'Hezbollah's propaganda war' against Israel, saying 'They have succeeded in driving us towards despair' (*Yediot Ahronot*, 25 April 1997, n.p.). The paper quoted an Israeli military psychiatrist as saying that 'Hezbollah's propaganda war' had been far more effective on the Israeli soldiers than the military one:

> The main targets for the Israeli air force at the moment are Hezbollah's TV and radio stations' transmitting areas – Israeli intelligence is planning to hit the Manar TV station and Al Nour radio station – and this indicates the real danger Hezbollah's [propaganda war] is having on the morale of the Israelis. Sixty-five percent of the Israeli soldiers that serve in south Lebanon are less determined to fight after watching the video tape Hezbollah released about its 'martyrdom battalion' while preparing for new operations in south Lebanon.
>
> (ibid.)

Elihu Katz, the Israeli media scholar, told Saad Hamad, Jerusalem correspondent of the pan-Arab newspaper *Al Hayat*, that the images Al Manar broadcast, which were then re-transmitted on Israeli TV (Channel One), highlighted and drew Israeli public opinion and attention to what exactly was happening in south Lebanon. He believed that these images had deepened the feeling of Israeli public opinion about the pointlessness of staying in south Lebanon, especially with the April Understanding that bounded the Israeli army's freedom of movement. He explained that these pictures were seen as 'bloody clear evidence on the situation' (Hamad, *Al Hayat*, 16 April 2000, n.p.).

Katz was referring to the fact that the Israeli army occupation of south Lebanon was not bringing security and strength to Israel, but rather images of death and humiliation. However, Tamar Liebes, professor of communication studies at the Hebrew University in Jerusalem, pointed out that it was very difficult to define how far these images affected Israeli public opinion so that it became largely in favour of immediate withdrawal from south Lebanon. She explained that no surveys had been conducted within Israeli society on this shift of position, and if this shift happened it would be difficult to identify what really made it take place.

Nonetheless, Liebes did not exclude the possibility that the Israeli audience's discovery of what was happening on the battlefield (watching wounded soldiers so close up and hearing their moans) had added to the cumulative process that led Israeli society to conclude that staying in Lebanon with such losses would be useless (ibid.).

## The Media Relations Centre

Hezbollah's liaison officer for all Lebanese, Arab and international media outlets, Haidar Dukmak, speaks of two phases of change that the media relations unit went through. In the early organisational structure, this unit was called the Central Media Unit. Between 1987 and 1996 it was responsible for all Hezbollah-affiliated media outlets: Al Manar, Al Nour (the radio station), *Al Intiqad* (the magazine) and Hezbollah's official internet website. It was also responsible for what Hezbollah calls the 'popular media': posters, regional parades, political festivals, sports and cultural activities and banners (Dukmak, interview with author, 2004).

Later, in 1996, the centre witnessed 'a restructuring phase' when Al Manar and Al Nour stopped being under the auspices of the Central Media Unit and became solely run by an elected board of directors in accordance with the Lebanese Audio-Visual Law (see Chapter Five on this). Also, delivery of Hezbollah's political messages to party members and supporters was no longer centralised. This responsibility was transferred to the regional party groups across the country (ibid.).

The Central Media Unit instead became responsible for organising relations with other media outlets and journalists, whether Lebanese, Arab or international. They became the source of information on Hezbollah and the resistance for all media outlets (Ez-Addine, interview with author, 2004). As mentioned, the resistance's videotapes, filmed by the Military Media Unit (identified as a separate section within the military apparatus of the resistance), would come to the central office first and would then be distributed to other stations and news agencies.

However, Al Manar came to have direct access to the Military Media Unit. Thus, the central office's responsibilities could be summarised as:

- issuing detailed press releases on the resistance's military operations and Hezbollah's political statements;
- establishing contacts with media institutions all over the world, inviting foreign and local journalists to meet leaders of Hezbollah and arranging visits to the Islamic resistance's military positions on the front lines in south Lebanon;
- establishing several web pages and exploring 'third wave propaganda', as defined by Taylor (2003). This is propaganda and counter-propaganda waged on the net, which is beyond the scope of this study.

Because of this re-structuring, the central media office was re-named in 2000 the Media Relations Centre. The emphasis of its work was on the relationship with other media outlets and journalists from all over the world.

## The Hebrew Monitoring Unit

Al Manar used to broadcast news flashes in Hebrew after every resistance operation against Israeli soldiers in south Lebanon. They also re-broadcast every commentary the Israeli TV or press presented on the 'failures' of the Israeli army and the 'abilities' of the resistance. They also broadcast what Israeli TV had re-broadcast from Al Manar in Hebrew, subtitled in Arabic, such as clips and films of military resistance operations.

The target of these broadcasts was the Lebanese domestic audience, particularly as these re-broadcasts indicated that the 'enemy' was admitting to the abilities of the resistance fighters. Importantly, they were also intended to raise the morale of the fighters themselves, and their families, and to encourage new people to be recruited to the resistance.

Further, two working units were created to monitor Israeli media outlets, to transcribe and translate whatever related to Lebanon, Hezbollah and the resistance. One unit came to be based at Al Manar and the other in the Military Media Unit (MMU). However, staff in the two units became integrated and could work interchangeably in either unit (anonymous member of MMU, interview with author, 2003).

The team of translators came to consist mainly of ex-detainees from Israeli prisons, who had (perhaps ironically) spent their years in detention studying Hebrew. One of the programmes they transmitted became called *The image coup* – highlighting problems in Israeli society and playing clips that demonstrated this, taken from Israeli TV. The target audiences here were Arabs generally and particularly the Lebanese, to show that Israel's 'ideal' community, which 'Israeli propaganda' tries to emphasise, 'hardly exists in reality' (Al Manar website, 2000).

Such an ideal Israeli society is pictured as utopian, where there is no crime, no corruption but ultimate freedom of speech. What this programme sought to do was to demonise Israeli society through its own television material. The programme therefore highlighted crimes of rape, military censorship, official corruption and discrimination against non-European Jews and Arab Palestinians within Israeli society. Demonising the 'enemy' has been one of the basic tools of propaganda throughout history (see the history of propaganda, discussed in Chapter Two).

Some of the Hebrew clips were addressed to the Israeli soldiers' mothers: 'Why let your son die in south Lebanon? Stop him from joining the troops in the Lebanese occupied territories!!' Nayef Krayem says these were obviously designed to work on their emotions, addressing the core feature a propagandist should appeal to in order to influence their targets. The clips were seen in Israel through both Manar and Israeli TV. Israeli TV used to show the Hebrew clips made by Al Manar and make comments on how the Hezbollah media were developing (Israeli Channel 2, September 1996), which for Krayem was a bonus. The Israelis were presenting the resistance with free publicity:

> We used to produce a new clip whenever we saw the old one on Israeli TV, which we monitor 24 hours a day. The Israelis later stopped broadcasting our clips, but the press kept writing about them.
>
> (Krayem, interview with author, 2000)

Muhammad Budiar, who works at both Al Manar and the Military Media Unit as a translator (from Hebrew to Arabic and vice versa), is considered by Al Manar as an expert on Israeli affairs and his analysis is seen as essential. He was detained in Israeli prisons for 10 years after being captured while conducting an operation against the Israeli army in south Lebanon. He obtained a degree in political science from Tel Aviv Open University during his years of detention.

Budiar speaks of eight individuals working in both Al Manar and the Military Media Unit on monitoring the Israeli media and translating what is related to Hezbollah, the resistance and Lebanon. Six out of eight are former detainees in Israeli prisons; the other two had learned Hebrew in Lebanon (Budiar, interview with author, 2004). He reveals that the outlets that are monitored 24 hours a day are: news programmes of Israeli Channels 1 and 2, Israeli army radio, the Israeli Arabic radio station and the Russian Bet network (ibid.).

In addition to monitoring what the Israeli press say or write on Lebanon, Hezbollah and the resistance, the Hebrew unit monitors political developments in Israeli society. Some of Hezbollah's communiqués, activities and statements are produced to address weaknesses in the political institutions in Israel, aiming at demonising its supposed moral superiority. Taithe defines this as counter-propaganda, where one party denounces the other's lack of credibility and its dishonesty at all levels, including within their political and military institutions (Taithe and Thornton 1999: 1).

Throughout Hezbollah's media work, aspects of their strategy can be identified among the devices listed by the Institute for Propaganda Analysis as propaganda techniques (Jackall 1995: 217). Among these are: name calling (giving pejorative names to the enemy); transference (having religious leaders and government back their campaign); testimonials (making use of narratives, such as those given by people affected by the Israeli attacks); plain folks (we are all plain folk, identifying true-life stories from all sections of Lebanese society and their involvement in the struggle – which underlines that this does affect all parts of society); the band wagon (adjuring everyone to become involved – follow us, everybody is doing it); targeting the emotions of all parties (as mentioned, this seeks to appeal to such people as the mothers of the Israeli soldiers).

However, the main feature that characterised their media performance was the credibility of their messages, which was also identified as a main feature in the TL journalists' performance presented in Chapter Six. Credibility was expressed mainly in what

Hezbollah media people and Al Manar journalists identified later as 'media traps', meaning footage of operations taken by resistance cameramen and only revealed to counter an Israeli army denial that such military operations had taken place. By revealing the real footage of certain losses denied by Israel, Al Manar and Hezbollah media people were undermining the credibility of the 'enemy' and keeping their own credibility high.

Being truthful and credible are two essential features of the liberation propaganda this book is exploring. This chapter shows examples of how devices like media traps were used, illustrated by Al Manar's coverage of certain incidents, mainly in south Lebanon between 1997 and 2000.

## Coverage by Al Manar

Assayed[8] Hassan Nasrallah said on the eve of the liberation celebrations on 25 May 2000, 'If it was not for Al Manar, the victory would have not been achieved'. Al Manar was the prime place where all the media strategy devices were put into practice.

This section looks at the coverage of certain incidents in the three years prior to the liberation. These incidents are considered landmarks in the development of Hezbollah's media strategy, which worked alongside its military achievements in building up to victory in the year 2000 (Al Huseini, interview with author, 2003). Thus, the incidents are presented chronologically to reflect how Hezbollah media strategy developed.

The incidents covered are: the killing of collaborator Salim Risha on 20 October 1997; the Beir Kalab operation on 27 February 1998; exchanging detainees and martyrs in June 1998; the killing of Eretz Gerstein, head of the Israeli army in south Lebanon, on 28 February 1999; Israeli attacks on Lebanese power stations in June 1999; capturing the Sujud position on 27 April 1999; the Beit Yahoun operation on 15 May 1999; the killing of Akel Hashem, second-in-command of the South Lebanon Army (SLA), commander of SLA Western Brigade, on 30 January 2000; reports on surrendering collaborators in January 2000; and the liberation on 23 and 24 May 2000.

In addition, some of the Arabic and Hebrew clips broadcast are presented in detail. What follows is a detailed account of this coverage.

## The killing of collaborator Salim Risha

On 20 October 1997, the Islamic resistance conducted an operation targeting one of the main figures in the SLA, Israel's proxy militia in the occupied territories of south Lebanon. Salim Risha, who had direct relations with the Israeli army and was accused of running an intelligence network for the Israelis outside the occupied territories, was killed.

It was a sophisticated operation and Al Manar devoted time and space to explain in detail what had happened and what the resistance achieved by killing the man known as 'collaborator Salim Risha'.

> The Islamic resistance has achieved a new security breakthrough inside the enemy's military and intelligence institutions. This is shown in the accurate and precise operation conducted today inside the occupied territories and targeted at Salim Risha, the head of Jezzine sector, and his bodyguard.
> 
> (Al Mousawi, Al Manar news, introduction, 19:45, 20 October 97)

These words aimed to emphasise the achievement of the Islamic resistance fighters who were often referred to as *mujahedeen*, which gave the battle against the Israelis a divine connotation of those who fight evil and oppression. The operation, which was filmed minute by minute from a distance, was also used to emphasise the weakness of the Israeli army (which was referred to as 'the Zionist forces/army') and the problems its collaborators were facing in south Lebanon – in this case, their inability to stop the resistance from targeting and killing high-ranking SLA people.

The resistance was clearly emphasising the failure of Israeli intelligence in south Lebanon to protect their soldiers, officers and their collaborators from its operations.

> Zionist sources spoke of problems the Zionist forces are facing in South Lebanon. That is what the enemy's government is discussing today. Salim Risha, who is directly connected to the Mossad [Israeli intelligence] and runs an intelligence network outside the occupied areas [of south Lebanon, which were known as the liberated parts of Lebanon] ...
> 
> (Al Mismar, ibid.)

# Liberation Media: Hezbollah and Al Manar, 1997–2000

This editorial statement, which reflects Hezbollah's political position – according to Hussein Rahal, Al Manar's head of news 1997–9 (interview with author, 2004) – was followed by a detailed report showing, minute by minute, how the van that carried Risha exploded when targeted by a side-road bomb. The report covered in detail the resistance communiqué that explained how the 'collaborator execution' took place. It also revealed that the 'enemy's radio and the collaborators' radio stations admitted the killing of Risha'.

The report included written information on the personal history of Risha, when he was born, his mother's name, and that he was prosecuted and given a life sentence by a Lebanese court for collaborating with the occupation forces and being responsible for the deaths of many civilians and resistance fighters. This information was provided to make clear that the target had been thoroughly studied and the killing was not random. The report went on to count the number of Mossad operations he was involved in and the names of Mossad officers he used to meet (Amhaz, Al Manar news, 19:45, 20 October 1997). The report was careful to point out that the road bomb was planted on the outskirts of Jezzine, in a remote and unpopulated area.

This kind of coverage targeted members of the South Lebanon Army (SLA), the Israeli proxy militia in the occupied zone, and their families, but also the Lebanese sectors outside the occupied territories. It is a message of capability, strength and justice to the Lebanese audiences, as Rahal pointed out (interview with author, 2004).

## The Beir Kalab operation

This operation, on 27 February 1998, was labelled a 'media trap'. Islamic resistance fighters attacked the Israeli and SLA position of Beir Kalab in the occupied zone in south Lebanon. The resistance announced that they had been in control of the position for some time, killed and injured many 'enemy' soldiers and planted the flags of the resistance on top of its barracks. Al Manar broadcast some general shots of the position, which did not show the fighters breaking into it.

The Israeli army denied the killing of its soldiers and the planting of the resistance flags, and said that the army managed to kill two of the attackers and the other two ran away (*Al Liwaa*, 4 March 1998, n.p.). They claimed it was a fabricated operation and that the footage Al Manar broadcast had been used before and was of previous operations that took place a year earlier (ibid.). At that point, Hezbollah's Military Media Unit released the detailed footage of the operation and the surveillance that preceded the operation.

Al Manar was the first to broadcast the images, with a detailed explanation from the leader of the resistance group. Al Manar's introduction to the breaking news emphasised the superiority of the resistance, its credibility and the weakness of the 'enemy':

> A new defeat hit the enemy today after the resistance dragged them to another media trap. This trap revealed the volatility of the Zionist Army, especially in relation to Israeli public opinion. They are faced day after day with one defeat after another. These live images and the explanation from the leader of the group that conducted the Beir Kalab operation indicate, without any doubt, that the Islamic resistance has taken the initiative in overcoming the dangers and surprise the occupation forces inside their positions through monitoring and surveillance, as is shown in the following tape.
>
> (Reslan, Al Manar breaking news, 2 March 1998)

At this point the audience saw the leader of the militant group that attacked Beir Kalab standing in front of a big screen in a dim room, explaining to the reporters every image that ran on the screen. During this time we could only see his back and hear his voice.

> This is when I asked brother Hamza to go with the camera and explore the area around the position. [He is explaining minute by minute what they were doing. The attack was all recorded on tape.] The cameraman suffered a leg injury, but he continued filming. Now they are inside the position. [We can hear the sounds of battle.] The cameraman is now crawling to get nearer to the resistance fighters to get better images. This is the Sujud position, which contradicts the enemy's lies that this was an illusory attack [real-time sound, the fighters crying *Allah Akbar*, 'God is Great']. Here we can see the *mujahed* [fighter] planting the flag of Hezbollah inside the position and handing the other flag to his brother to plant on the other side. We destroyed the barracks and then we withdrew. While we were withdrawing the Israeli army started bombing the position heavily. Brother Murtada

was martyred and the head of his team, brother Hamza, was injured.

(Abu Yasser in Al Manar breaking news, 2 March 1998)

Abu Yasser, as he was introduced, moved on to specify in detail what these barracks contained and the amount and kinds of weapons that they found there. He then explained the plan of attack on a map.

In an interview with *Assafir* newspaper, one of the cameramen involved in the Beir Kalab operation revealed that three cameramen covered the operation, of whom two were responsible for filming outside the position and the third was responsible for filming inside the barracks. He explained that one of the cameramen was, during the surveillance operation, only 15 metres away from one of the soldiers, but the latter could not see him because he was camouflaged (*Assafir*, interview with Marmal, 10 March 1998).

This was a show of ability and credibility. It was mainly aimed at demonstrating to the Lebanese public that the resistance was able to destroy the best defences and fortifications of the 'enemy'. It also aimed at demonising the 'enemy' by undermining its credibility and accusing it of deception. Because Hezbollah media people were aware that Israeli TV would re-broadcast the tape of the operation or would talk about its existence, the disclosure of the tape aimed at undermining the Israeli army's credibility in the eyes of the Israeli public.

Whaley (in Lasswell et al. 1980: 341) spoke of how important and dominant the element of deception is in what he called propaganda efforts to control and influence public opinion. By showing the operation tape on Al Manar, the resistance had countered the 'enemy' propaganda and revealed the Israelis' 'deception'. This is what Hatem identifies as 'psychological warfare'. He believes that in applying counter-propaganda during confrontations and conflicts to influence mass opinion, propagandists need to calculate and manage psychological effects (Hatem 1974: 58).

## Exchanging detainees and martyrs

On the evening of 5 September 1997, 16 Israeli commando soldiers from the Special Forces fell into an Islamic resistance bomb trap near the village of Ansariyeh, north of Tyre, 20 km from the occupied zone in south Lebanon. The unit had landed on the Adloun beaches after midnight in an attempt to reach the adjacent village of Ansariyeh and kidnap, or kill if necessary, one of the resistance leaders (*Ha'aretz*, 7 September 1997: n.p.). Twelve Israeli soldiers of this unit were killed and the others injured.

The Israeli rescue forces that flew to the scene were then subjected to heavy fire from resistance fighters and the Lebanese army. The Israeli helicopters had to leave without being able to collect all the remains of their dead soldiers. The resistance celebrated what it called the Israeli forces' defeat and presented to the public through Al Manar TV some of the Israeli soldiers' remains and the weapons left behind (Al Manar news, 5 June 1997). Again, the aim behind broadcasting and distributing these images was to show strength and ability.

Eight days later Hadi Nasrallah, the son of Hezbollah secretary-general Assayed Hassan Nasrallah, was killed during a resistance operation in the occupied zone. Hadi's body was taken hostage by the Israeli forces. The whole country showed sympathy and unity with Hezbollah and its leader (Shararah 1998: 180). On that day, Nasrallah had to deliver a speech 'in memory of the resistance martyrs' at a festival in the southern suburbs. Nasrallah spoke for more than an hour, emphasising the fact that nothing would stop the resistance from continuing the fight to liberate the occupied lands in south Lebanon and free Lebanese prisoners from Israeli jails. The speech was broadcast live on Al Manar TV.

Nasrallah told Talal Salman, publisher of the Lebanese daily *Assafir*, that while delivering his speech he was sweating because of the large number of television crews' spotlights. Despite this, he refused to wipe his sweat on television so the Israelis wouldn't think that he was weeping for his son. He told Salman that he wept in silence, as any father would do in such circumstances, but he didn't want the Israelis to use his tears in public as a sign of weakness or defeat (Salman 2001: 38).

In the same month, negotiations to exchange the remains of the Israeli soldiers – with Lebanese prisoners and bodies taken hostage by Israel – were started through a third party, the International Red Cross (Sharara 1998: 216). To the Israelis' surprise, Nasrallah did not put his son's name ahead of other resistance fighters' bodies.

> He [Nasrallah] has been transformed into a 'national symbol', says Avigdor Kahlani [former Israeli army general

and Public Security Minister at the time]. He reveals: 'We kept his son's body, but nothing changed'. The Western correspondents see in Assayed [Nasrallah] more than a symbol; he is charismatic, articulate, straightforward and a mastermind in politics. With Hassan Nasrallah the political scenery seems to be different. He is ready to accept and answer any question, no matter how complicated or critical.

(Al Bourji, *Al Kefah Al Arabi*, 18 March 1998)

Nine months later, on 25 June 1998, the exchange took place. It was regarded as a 'victory', being achieved by the combined group efforts of the government, the Lebanese army and the resistance, supported morally and financially by Lebanese people. Forty martyrs and sixty detainees were released. Some of them belonged to other Lebanese parties, such as the Communist Party and Amal movement.[9] The relationship between the Ansariyeh operation and the exchange deal was made clear in Al Manar's coverage of the event:

After 9 months the Islamic resistance *mujahedeen* followed their achievement in Ansariyeh with a new one. From the heroic operation of Ansariyeh crawled the beams of freedom for the detainees in the Israeli detention camps. Because of the fighters' blessed heroism in Ansariyeh it was possible to bring back the martyrs to their motherland ... Because of the resistance fighters' bullets, explosives and their open eyes in Ansariyeh, Lebanon was able to receive in Kfar Falous and Majdalyoun [two towns on the border of the occupied zone] today the group of *mujahedeen* freed from their detention. Before that they received their resistance martyrs at Beirut airport.

(Al Mousawi, Al Manar news introduction, 27 June 1998)

The first report in the news programme was a report on Hezbollah Secretary General Assayed Hassan Nasrallah visiting the place where the fighters' bodies, retrieved from Israel, were kept. Among them was the body of his son Hadi Nasrallah. The anchor praised Nasrallah's courage and the credibility that lay in his leadership:

for him [Nasrallah] to receive the body of his own son [Hadi] today with the bodies of those martyrs brought back home, is an indication of truth and honesty in his leadership. For ten months the 'father–leader' had been waiting to be reunited with his son who was martyred in Jabal Al Rafee on the 13th of September 1997.

(Al Mousawi, Al Manar news introduction, 27 June 1998)

The report took us inside the Imam Al-Mehdi School in Ouzai, on the outskirts of Beirut, where 28 coffins were laid out in a row. Outside the school we saw men preparing for the funeral. Then a small convoy of cars arrived carrying, among others, the Secretary General of Hezbollah, Assayed Hassan Nasrallah. The coffins carried the Hezbollah fighters who had fallen in past battles with Israeli forces in south Lebanon. They were among the forty Lebanese fighters whose bodies were brought back to Lebanon on that day.

We saw Nasrallah entering the hall in 'solemn dignity', as expressed by Al Manar, accompanied by Jawad, his younger son. The report followed Nasrallah's steps in detail:

> He stopped before each coffin and offered the *Fatiha* [the Muslim equivalent of the Lord's Prayer] until he reached the one marked 13. He beckoned an aide and spoke to him in a whisper. The aide summoned two workers of the Islamic Health Association [Hezbollah's health organisation]. They opened the coffin, exposing a body wrapped in a white shroud. Sheikh Nasrallah's eyes closed, his lips trembled as he offered the *Fatiha*. Slowly, he bent over and tenderly stroked the head of Hadi Nasrallah, his eldest son, who was 18 years old when he died in battle. Jawad, the younger son stood still and pale next to his father. A deep silence fell on the room while his right hand rested on his son's chest.
>
> (Al Manar news, 27 June 1998)

The report praised the secretary-general's thoroughness and selflessness:

> The secretary-general meant to read the *Fatiha* over every coffin before he went to see his martyr son Assayed Hadi. There he stood strong, whispering to his son and touching his virtuous body from above the shroud [*Kafen*] before he

left him with a smile that carries all the determination of a leader.

(ibid.)

Journalists like Iqbal Ahmed of *Al Ahram Weekly* described the event that she witnessed on television as an 'awesome scene' (Ahmed, *Al Ahram weekly*, 30 July 1998: n.p.).

To express the solidarity and support the resistance received from the Lebanese army and government, the martyrs were given an official military welcome at the airport and were saluted by an army brigade before moving their coffins into the ambulances. The president of the republic, the House speaker and the prime minister were all at the airport to receive the bodies of the resistance fighters. This honorary ceremony was broadcast live on Al Manar TV where emphasis was given to the high position these fighters occupied in the hearts of the Lebanese and Arab peoples and 'in God's heaven' (Al Mousawi, Al Manar news, 27 June 1998).

Ellul (1965/1973) speaks of symbols as one of the two most favourable elements of propaganda that emerge from mass society. Nasrallah plays the role of a national symbol. He is respected and trusted, and thus accepted and believed. By allowing his son to take part in fighting the Israeli occupation in south Lebanon, he is seen as a credible leader who is treating himself and his family on equal grounds to those who follow and support his calls. He has identified himself as a leader with other resistance fighters' families. Al Manar's coverage aimed at highlighting this fact.

They were applying what Jackall identifies as 'the plain-folks device' in propaganda – a device aiming at allowing leaders to win confidence by appearing to be like them: 'just plain folks among the neighbours' (Jackall 1995: 220). Al Manar did not have to fabricate this fact, it was there and they succeeded in giving it prominence. Pratkanis and Aronson point out the importance of having an authoritative figure that people are willing to believe if a message is to be accepted by them (Pratkanis and Aronson 1991). Nasrallah as a symbol has been used to instil a massive wave of patriotism and heroism among a national audience in order to achieve a common objective. This is what Jowett and O'Donnell assert to be one purpose of propaganda (Jowett and

O'Donnell 1999). The objective here is to liberate the occupied land in south Lebanon from the Israeli occupation forces and their allies.

Additionally, by highlighting the role the government and the Lebanese army played in achieving the exchange deal, Al Manar was trying to emphasise that the resistance (and thus Hezbollah) is not alone in its struggle to liberate the land, thus calling upon all sectors of the Lebanese society to join and help the resistance in every possible form.

## The killing of Brigadier-General Eretz Gerstein

On 28 February 1999, Israel lost its highest-ranking officer in Lebanon. The Islamic resistance killed Eretz Gerstein, head of Israeli forces in the occupied zone in south Lebanon, along with three other officers. They were killed by a roadside bomb as his car passed in a military convoy. The incident came hours after hundreds of Lebanese youth and university students removed a fence put in place by the Israeli army to separate Arnun village from the neighbouring liberated villages and claim it as part of the occupied zone.

On that day, Arnun was witnessing a huge national celebration and most television stations were covering these celebrations live. I was reporting live from Arnun when we heard the news from Al Manar journalists in the village that the resistance had succeeded in killing the highest-ranking Israeli commander in south Lebanon. News of the operation resulted in more celebrations among thousands of Lebanese who marched to Arnun from all parts of the country to celebrate what was then called the liberation of Arnun. However, we had to cut short the celebrations and remove all the live coverage equipment in response to a request put to us by Lebanese army officers. They feared that Israeli retaliation might target the huge civilian gathering in Arnun.

While most of us at Arnun were still guessing who the targeted Israeli officer was, Al Manar had the full story:

> A new victory has been achieved for the resistance, a unique victory for Lebanon, and a setback, a defeat for the enemy. The head of the Israeli enemy in South Lebanon was crushed at the feet of the *mujahedeen* and was burned in the fire of their explosives. The echo of this operation was huge. It went beyond Lebanon, around the Arab world and to the

world in general. Eretz Gerstein, the head of the occupation forces in South Lebanon, was killed today, with three of the collaborators' leading figures, on the road between Hasbiah and Marj Ouyoun [in the heart of the occupied zone]. The *mujahedeen* revenge in killing him for the children of Lebanon, the victims of the Zionist massacres, to the martyrs of Kfour [where five resistance fighters were killed by roadside bombs planted by Israeli forces] and all the resistance *mujahedeen*.

(Al Dhaini, Al Manar news, 28 February 1999)

Clearly, the rhetoric used in this introduction is one of ringing victory. No line is drawn between the resistance and the television station. They were part of 'us', against 'them' or the 'other',[10] which stands here for the occupation forces.

In addition to the great sense of victory, revenge and power, the introduction included clear praise for the good intelligence network the resistance had established in order to accomplish its mission. The images that were played during the anchor's voiceover marked Israeli losses during the operation:

... [pictures of helicopters, then soldiers walking near an ambulance. Some people are standing by an electricity pillar pylon crying loudly, while a policeman is trying to calm them down.] Reuters, AFP and Associated Press revealed the killing of Gerstein, according to well-informed sources in the Lahed Militia. While security sources from the occupied zone spoke of 5 enemy soldiers being killed, AFP has mentioned in a telegram from Marjayoun the death of 4 Israeli officials in the attack [footage of an Israeli soldier crying]. Associated Press pointed out the fact that Gerstein is the highest-ranking officer killed in Lebanon since the 1982 [Israeli] invasion, when the resistance killed General Yukteel Adam in Khaldeh [south of Beirut].

(Al Mousawi, ibid.)

Anchor Hussein Al Dhaini read word for word the Islamic resistance's communiqué on the operation. File pictures of Gerstein were used with the voiceover of Dhaini. Al Manar identified itself as the 'channel of the resistance', thus communicating the fact that resistance messages, ideas and ideologies were part of its responsibilities.

Again, the message here was one of strength, capability, power and supremacy.

The news programme went on to present what the Israeli media had said about Gerstein when he undertook his responsibilities as a leader of the occupation forces in south Lebanon, and how they had said it. By doing so, Al Manar was trying to emphasise to Lebanese audiences that Gerstein was not a low-ranking officer and that he belonged to the Israeli army elite, which allowed the resistance to claim his killing as a military achievement.

A file report presented by Hakam Amhaz (Al Manar news, 28 February 1999) referred to the fact that Gerstein was not the only officer that the resistance had killed. He went on to list all Israeli officers killed or subject to such attempts by the resistance. Among them was Gerstein's predecessor, Eli Amitai. The archive footage used was taken from Israeli TV and the Lahed militia's television station.

Al Manar's intensive coverage of Gerstein's killing was picked up by Israeli Channel 2, which in return was monitored and re-broadcast by Al Manar TV:

> The battle has moved to the media front. The enemy's TV was monitoring Al Manar transmissions all day yesterday on the killing of the Zionist General Eretz Gerstein. More in this translated report...
> (Al Mousawi, Al Manar news, 29 February 1999)

Israel's Channel 2 dedicated four minutes to analysing Al Manar's coverage. The screen was divided into two windows, one with the anchor and the other with a military analyst:

> Anchor: Hezbollah has expressed its exultation at what happened today.
>
> Analyst [full screen]: Hezbollah television transmitted and repeated this news all afternoon yesterday, and because of this I have to say that there was clear pre-planning for the 'assault' on General Eretz Gerstein in particular. What I mean is that what happened was not a coincidence and that they have been monitoring him and investigating his movements...
>
> Anchor [interrupting him]: Is this because they were transmitting information on him and details of his biography?

Analyst: Yes, since Al Manar's first breaking news in the early afternoon they spoke for 20 minutes on Eretz Gerstein's life as part of the well-documented archival material, and this is not an easy process you can do in one day. What they have broadcast has to do with various occasions and various tours he has conducted since he was appointed to this position a year ago, including recorded material from Israeli TV.

(Israeli Channel 2, on Al Manar news, 29 February 1999)

The Israeli anchor repeated Al Manar's story on how and where the incident took place:

According to Hezbollah, this was done with two explosive packages: the first exploded at 11.50 [ten minutes] before noon and killed the four, and the second was at 12.15 exploded in one of the jeeps a kilometre away from the first explosion.

(ibid.)

Then he asked the audience to listen to the anchor that broadcast this on Al Manar.

Kawthar Al Mousawi's introduction, presented earlier, ran with Hebrew subtitles. The piece that Al Manar re-ran from Israeli Channel 2 ended with the Israeli military analyst highlighting the effectiveness of the Hezbollah intelligence network inside the occupied zone.

What is important is that the operation was conducted inside the security zone that lies completely under Israeli control. We know two important points from the past: one is that Hezbollah has very effective intelligence and that they clearly have intelligence agents inside this area. These members gather intelligence information and take it to the leadership in south Lebanon and based upon that information Hezbollah plans its operations.

(ibid.)

Through re-broadcasting the Israeli TV analysis, Al Manar wanted to emphasise the resistance's superiority in 'the words of its enemy'. Such words proclaiming their effectiveness were viewed as words of praise. And, coming from 'the enemy analyst's mouth', they were believed to strengthen the credibility of the resistance in the eyes of Lebanese and Israeli audiences. This act is related to counter-propaganda techniques, as when the propagandist Goebbels (Doob 1995: 204) suggested using enemy propaganda to diminish the enemy's prestige. However, what was happening here was not that the enemy's propaganda was used, but that the enemy's admission of failure was used and highlighted.

*Ha'aretz*, the left-wing Israeli daily, wrote on 8 October 1999, six months after the killing of Gerstein, that the incident was a defeat for Israel. Shohat Orit of *Ha'aretz* expressed his belief that the Israeli involvement in Lebanon was not a 'stunning military achievement, but rather a crushing moral defeat' (Orit, *Ha'aretz*, 8 October 1999). He explained that the 'victories' Israel claimed in Lebanon were 'ephemeral and accidental' and they would last only until the death of the next senior Israeli army officer or until the number of Israeli soldiers killed in Lebanon exceeds what he described as 'the emotional capacity of Israeli society' (ibid.).

Five years later, Daniel Ben-Simon of *Ha'aretz* described the death of Gerstein as a means for Barak to withdraw from Lebanon.

> Gerstein is considered one of the unnecessary victims of an unnecessary war that exacted the deaths of more than 1,000 Israeli soldiers. The senior officer's death shocked the country's leadership and served as a catalyst for Prime Minister Ehud Barak's decision to withdraw from Lebanon.
> (Ben-Simon, *Ha'aretz*, 22 November 2004, n.p.)

The *Ha'aretz* journalists' comments illustrate the effect that news of Israeli human losses in south Lebanon had on Israeli political and civil society.

## Capturing the Sujud position

This was the third media trap that Israel fell into, after the Debshe and Beir Kalab operations mentioned earlier. The resistance attacked the Sujud position (a fortified, strategically positioned military installation on a hilltop) in memory of the April 1996[11] martyrs. They marched into the position and planted the resistance flag on top of it.

However, the Israeli army denied the operation had taken place and claimed that the resistance had fabricated the operation (Smaha, *Al Hayat*, 20 May 1999). The head of the military media unit, Haj

Maitham,[12] believed that the Israelis denied the operation when they saw the first images Al Manar broadcast on the operation. They were general shots of the position from a distance. 'What they did not know is that we had detailed footage of the operation filmed by the military media unit cameramen' (Maitham, interview with author, 2004).

The 'media trap', as Maitham branded it, was staged by Al Manar TV in three stages. First Al Manar announced on 27 April 1999 that the operation had taken place that day and declared that they would broadcast the footage as soon as they received it.

> The [Islamic resistance] strike took place as the head of Israeli military intelligence was still issuing his threats against Lebanon. The Zionist leader threatened to target positions deep in Lebanon if the moral and political support given by the Lebanese Government to the resistance changes to logistical support. In this context, the resistance *mujahedeen* targeted one of the enemy's positions in Sujud. They defeated it and planted the resistance flag on top of it. We will be with you with live footage on the confrontation as soon as we receive it.
> 
> (Areslan, Al Manar news, 27 April 1999)

This was presented without any footage. Then, in a later bulletin, Gada Assaf Nemer repeated the news of the capture of Sujud, introducing a detailed report of the resistance communiqué on the operation.

> It was a hot southern day. Air raids and random military aggression injured a mother and her son in Jarjouaa [a southern village in the liberated central sector of south Lebanon]. The Islamic resistance raised its flag another time on top of the Sujud position. The enemy is trying to minimise its casualties, only admitting to six injuries among its soldiers and three [SLA] collaborators.
> 
> (Nemer, Al Manar news, 27 April 1999)

Bahaa al Deen Al Nabulsi read the communiqué, accompanied by general shots of the Sujud position from a distance. The communiqué emphasised that the operation was set off in response to Assayed Hassan Nasrallah's orders, issued 24 hours earlier.

The third stage came on the second day of the operation. This news report had step-by-step footage of what they called 'a triumphant raid' on the Sujud garrison. Areslan was guiding the audience step by step through the footage in live narration, which was intended to assure the viewer of the genuineness of the footage. The report intended to dismiss Israeli denials that the operation took place and their claims that Al Manar's images of the operation were fabricated.

> The camera is monitoring the Israeli position minute by minute, observing the movements and preparations of the enemy. [10:11 camera time slot appears on the screen, with complete silence.] In these scenes [12:30], you can see the precise surveillance through the military media camera. Also you can notice the time difference between the scenes. The reinforcements are well focused and obvious in these images.
> 
> Spiral razor-wire fences, huge reinforced buildings and small hidden underground facilities; in addition you can see the monitoring positions and the land mines planted around the position. The Israeli warplanes are in the sky, and so are the drones, but the *mujahedeen* [fighters] are disguised in colours that match the colours of the land where they are hiding. They cannot be recognised from the sky...
> 
> (Areslan, Al Manar news, 28 April 1999)

Areslan continued his narration to indicate how close the fighters were to the position. He then mentioned that the order to open fire came at 4 o'clock in the afternoon from the resistance leaders.

> [Sounds and pictures of shooting and fighting] We notice here the accurate shooting of the fighters' fire in hitting the barracks. And in a few moments they were able to silence all sources of fire from the enemy. [Clear sound of resistance fire] The orders are given to the combat groups to move forward into the position. Here we can see one of the fighters moving forwards towards the highest point in the garrison, overcoming the obstacles of the barbed wire and the land mines, opening the way for the other resistance teams to conquer the position where the enemy has always felt proud of its defences. [Images with sound are running...a group

of fighters is moving forward...one of them is carrying a Hezbollah flag and waving it and we are still hearing gun shots.]

(ibid.)

The camera and the narration followed the fighters till they planted the flags and withdrew 'victoriously. The flags remained waving on the top of the hill till the late hours of yesterday' (ibid.).

While conducting the operation, the fighters were calling the name of the Shiite religious and historic imam, Imam Hussein (grandson of the Prophet Muhammad), whom they believe to have fought and died for justice and against oppression.[13] Calls of *Allah Akbar!* ('God is Great') accompanied all their steps and movements while destroying the entrenchments. The fighters were saluting the Hezbollah banners as they were planted. According to Haj Naser, one of the cameramen involved in filming resistance operations, the filming aimed to reflect their confidence, heroism and power in the face of the Israelis trying to destroy their morale. On the other hand, the filming and broadcasting of certain operations tended to emphasise the ability of resistance fighters to defeat the Israeli army, which helped in raising the morale of the Lebanese people (interview with author, 2004).

Naser added that 'these pictures show that we are the land owners who carried their guns to reclaim the land from its aggressor' (ibid.). He feels he is a fighter and a cameraman at the same time. However, his priority during operations was to film and not to fire. The gun that he carried was only for defence, if subjected to life-threatening actions by the 'enemy's soldiers'. He called himself a 'resistance cameraman'. The cameraman's role within the resistance group was seen as highly important, and the fighters would try to protect the cameraman (ibid.).

The camera proved to be a primary weapon, which the resistance used cleverly to demonise the enemy's credibility, and it was the main tool used to achieve credibility for the resistance. It was the tool that could propagate to the home front the idea of the capacity of the resistance and also to undermine the 'enemy's' credibility and superiority in the eyes of its own people.

Nayef Krayem, former head of Al Manar, explains that they had monitored the Israeli army's behaviour for a long time and they were aware of their usual responses to any military losses. He adds that the resistance knew they would deny true army losses. The only way to counter Israeli army denials was to have proof of them, and the operations' footage was that proof (interview with author, 2000).

Sujud was liberated ten months later, on 4 February 2000, after the resistance had claimed the position 6 times and conducted 33 traps, 33 explosions, 9 sniper operations, 475 attacks, 2 Katyusha shellings and 241 mortar shellings – a total of 793 operations. These numbers were repeated several times a day in a clip prepared by Al Manar following the Israeli army withdrawal from the position (Al Manar, clip, February, 2000). The images of fighters waving and planting flags inside or on the top of this position marked the role the camera played in achieving this 'victory'.

The resistance camera was a major player in the resistance's media war against Israel. One objective of this war was to undermine Israel's army motto: 'The army that could not be defeated' (Krayem, interview with author, 2000).

## The Beit Yahoun operation

On 15 May 1999, the resistance fighters attacked the occupation forces' position at Beit Yahoun in the occupied zone in south Lebanon. The position was heavily reinforced. It served as a protection point and controller for the main Israeli military crossing point between the occupied zone and the liberated areas in south Lebanon. It controlled the movement of residents of the occupied towns and villages on their visits into and outside the occupied territories.

The fighters regained the position from the Israeli soldiers and their collaborators (the SLA), captured two of them and a troop carrier, and drove that to the liberated areas after attacking the crossing point and clearing the way for a troop carrier to cross.

The event was filmed by the military media cameramen, and the communiqué of the resistance on the operation came to match the pictures, frame by frame. This operation generated a 'media event'[14] on Al Manar.

This took place two days after the operation. A parade was organised in the southern suburb of Beirut to celebrate what became known as the 'the conquest'. Thousands of resistance supporters gathered in the town of Haret Hreik in the southern suburb, celebrating the *mujahedeens*' ability to capture the troop carrier and drive it safely to where they were gathering. Al Manar cut all its regular programming to transmit live, from an early hour, footage of the supporters marching towards the gathering point, with live commentary from a spot overlooking the square where the gathering was taking place.

As mentioned, the operation itself was covered extensively on Al Manar the day before. The prime-time news on the night of the operation started with the story of the operation. The first two lines of the introduction made clear reference to historic events in the Arab–Israeli conflict, pointing out that the Beit Yahoun operation took place on the same day that Palestinian Arabs were deprived of their homeland (see Chapter Four). The introduction read as follows:

> First Anchor: Kawthar Al Mousawi
>
> The 15th of May – the day of *Al Nakba* ('the catastrophe') for the Arabs in occupied Palestine – has been transferred by the Islamic resistance *mujahedeen* to a date of *Nakba* ('catastrophe') for the occupation forces in South Lebanon. The *mujahedeen* scored a triple strike today. The resistance heroes attacked and broke into the Beit Yahoun position. They took over a [Israeli] troop carrier and detained two collaborators from the Lahed militia. They drew the first out from inside the position and hunted the second on their way out from the occupied zone into the liberated areas...
>
> Second Anchor: Hussein Al Dhaini
>
> The collaborators had yet not woken up from the preliminary attack on their position in Beit Yahoun, when the Islamic resistance *mujahedeen* broke into their position and planted the Hezbollah flag. Factual details and footage of them breaking into the Beit Yahoun position will be given in the next report.
>
> (Mousawi and Dhaini, Al Manar news, 15 May 1999)

The report that followed gave a full presentation of the resistance's communiqué. It was accompanied by pictures taken by the Military Media cameramen. It sounded as if the words were written for the pictures, because every word read out matched with the pictures shown. The first images of the fighters storming into the position matched with a Koran verse that promises sinners and oppressors God's punishment, even if they were hiding 'behind reinforced castles', a phrase used in the opening sentence of the communiqué. So the written communiqué or statement gained visual authority.

This was one of the few operations when the footage was released on the same day as the shooting. Haj Maitham, head of Hezbollah Military media unit, explained that the resistance leaders usually needed time to edit the pictures and remove whatever might jeopardise the security of their work; thus they tended not to release the footage immediately. However, the timing of the operation of Beit Yahoun was important because of its historical connotations. That was why they had to release it on the same day (Haj Maitham, interview with author, 2004).

It was also important to show the troop carrier being captured and that it had left the occupied territories. The resistance communiqué broadcast on Al Manar gave evidence of the ability of the resistance to drive the troop carrier safely outside the occupied zone:

> Meanwhile, another group from the resistance was attacking the Beit Yahoun check point and destroying it over the heads of its members, opening the way for the fighters to drive the troop carrier towards the liberated areas. [Ambience, images of the carrier driving fast on the road towards the liberated areas. The resistance fighters are taking the captured SLA soldier away from the position.] ...
> (Al Hajj Hassan, Al Manar news, 15 May 1999)

The Islamic resistance's communiqué ended by promising all Lebanese detainees in Israeli prisons that the resistance fighters would not sleep until they had freed them and brought them back to their families. The same communiqué referred to the fact that Israel had admitted the attack and acknowledged the injury to one soldier, while the collaborators had admitted the capture of one militia member and the injury of seven others in a series of attacks that targeted their positions in the central sector of south Lebanon.

It should be mentioned that most of the resistance's communiqués tended to state the number of casualties the 'enemy' would claim – to emphasise the deception in the 'enemy's' story. They were aiming at destroying the 'enemy's' credibility.

Doob revealed that Goebbels, in his principles of propaganda campaigns, stated that 'credibility and intelligence, determine whether [an enemy's] propaganda materials should be censored' (Doob 1995: 203). The 'enemy's' communiqué was recalled here and used to harm its credibility.

The story did not end there. Two days later, Al Manar went live to cover the mass ceremony outside Hezbollah headquarters in Haret Hreik (southern suburb of Beirut) celebrating the capture of the M113 troop carrier. Again, Al Manar's reporter at the time, Abass Naser,[15] who was doing the live commentary from a spot overlooking Hezbollah's headquarters, made links between this event and others that marked the history of the Arab–Israeli conflict. Naser's tone and words were sharp and full of excitement, praise and pride. He sounded as if he was talking to himself first, only then addressing the audience of Al Manar.

> The day of shame and dishonour, the day when the enemy tried to drag Lebanon into signing an insulting and offensive treaty with them.[16] God's glorification, the phrase *Allah Akbar* ['God is Great'] is on everybody's lips. [Crowds of thousands of people surrounded the carrier. On it were fighters wearing their military fatigues, black berets and black sunglasses. People were throwing rice on the carrier, and a clergyman climbed to the top of it and stood there with the fighters. People were carrying the flags of both Hezbollah and Lebanon.] *Allah Akbar* is uttered by thousands of people who have been waiting here for hours to receive the captured Zionist carrier. [General wide shot of the place of gathering, showing the huge number of people assembled there. Patriotic hymns are played in the background.]
> 
> (Naser, Al Manar, 17 May 1999)

Later in his commentary, Naser informed his audience that the fighter who was driving the carrier was the same person who had driven it from the Beit Yahoun position to the liberated areas. He also told his viewers that the fighters standing on top of the carrier were those who conducted the operation. The whole coverage was implying that the act of resistance is an act that everyone could do.

Thus, the coverage relates to 'the band wagon' propaganda device that Jackall discussed. It is a device that 'makes us follow the crowd, to accept the propagandist's programme en masse. Here his theme is: "Everybody's doing it"' (Jackall 1995: 222).

Naser's commentary also drew references to other 'heroic' operations that would make 'the defeat of the Israeli Army in south Lebanon close at hand'.

> What shame the enemy and his collaborators are living this year, from the defeat of Burkat al Jabour to the failure of the enemy's air force in chasing one *mujahed* [singular of *mujahedeen* in Arabic] in Markaba, to the killing of their leader Gerstein and his escorts, to the targeting of the collaborator Joseph Karam Aloush, and then the killing of his successor Muneh Tuma, to the capture of four collaborators in different places and, last but not least, the defeat of the military machinery and its falling into the hands of the resistance fighters and to... and to... and the list will not end. The fighting [*al Jihad*] has not ended. What an honour and ultimate superiority the resistance and its people are living with today. The people have gathered here today to express their pride and to call upon the resistance to continue the fight till the land is liberated. [Sounds of the crowd.]
>
> (ibid.)

The coverage of the ceremony continued, and the disguised fighter driving the carrier stepped down, carrying a machine gun. He was marching, his head up, towards the secretary general to present the vehicle and the machine gun captured from the Israeli army in Beit Yahoun. The crowd was hailing and saluting him till he stood in front of Assayed Hassan Nasrallah, Secretary General of Hezbollah.

At that moment, the crowd went silent. The fighter presented the machine gun to Nasrallah and addressed him, saying: 'To the master of resistance, their weapons are under your feet'. Nasrallah hugged him and decorated him with a resistance medal.

All was prepared and set to show the respect and pride the resistance fighters were surrounded by. According to Ez-Addine, former head of the Hezbollah media relations centre, the resistance managed to portray its superiority over Israeli soldiers in films shot during operations or during resistance festivals (interview with author, 2004) and this was one of them.

## Targeting the power stations

On 24 June 1999, Israel launched a nine-hour attack on Lebanese civil structures, from bridges to power stations. The most affected were the two main power stations that supply Beirut with electricity. Those two stations were still recovering from the April 1996 attacks, which had left them severely damaged.

According to Bechara Merhej, a member of the prime minister's parliamentary group at the time, Israel aimed, through this attack, to send a message to both the Lebanese government and people, saying: 'If you want to keep supporting the resistance, you have to pay the price' (Merhej, Al Manar news, 25 June 1999). He added, 'Israel wanted to create a dispute between the resistance and the people' (ibid.).

The nine-hour long night-time aerial blitz killed eight people, wounded 62 and left much of the country's electricity, telecommunications and road networks in a mire. The attack on Al Jamhour power station, some 10 km (6 ml) east of Beirut, killed five fire-fighters who were trying to put out the blaze when the warplanes bombed the plant for the third time. Hours later they bombed Bsaleem on the outskirts of Beirut. The attacks injured 18 fire-fighters and civilians living near the stations.

Al Manar's coverage reflected the collective damage these attacks were causing for all Lebanese, arguing that the only response would be more resistance operations against the occupation until they left south Lebanon.

> The nine-hour siege that the Zionist enemy orchestrated against the civil infrastructure in Lebanon caused many wounds on the Lebanese side, but at the same time lifted up the people's resolve in the face of the challenge the occupation is imposing by terrorism and fire. The air raids, which every member in the Zionist government refused to acknowledge full responsibility for because of its implications on the international level, revealed deep disagreements within the Israeli Government regarding the way to deal with the situation in South Lebanon.
> (Al Dhaini, Al Manar news introduction, 25 June 1999)

Israel 'unleashed' its fighter jets hours after Hezbollah resistance fighters fired Katyusha rockets into northern Israel, 'in retaliation against the Zionist state's week-long raids on southern villages which wounded six people' (*Al Ahram Weekly*, 1–7 July 1999). Al Manar's introduction to its prime-time news of 25 June 1999 asked the question of whether the attacks on Bsaleem and Al Jamhour were 'a message or revenge of some helpless, vindictive nature?'(Areslan, Al Manar news introduction, 25 June 1999).

The report on the destruction of the power stations featured the blood of the fire-fighters mixed with the water they were using to put the flames out. The language used was full of anger and condemnation:

> More than 15 hours have passed since the Zionist aggression that targeted Bsaleem and Al Jamhour power stations and the smoke of fire was still coming out of the generators and the blood of the five fire department martyrs is mixed with water on the country's soil, witnessing the enemy's vindictive hostility and crimes. This aggressive crime is not an Israeli political message to Lebanon, but a desperately vengeful act.
> 
> (Amhaz, Al Manar news, 25 June 1999)

Hakam Amhaz, who reported the raids, paid tribute to the five martyrs by name and revealed that the fire-fighters took six hours to put the fire out. He then specified the amount of damage caused to the generators and asked how long it would take to repair them – and at what cost? Amhaz revealed the role the Lebanese army had played in clearing the destruction from the power stations, emphasising the argument made earlier that the army and the resistance were united in fighting the Israeli aggression (Al Manar news, 19:45, 25 June 1999).

The report was followed by details of an alternative plan to enable Beirut and neighbouring districts to have electricity and phone lines, as if to say, 'we will not be defeated'. A statement from Naser Al Saidi, finance minister at the time, came after. He called upon people to take part in civil and economic resistance and to stand side by side with the military resistance (Al Saidi, ibid.).

According to Amhaz, one of the main aspects that Al Manar's reporters have to consider in their reporting is national unity. This is revealed through the emphasis on the aggressive nature of the Israeli attacks, which do not differentiate between sectors of Lebanese society, and the focus on the fact that destroying the prosperity of Lebanon was their main aim. Amhaz points out that the resistance has always been portrayed as the defenders who fight back against the Israeli aggression (interview with author, 2004).

This relates to Goebbels' propaganda principle 18, which states that 'propaganda must facilitate the displacement of aggression by specifying the targets of the Hatred' (Doob 1995: 214). The hatred here is directed at the Israeli army for its aggression against the Lebanese civilian infrastructure. The emphasis is on national unity against one aggressor, thus giving legitimacy and support to resistance actions, which should not come under negative scrutiny from its own people.

This was how the Islamic resistance response to the bombings was portrayed: 'The Islamic resistance retaliated by firing rockets at settlements in northern Israel and killing two people' (Al Manar news, 25 June 1999). Hezbollah gave its own warning: the only way Israel can protect its northern settlements from attack is by renouncing the attacks on civilians and civilian installations in accordance with the April 1996 Understanding. Hezbollah's secretary general, Assayed Hassan Nasrallah, was quoted on Al Manar saying: 'The cease-fire bans attacks on or from civilian targets on both sides of the border but permits the resistance to launch operations against Israeli troops in south Lebanon' (Nasrallah, Al Manar, 26 June 1999). Emphasis was also put on reporting the reaction of the Lebanese prime minister at the time, Salim Al Hoss, who said that the government would continue to resist attempts to change the accord and back resistance groups as long as Israel was occupying Lebanese territories (Hoss, ibid.).

The propaganda 'transfer device' that Jackall identified can be seen here. It is a device by which 'the propaganda carries over the authority, sanction, and prestige of something we respect and revere to something he would have us accept' (Jackall 1995: 219). Thus, figures of authority were quoted defending the right of the resistance to fight the occupation and to liberate the land. In a multi-sectarian country it is important to have all religious groups supporting such military acts of resistance conducted by one sect and not the others. Al Manar was giving prominence to the support the resistance was getting from other groups and was emphasising the importance of national unity and solidarity with the resistance.

## The killing of Akel Hashem, the SLA second-in-command

On 30 January 2000 the resistance killed Akel Hashem, who was known to be the most prominent candidate to replace Antoine Lahed, commander of the South Lebanon Army, Israel's proxy army in the occupied territories. Hashem was killed by a well-concealed bomb set off by remote control inside his ranch in the occupied zone.

According to Naomi Segal, of the *Jewish Telegraphic Agency* (4 February 2000), Ehud Barak, Israeli prime minister at the time, called the killing of Hashem a 'difficult and sad' loss for Israel. He said he had known Hashem for more than 20 years and that his killing would be avenged (ibid.).

Hezbollah hailed the killing of Hashem as a breakthrough (BBC News, 30 January 2000). It was a breakthrough on two levels: the intelligence and the media. Hashem had been tried and sentenced to death in absentia by a military tribunal in Lebanon for his role in the Israel proxy militia, the SLA. The resistance was not just able to track him down and kill him, but also filmed the operation as it took place, step by step, for more than six hours. This was then edited and broadcast on Al Manar as a three-minute story on the 'execution of collaborator Akel Hashem'. The narration came to match the pictures the resistance cameramen filmed on the spot:

> The resistance has followed him for a long time through a precise and close surveillance of his movements at his private ranch in Debil, away from people's eyes. Collaborator Akel Hashem appears in the middle of the circle. Beside him stands one of his assistants; also you can see a watchdog moving away from them [silence, then background sound]. So collaborator Akel Hashem is walking in his country house, in the midst of very tight security measures. As we mentioned earlier, a trained watchdog that can detect explosives accompanies him. As you can also see, his assistant and bodyguards are surrounding him. Now you can see beside Hashem an armoured Hummer Jeep that Israel gave him for more security protection. [Silence] The resistance camera is following Akel Hashem closely. This is a clearer picture of the farm that Akel Hashem uses as a refuge away from people, for his own pleasure and rest. [Silence, background sound] He is talking now to his

assistants near the Hummer Jeep. He is preparing to leave the place.
(Al Mismar, Al Manar news, 30 January 2000)

There was emphasis on the watchdog that could sniff out explosives, as if saying that even this trained dog could not detect the resistance's explosives. The report highlighted the tight security measures, which provided evidence that the resistance fighters were able to outwit the collaborator's security personnel. The story continues to underline the fact that Hashem's ranch stood remote from any residential areas. Referring to this fact implied that the resistance had considered the safety of the civilians in the area.

> A few moments from now, we will see the explosion that took the life of Hashem to what is his dreadful fate, going to hell. The place at which the explosion happened is well away from civilian residential areas. It is on the outskirts of Debl village. Moments later, the explosion takes place.
> (ibid.)

Two days later, on 1 February, Al Manar aired a five-minute report of an interview with both the guerrilla commanders who masterminded the attack that killed Akel Hashem. The fighters, who were only identified as Jawad, 25, and Hadi, 28, wore military uniforms and black berets, and both kept their backs to the camera as they spoke. Jawad said:

> I led my squad through Israeli defences and reached the vicinity of Akel's ranch-house in Debl before dawn. We laid the explosive charges in a semicircle in the garden and withdrew to a hideout about a hundred feet [30 m] away... Shortly after, Akel came out of the house and paced back and forth in the garden as two body-guards with police dogs watched at a ten metre [33 ft] distance... Family members quickly came to keep him company and we had to wait until they returned to the house to detonate the charges by remote control.
> (*mujahed* Jawad, interview with Al Manar, 1 February 2000)

Both Jawad and Hadi said they retreated from Debl half an hour after the explosion took place, implying that there was no immediate danger to their safety. While narrating their story, the two fighters were talking with confidence and certainty. There was no hesitation in their voices, an image most resistance fighters tend to have when seen on screen.

Killing Akel Hashem and presenting the details of his 'execution' on television aimed to send a message to other collaborators that they would not escape the resistance's punishment (Rahal, interview with author, 2004). The film of Akel Hashem's assassination was used later in a clip produced on Al Manar and was repeated over and over again. The clip had Akel Hashem telling his fellow collaborators on SLA television (also known as the Lahed Militia TV):

> We believe in the Israeli Government and in the Israeli Defence Force. Hezbollah hides many of its casualties and its victories are illusory. In contrast to what they say, the South Lebanon army is not falling apart. The South Lebanon army is not a mat they step on. The South Lebanon Army will cut any hand that comes near it.

At this point the picture of Hashem faded into images of the explosion that killed him at his ranch. The image faded again into a fighter rising up from the bushes, holding his gun and aiming it. This image of the fighter was sound-bridged with Nasrallah saying: 'The resistance should sentence those collaborators with the toughest verdicts for being traitors to the Lebanese people, their country and their nation'. The clip ended with the slogan 'To hell, their worst fate' (Al Manar clip, February 2000).

However, collaborators were later given the chance to surrender to the resistance and to the Lebanese army prior to the liberation day, a call initiated by Hassan Nasrallah, Secretary General of Hezbollah.

The killing of Akel Hashem, having the process filmed and broadcast, emphasised that he was a traitor and could not escape the death sentence, and was intended to undermine the authority and morale of the SLA. The name-calling device presented by Jackall was implemented here. It is 'giving "bad names" to those individuals, groups, nations, races, policies, practices, beliefs, and ideals that he [propagandist] would have us condemn and reject' (Jackall 1995: 218). The coverage thus also aimed at undermining the ability and credibility of SLA leaders and their masters, the Israelis, to protect their proxy militia in south Lebanon.

## Liberation coverage

By February 2000, Israeli soldiers serving in south Lebanon were calling for an immediate withdrawal from south Lebanon (*Al Anbaa*, 10 February 2000). Israeli radio quoted one soldier as saying 'I don't want to be the last soldier to be killed in south Lebanon' (ibid.), while another said 'We cannot win this war. We are many, they are few and we cannot control them...there is nothing for us to win if we stay in south Lebanon' (ibid.).

The Lebanese daily *Addiyar* gave prominent space on 27 February 2000 to discussing an Israeli documentary, made by one of the soldiers who served in Lebanon and broadcast on Israeli TV. The documentary reveals that the Israeli newspaper *Shaair* had published lately obituary announcements for some of the Israeli soldiers who had died in south Lebanon. They posted the pictures of the dead soldiers and left an empty frame at the end of the sequence with a question mark, as if asking who would be next. The newspaper revealed that they had received permission from the dead soldiers' families to put this question mark.

Hezbollah's media personnel believed that, in addition to their military achievements, part of the fear expressed by Israeli soldiers and their families was caused by, or came as an answer to, the media campaign launched by Al Manar TV. The core aspect of this was the number of clips produced by Al Manar in Hebrew – addressed to Israeli soldiers in south Lebanon (Al Manar, February 2000).

One of these clips repeated in Hebrew the slogan 'Why do you have to wait till June to leave Lebanon? Why be the last soldier to be killed on our land?' while another shows the bodies of Israeli soldiers and the moaning of the wounded after the bombing of their positions in the occupied villages. The clip ends with the slogan 'Lebanon is a cemetery for Israeli soldiers' (in Arabic and Hebrew). About this, the Head of Al Manar at that time, Nayef Krayem, said:

> The audiences targeted by these clips are the locals and the Israeli soldiers, their mothers and leaders. Locally we wanted to say that this is an enemy that can be defeated – after decades of Israeli propaganda asserting that their army could not be beaten. Concerning the Israelis, we wanted to make the soldiers feel insecure and losing their faith in their

leaders, and for their mothers to put more pressure on the
Israeli Government to withdraw from south Lebanon. We
wanted to make both audiences aware that liberating our
occupied land was indisputable.

(interview with author 2000)

The words of the Israeli soldiers, quoted above, meant that Al Manar had achieved one of its objectives: to bring insecurity and fear to Israeli soldiers serving in south Lebanon. The soldiers were clearly affected by the content of Al Manar's clips. Goebbels' fourth principle of propaganda was met here. He stated that 'propaganda must affect the enemy's policy and action' (Doob 1995: 197).

Meanwhile, the Four Mothers movement in Israel was growing. It had been started on 4 February 1997[17] by four mothers of Israeli soldiers serving in south Lebanon, and grew to become, as the *Jerusalem Post* put it, 'one of the most successful grass-roots movements in Israeli history'.

> Extensive media coverage, mounting casualties in Lebanon and, ultimately, Prime Minister Ehud Barak's election promise to withdraw the army from the security zone all helped galvanize more support for the movement and its goals. It soon counted among its members not only mothers, but fathers, sons and citizens from all over Israel, and at one point it collected 25,000 signatures for a petition to withdraw from Lebanon.
>
> (Frucht, *Jerusalem Post*, 8 June 2000)

According to Frucht of the *Jerusalem Post*, the movement gained respect and support for being mothers in the first place and for being connected to highly-placed individuals:

> They were mothers of soldiers serving in Lebanon and among their ranks were bereaved mothers who had lost their sons in Lebanon. That touched a deep chord in Israeli society...A more prosaic explanation is that these women ultimately won respect and attention because they were well connected. Many not only had sons serving in elite units in Lebanon, but had husbands in the military as well. At one point, for instance, the Four Mothers movement included

the wife of OC Northern Command, Maj-Gen. Amiram Levine.

(ibid.)

Lemish and Barzel, in their article 'Four Mothers, the womb in the public sphere' (2000), quote a letter sent by one of the mothers called Zabarie to an Israeli weekly, *Ha'ir*. The letter reads:

> Woman, mother! Why do you give them your son, so they would sacrifice him? Your flower is 18, and he is the most important thing for you in the world – more than yourself. You won't eat because of him. You won't sleep because of him. And now, you let him go straight to hell, instead of telling him: 'My child, they die there! Don't go there!' ... Lebanon is a monstrous altar. Tell him the truth, don't let him go so easily. Don't give them your child. He wants to live.
> (Zabarie in *Ha'ir*, 7 February 1997, quoted in Lemish and Barzel, 2000, Vol. 15(2): 148)

According to Krayem, Al Manar were aware of the mothers' movement, who had contacted him personally via e-mail and tried to open a bridge of dialogue between them and the resistance leaders through Al Manar. Because of this, some of the Hebrew clips were addressed to the soldiers' mothers: 'Why let your son die in south Lebanon? Stop him from joining the troops in the Lebanese occupied territories!!' Krayem said these were obviously meant to work on their emotions, addressing the core feature that they should appeal to in order to influence one of their targets (interview with author, 2000). As mentioned before, the clips were seen in Israel through both Al Manar and Israeli TV, which used to copy the clips and re-broadcast them as news stories.

Meanwhile, the Israeli army's proxy militia (the SLA) was collapsing; many of its members were fleeing from their military positions towards the liberated areas (*Al Diyar*, 27 February 2000). All of this led to the sudden decision by the Israeli Government to complete its withdrawal from south Lebanon, but without any negotiations that might lead to pre-conditions, on 25 May 2000.

The withdrawal started on 21 May. Positions and villages were emptied one after another, leaving the collaborators' militia behind unable to keep its positions in the face of local inhabitants and those who marched from the liberated areas towards the occupied villages, towns and cities that some had not even had the chance to see before, because the occupation had lasted for 22 years.

For Lebanon in general, and Hezbollah in particular, this was victory. The time for celebration had arrived. Al Manar spread its reporters in several positions at the checkpoints to the occupied zone and dedicated its air time to the 'first returnees' trip' as it was known. There was just one news item on their news programmes' running order: the liberation.

> Welcome to this detailed bulletin that is dedicated to the day of Liberation.
>
> The returnees to their liberated villages spent a busy day celebrating the Liberation (wedding) ceremony, while the collaborators spent a bitter day on the edge of the abyss. Most of the central sector areas were reunified with the other parts of the country in less than 24 hours – after 22 years of defiance and resistance.
>
> (Areslan, Al Manar news, 24 May 2000)

Images of people singing, hanging onto cars and vans with flags of the resistance and Lebanon, expressing their joy and happiness with words, flowers and symbolic rice, filled the television screen.

> Hours were enough after yesterday's vehement scenes to break the chain of the Zionists and their collaborators, the Lahed Militia. Village after village fell into the hands of the massive flow of our citizens who announced, through ululating and shrill calls to God the Great, the end of an occupation and the beginning of a new era. By liberating their land, the Lebanese today have brought victory and pride and added to the history of Arab defeats of Israel.
>
> (Naser, Al Manar news, 24 May 2000)

Scenes of massed crowds marching towards their villages were all over the screen. Some people were crying, others were throwing rice over the returnees' heads,[18] hugging and kissing them and waving the flags of Lebanon and Hezbollah. People were jubilantly uttering welcoming and victorious phrases to the camera: 'Thank god for your safety and return', 'God is Great', 'The village is full of light with your presence and we missed you'. In another scene three old women came towards an Al Manar reporter and sang him songs of joy, asking him to give their greetings to Assayed Hassan Nasrallah.

People were conveying their euphoria and jubilation all through the day to the resistance and its leader, Hassan Nasrallah. Hezbollah was again the centre of focus for Al Manar's coverage to express the support the resistance were getting from the Lebanese people. Shouts of 'May God protect you and may God prolong your life' were addressed to Al Manar reporters and the resistance leaders. Through this coverage, Al Manar was also trying to ensure the unity of the people and that the taking over of the villages and towns from the Israelis was going as smoothly as possible.

There were many references to the fact that the resistance did not take revenge on any of the collaborators. They were either surrendering or fleeing towards the Lebanese–Israeli border, leaving their offices and machinery behind them. In less than 24 hours, the villages of the central sectors were liberated. It was a 'smooth Liberation', as Assayed Hassan Nasrallah put it that day.

> If the Zionists knew what would happen to them in Lebanon, would they have thought of entering this exceptional country? If Lahed militia members were expecting what their fate would be, would they have started their collaboration with an enemy that throughout history fought everyone who was different to them? Only the resistance was sure of the end and, based on that, chose the clear course of Liberation. Victory was its ally.
>
> (Naser, piece to camera, Al Manar news, ibid.)

Coverage from various villages and sectors followed. The most emotional moments were when the people knew that the Israeli soldiers and the collaborators had left the Khiam detention centre without setting the detainees free. The people, with camera crews, crawled towards the centre and broke into the cells where the detainees did not know what was happening outside. Suddenly, those who had been behind prison doors were celebrating their freedom.

That day, 25 May, was named Liberation Day and was announced by the government as a national day that Lebanon would celebrate every year. Additionally, Al Manar gained its celebrated name as the resistance television station by officials, journalists, academics and ordinary people.

## Reflection and conclusion

The only thought that came to my mind on 24 September 2006, standing on the rubble of the Al Manar complex in Haret Hreik in the southern suburb of Beirut, was: 'This is the evidence that Al Manar's media campaign or psychological warfare against the Israeli army was effective.' This is a huge assumption on my behalf, but it was also what most of my colleagues in Lebanon believed.

In our informal discussions following the July 2006 war there was huge sympathy for Al Manar. Israel, by bombing Al Manar's headquarters and the transmitters of the Lebanese Broadcasting Company (LBC) and Tele Liban, declared its military war on the media in Lebanon. Al Manar journalists were embraced, and technical help and support were given by most Lebanese television stations to Al Manar to help keep its broadcasts on air. Al Manar's broadcasts were interrupted for less than two minutes after the Israeli F16 jets flattened the complex to the ground.

Journalists from Al Manar reassured me that, because of earlier threats from the Israeli army to bomb their station, Al Manar had an evacuation plan ready. They had prepared an alternative centre to broadcast from if they should feel that the danger was close. Only two technicians were wounded in the attack on Al Manar. Soon after Beirut airport was attacked, the evacuation plan was put to action. It was not long after they attacked Beirut Airport[19] that they hit Al Manar's top floors, 'clipping off its antenna with a missile, but failing to put the station off air' (Fisk, *The Independent*, 14 July 2006). A few hours later, the station's headquarters was demolished.

Avi Jorisch, of the Washington Institute for Near East Policy, published a study on Al Manar in 2004 in a book titled *Beacon of Hatred: Inside Hizballah's Al Manar Television*. Jorisch refers to Al Manar ('Beacon' in English) as the beacon of hatred. He accuses Al Manar of inciting hatred against Israel and the United States. Jorisch attached a CD-ROM at the end of his book, containing what he called 'real Al Manar footage'. He used this footage as evidence of what he calls the 'beacon of hatred'. Most of these are clips that my study looks at as part of Hezbollah's psychological war against Israel.

Inciting hatred against the enemy is one of the key points in propaganda techniques. Al Manar, and subsequently Hezbollah, wanted to channel hatred in one direction – at the 'enemy' – Israel. The resistance was seeking domestic and Arab support to achieve its aim of liberating south Lebanon. Jorisch made his study look as if he had achieved a breakthrough with his discoveries inside Al Manar. However, as revealed in his study, Al Manar's staff and personnel received Jorisch and gave him full access to the television offices. He conducted interviews with Al Manar journalists and administrators, and they were clear about their aims and targets: they were trying to influence the public, both inside Israel and in Lebanon, in order to achieve the ultimate goal of liberation.

After the liberation, their target audience on the satellite channel was the Palestinian public. They were aiming at gaining support for the Palestinian resistance. As for the United States, the Al Manar campaign focused on the US military and financial help that made it possible for Israel to maintain its occupation of Palestinian territories. Jorisch recommended that the United States put Al Manar on its list of terrorist organisations (Jorisch 2004: xvi) and that is what happened.

Al Manar was put on the US state department's list of terrorist organisations in 2004, the first media institution to be placed on the list. The reasons that Jorisch argued in his study, why Al Manar should be banned, were its planned and structured campaigns to influence the Lebanese public to unite and support the resistance in its fight to end the Israeli occupation of south Lebanon.

A unified mass society or group and a feeling of togetherness are essential elements to the kind of propaganda this book is exploring, and which both Al Manar and TL journalists were trying to achieve. What was new in the Al Manar media campaigns, and which complemented TL's campaign, was that Al Manar tried to undermine the occupation forces' ability and credibility with images of killed and wounded soldiers, as well as with its media traps (explained earlier in this chapter).

Accordingly, the Al Manar and TL media campaigns both matched the positive understanding of propaganda discussed in Chapter Two. What they realised were campaigns that achieved, and intended to achieve, collective national public support for a cause or a mission, with the mass media being a core tool in disseminating political, social and patriotic messages to the public. In addition to this, Al Manar's media campaign sought to bring national unity and support for the resistance groups fighting the occupation forces within the sovereign, independent state of Lebanon. This summarises the core aspects of liberation propaganda explored in Chapter Two. We will come back to it later, in the summary of this chapter.

Al Manar journalists, like those of TL, believed that they were fighting for a cause with right on its side, and consequently none of them claimed impartiality. For them, being one-sided did not affect their professionalism. They were on the side of the victims. Objectivity for them too was not a norm that exists in a vacuum. For them, objectivity becomes negotiable when a journalist is faced with aggressive acts against his or her own people.

'Being fair and being objective are not the same thing', Amira Hass of the Israeli daily *Ha'aretz* told the independent veteran Robert Fisk (Fisk 2005: 558). Hass, who lives among the Palestinians in Ramallah and writes a daily column of what she describes as 'life under occupation' believes that 'there is a misconception that a journalist can be objective' (ibid.). She says: 'Palestinians tell me I'm objective, [and] I think this is important because I'm an Israeli. But being fair and being objective are not the same thing' (ibid.). In a later narrative, Hass, a critic of the Israeli occupation of the Palestinian territories, admits that she herself as an Israeli could not be objective towards those who commit suicide attacks against Israeli civilians, nor to their families (ibid: 559).

Al Manar journalists, like TL journalists, did not have this clear-cut differentiation between objectivity and fairness. In their own understanding, they were objective by being factual, by being fair to the victims of an 'aggressive occupation'. The word 'objectivity' was not dismissed, but it was related, as Iskandar and El-Nawawy suggested (in Allan and Zelizer, 2004), to their collective religious, cultural, social and ideological backgrounds. It was also related to their audiences' sensitivities and historical collective memory. Their objectivity was 'positioned' or 'contextual', as Iskandar and El-Nawawy (2004) put it. Al Manar journalists were aware that they were part of a planned and structured campaign targeted at concentrating the clear loathing among the Lebanese people towards Israel – which, after the 1996 events, hardly needed much effort – and support for the resistance.

They were aware of the campaign aimed at maintaining national unity – and which could protect and promote the resistance till it achieved its goal of liberation.

However, most of them didn't need instructions how to report and what to say or not say. It was, as in the TL journalists' case, a personal commitment to what we all believed to be a 'sacred cause'. However, for Al Manar journalists, it was not just a patriotic, nationalistic commitment that was guiding them, but also a religious Shiite ideology, which demanded that they fight oppressors and aggressors, and never accept humiliation or subjugation (Amhaz, interview with author, 2004).

'Propaganda' as a term was dismissed by Al Manar journalists, even though its literal translation in Arabic, *Al Diaayah Al Siyasiah*, was the name given to a section in Al Manar dedicated to producing the video clips mentioned earlier in the chapter (Hmayed, interview with author, 2004). The propaganda that they denied, as did the TL journalists, was the propaganda of deception. Those in higher administrative positions preferred the term 'psychological warfare'. However, it can readily be seen that many of the propaganda techniques and principles discussed in Chapter Two were at the core of their conduct. Moreover, what they were doing was another, different and much more deliberately orchestrated version of what I have defined as a very specific kind of liberation propaganda.

The propaganda they were conducting was of two kinds: propaganda targeting 'the home front' and propaganda targeting 'the enemy'. Many of Goebbels' principles have been identified in the media coverage of Al Manar, and the most important among these was the pursuit of credibility. To achieve that, their propaganda output had to be true and not false, as Goebbels (quoted in Doob 1995: 199) put it. However, Al Manar's propaganda was white and not black, which contradicts another principle of Goebbels. Jowett and O'Donnell (1999) state that, if propaganda devices are spotted through an analysis of media messages, then they fall into three categories:

> Propaganda is also described as white, grey, or black, in relationship to an acknowledgement of its source and its accuracy of information. White propaganda comes from a source that is identified correctly, and the information in the message tends to be accurate...Black propaganda is

credited to a false source and spreads lies, fabrications, and deceptions. Black propaganda is the 'big lie', including all types of creative deceit... Grey propaganda is somewhere between white and black propaganda. The source may or may not be correctly identified, and the accuracy of the information is uncertain.

(ibid: 12–15)

According to Jowett and O'Donnell, national celebrations with their 'overt patriotism and regional chauvinism, can usually be classified as white propaganda' (Jowett and O'Donnell 1999: 21), and this characterises most of the Al Manar coverage. Jackall (1995) presents the devices that the Institute for Propaganda Analysis use to detect propaganda. They call them 'the seven common propaganda devices' (see Chapter Two). As demonstrated earlier in this chapter, all have been detected in Al Manar's coverage except for one: the card-stacking device in which the propagandist employs all the arts of deception to win people's support for himself, his group, nation, race, policy, practice, belief or ideal. 'He stacks the cards against the truth' (Jackall 1995: 221).

Al Manar journalists were giving their account of what happened; they were not fabricating stories or being dishonest with their audiences. They were glorifying certain incidents and giving them prominence and importance through repetition and space, but none of those incidents was made up. They were factual, and thus the reporters believed that they were being fair to the victims of the occupation.

Jeremy Bowen, BBC Middle East editor, wrote in his book *War Stories* (2006) that every journalist starts from somewhere. He believes that no human being can be truly objective. Bowen explains that it is impossible because 'we all have a series of experiences, from parents, from teachers, from what we have seen in the world, that shape the way we think'. For him 'every reporter, every morning, has to decide how to cover the story and those decisions don't come out of nowhere', but he concludes that this should not make a journalist biased (Bowen 2006: 124). Nor does it mean that taking up a position on an issue is a form of negative or unbalanced propaganda.

Al Manar journalists, like TL journalists, challenged the word 'biased' when applied to their coverage of a war affecting their own people and nation. Yet they also agreed that, if they were to be labelled biased, then, yes: they would confirm that they were biased 'towards the victims, the oppressed and those affected badly by the occupation'.

## Summary

Notions of impartiality, objectivity and balance are challenged in this chapter, as in the previous chapter, by journalists who believe that they were subjected to and affected by the same experiences as their audiences, so that distancing themselves from the suffering of their people would be difficult to achieve.

There was a deep sense of patriotism, nationalism and (among Al Manar journalists) religious commitment guiding them in their reporting. On the one hand, they were addressing the collective mind of people who were being subjected to the same conflict. Their objectivity was contextual in that sense. On the other hand, Al Manar journalists' national and patriotic commitment was a core aspect of the media campaign launched by Hezbollah and operated by Al Manar TV. This was a campaign planned and structured, firstly, to influence domestic audiences and maintain national unity, and secondly, to influence Israeli soldiers and their families – to raise their voices and to refuse service in south Lebanon; and this campaign was implemented to achieve liberation. Propagating the right and ability of the resistance to fight the occupation, and highlighting the fears and failures of the enemy's soldiers, were the aims of the Hezbollah media campaign against the Israeli army.

Thus, propaganda techniques were used. Taylor speaks of propaganda used for 'good reasons' (Taylor 1995: 6). Related to this, Hatem speaks of 'honest propaganda' and 'psychological warfare' when propaganda targets the enemy in wartime (Hatem 1974: 63), while Jowett and O'Donnell speak of 'white propaganda' which can characterise national celebration (Jowett and O'Donnell 1999: 12). The propaganda of Hezbollah and Al Manar is a combination of all these aspects – and therefore, as I have argued in earlier chapters, I call it liberation propaganda.

# REFLECTION: ACHIEVING LIBERATION PROPAGANDA

The day the Israeli army withdrew from south Lebanon on 25 May 2000, I called the late Lebanese prime minister, Rafic Hariri, to congratulate him on this historic moment. He responded by praising the role of the Lebanese media in contributing to liberation. At that point, I began to feel the need to ask questions about the role we, the Lebanese journalists, had played in achieving that liberation.

The most poignant question to me was whether or not we had conducted propaganda. If so, what kind of propaganda was it? Did it match any aspects of the twentieth-century propaganda models discussed in the West? Did it meet all the criteria, techniques and principles of such propaganda? And, if it was propaganda, what defined or distinguished 'our propaganda'?

What was very clear to me was that we journalists were deeply proud of the 'objective coverage' we had delivered, from 11 April 1996 right through to liberation day, 25 May 2000 – and yet Hitler's propaganda mastermind, Goebbels, had said that objectivity and propaganda do not go together (Doob 1995: 190). So what kind of objectivity were we adhering to? How then can journalistic norms and values fit together with certain kinds of propaganda?

To try to find answers to these questions, it seemed to me that a reflexive, ethnographic approach was essential – particularly, I would argue, because it offers the tools that help relate theory to practice. It allowed me, as a researcher, to distance myself from, look critically at and reflect on earlier events and performances in which I was a complete participant.

This approach enabled me to judge my performance by trying to match what I had learned in the West about being an 'objective reporter' with what I had actually done on the ground. Equally, I had to assess my colleagues' performance, to try to identify the trends and norms of their journalistic conduct in reporting military operations and the wars with Israel, and relate that conduct to propaganda techniques and principles.

I applied ethnographic principles and their related methodologies to explore the social, cultural, religious and political contexts in which we journalists operated, and thus to achieve the particular understanding of propaganda put forward here. This book has thus sought to establish how different cultural contexts might generate different understandings of the same set of news values, even while implementing those same news values. Therefore, journalistic norms of objectivity, neutrality and balance were explored in different contexts.

This research suggested that different interpretations of news values and norms might produce different journalistic performances and that contextualising these news values and norms is essential to identify the suggested propagandistic performances.

## Objectivity and war reporting

Journalism culture is studied in this book in relation to propaganda, and not as a sociological object in itself. Thus, defining objectivity was not the aim of this study, nor was defining the sociology of the Lebanese TV news room, though they were necessarily touched upon. Aspects of history, politics, society and religion that define the culture of Lebanese broadcast journalists have been discussed in this work to highlight the performance and techniques of Lebanese journalists and to gauge their congruence with normative propaganda techniques and principles. Therefore, the concepts of 'truth', 'impartiality', 'objectivity' and 'balance' were problematised here.

It seems that the work I and other Lebanese journalists were doing was clearly 'intentional' – our training, our experience as Lebanese citizens over the course of our lifetimes, our sense of the wrong being done to our country, all this made it possible for us to be quite sure and focused about what had to be done and could be done. What we did was therefore very much connected to our 'professionalism' and our role as 'disciplined' journalists and media personnel. This is why I was able to remain 'calm and professional' while covering the April 1996 events, as demonstrated in Chapter Six.

The 'truth' we were intent on showing was the Lebanese version of 'truth' at that moment – there is always another version (or several others) available. It was thus a 'positioned' truth, which then – because it is believed in so passionately and so nationalistically, because it is lived and embodied in daily encounters with shattered and innocent bodies – comes to seem an 'objective' truth.

This has much to do here with the way the body lives this horror – we also came to live the same horror as the victims of the Israeli assaults. Our normal sense of objectivity and distance was impossible in such a context, and the only truth that was even remotely possible was a positioned or contextual truth – as this book argues. Thus, seeing it as 'contextual truth' or 'contextual objectivity' could not have been achieved without the ethnographic approach that this study adopts. It is only afterwards and from a distance that I can see our 'contextual objectivity' for what it was.

The 'contextual objectivity' that we Lebanese journalists adopted when covering military incursions by Israeli forces in south Lebanon could be applied to war reporting in general – and it can be generalised to that. As we have seen, journalists reporting war when their own nation is under threat can hardly have any other kind of objectivity than precisely this. Journalists who encountered the horror of crushed, innocent bodies while covering wars could not have any other kind of objectivity but a 'contextual objectivity', and this is demonstrated in Chapters Three, Six and Seven.

Balance too became questionable when covering the massacres of innocent children and women, as illustrated and emphasised by the ITV news editor, David Mannion, in his commentary on claims of bias while covering the July 2006 Lebanon war (Mannion, *Broadcast*, 4 August 2006).

Along with objectivity, there is also the concept of impartiality. The terms 'positioned' and 'contextual' deny the very possibility of impartiality or a distanced position when making decisions in this kind of context (as illustrated in Chapters Six and Seven).

## Liberation propaganda

This book has sought to present the history, definitions, principles and analysis of the various notions of propaganda, as seen by the major scholars on this subject at different times in the twentieth century and the beginning of the twenty-first. Chapter Two, along with Chapter

Three, aimed to set out the theoretical basis for an analysis of Lebanese journalists' performance during the major incursions by Israeli occupation forces in south Lebanon. It looked at the different definitions and characteristics of propaganda and explored a new understanding of liberation propaganda.

As this study has demonstrated, propaganda has been seen and identified throughout its existence in very different ways. Some views of it are positive, but most of its connotations are negative. However, no one could claim a definitive description. This study has tried to restore Edward L. Bernays' argument – that 'the fine old word, Propaganda' in itself has certain technical meanings which, 'like most things in this world, are neither good nor bad but custom makes them so' (Bernays 1928: 20) – and then to use the word again in a positive sense to describe what might also be called a media campaign, or indeed something else.

To reinforce Bernays' point, this book has adopted Barlett's approach, which states that 'Propaganda must be defined by reference to its aims' (Bartlett 1942: 6). The propaganda this study has argued for fits within the framework of Ellul's propaganda of integration. 'Propaganda aims at making the individual participate in his society in every way' (Ellul 1973), but this can be accomplished even when the campaign is part accidental, part improvised, part an almost-unconscious (because professionally informed) response to desperate situations. 'Deliberate' here acquires context-specific meanings that do not entirely contradict its quasi-opposites 'automatic' and 'unwitting'.

Nevertheless, by 'propaganda' I mean a campaign that achieves, and was intended to achieve, a collective national public support for a cause or mission, with the mass media being a core tool in disseminating political, social and patriotic messages to the public.

In accordance with that, the idea of liberation propaganda this study has investigated is certainly of a media campaign that seeks to bring national unity and support for those resistance groups fighting occupation forces within a sovereign, independent state. It is a propaganda of integration, not (internal) subversion. It is an 'honest' (Hatem: 1974) or 'white' (Jowett and O'Donnell: 1999) propaganda. Its sources and aims are acknowledged. It is a propaganda that claims dependency on objective and factual information. It is a propaganda that aims at dismissing fear of the enemy and denouncing the enemy's credibility and abilities, at the same time highlighting the ability and credibility of the resistance groups and their leaders.

This honest propaganda therefore rejects Goebbels' assertion that 'objectivity has nothing in common with propaganda, nothing in common with truth' (quoted in Thomson 1994: 4). This propaganda uses national symbols, and draws upon the history of conflict between occupied and occupier, to achieve its fundamental goals.

Previous use of the term – 'liberation propaganda' – has been related to different contexts than this study. It was Gerhard von Glahn who first introduced the term, in an article submitted to the journal *Law and Contemporary Problems*. His article talked of the use of propaganda in foreign countries, as a device to abet and arouse 'revolutionary tendencies' and violence to overthrow their rulers (Glahn 1966).

It is very important to distinguish this use of the term 'liberation' from the one I wanted to develop. The propaganda this book has investigated is one conducted by domestic governments, alongside domestic resistance movements, with the aim of achieving liberation from a foreign occupying army. Indeed, it could be said that the liberation propaganda I described in Chapters Two, Six and Seven is something like a domestic variant of von Glahn's externally driven version.

What I have described is a propaganda that seeks loyalty, one that binds citizens to their governments and their resistance groups in their fight against a foreign enemy. It is a propaganda of integration; where it is a propaganda of subversion, it is subversive of the activities of a foreign enemy. It is, like most forms of propaganda, context-specific. It borrows some, and rejects other, aspects of the principles and tools of propaganda which have been identified in academic studies in the twentieth and twenty-first centuries.

With the Tele Liban journalists (see Chapter Six) there was no orchestrated and managed propaganda campaign – but the professionalism, shared ideas and ideals, shared experiences and shared dangers, and the interpersonal relationships did (and do) produce a very consistent common approach, one that is very deliberate in terms of personal commitment and therefore not unintentional – yet, in the case of TL, not one that was managed or planned.

In contrast, for Al Manar journalists (see Chapter Seven) the campaign developed to become both managed and planned, aiming at achieving a clear set of goals. It aimed to unify the nation in support of the resistance, to promote faith in the resistance fighters' ability to defeat the enemy army, to demonise the enemy's military capabilities and to make people believe that the dream of liberation was achievable.

As Chapter Four illustrates, the histories of the Arab–Israeli conflict – especially the Lebanese–Israeli conflict – continue to occupy much of the collective memory of the Lebanese people, including the journalists under investigation. Thus, history was used in the messages constructed to address both home-front audiences and Arab-speakers abroad, whom Tele Liban and Al Manar were able to reach through satellite broadcasts.

The conflict with Israel had clearly fractured Lebanon's stability and security, causing divisions among its many religious communities, which explains the emphasis that was placed, by both TL and Al Manar journalists, on the need to achieve national unity. Uniting the nation, as Chapters Six and Seven revealed, is what propaganda on the home front was aiming at, whether planned or unplanned.

Liberation propaganda is here defined as a national media campaign aiming to free occupied land from foreign occupation forces. It is propaganda to the home front that seeks to keep the nation united to achieve emancipation. It additionally aims at diminishing fear of the enemy and emphasising the ability and credibility of resistance fighters to lead the nation towards liberation. It is a propaganda that aims at demonising the enemy's abilities and credibility.

Significantly, liberation propaganda also seeks to establish fear of the resistance among the enemy audience – yet centrally it is a propaganda campaign that considers credibility and factuality as its main features. It is a propaganda campaign that dismisses deception and fabrication. It is a media campaign that does not contradict the journalistic norm of 'objectivity' in its 'contextual' form. It is thus a positive model of propaganda.

## Areas of future research

During the July 2006 war on Lebanon, Israeli jets deliberately targeted and bombed several Lebanese TV studios and transmission centres, including those of Tele Liban and Al Manar. Al Manar's headquarters in the southern suburb of Beirut was among the first set of targets. It was hit in two separate attacks, and the second attack destroyed the building completely. The air raid aimed to silence the voice of Al Manar and other Lebanese stations and stop it from reaching its audiences, whether local or via satellite.

It was when the images and stories of Lebanese journalists began to spread beyond Lebanon to operate in a global arena – using the power of those images to become 'propaganda' to non-home audiences – then the recognition of that power led to military attacks on the source of those images. These attacks were an innovation in this kind of media war – a war where media organisations became military targets because of their role in reporting images of destruction and innocent casualties. It was a war against reporters who were resisting military attacks on their country simply by doing their job in such a way as to hold the nation together.

What makes the notion of liberation propaganda particularly valid is the way the Lebanese media reacted to the Israeli attacks during the July 2006 war. All domestic political differences were put aside and all groups were following the same line of solidarity and calls for unity that had characterised April 1996 and the years that followed until Liberation day on 25 May 2000.

Hezbollah media people and Al Manar TV introduced new techniques to their propaganda campaign, techniques that deserve future analysis. For instance, the direct role that the television speeches of Hezbollah Secretary General Hassan Nasrallah's played in the propaganda campaign to the home and non-home audiences warrants research.

Moreover, the Lebanese Bloggers diaries that emerged daily from Beirut over the internet during the July war – such as those of Rasha Salti and Hanadi Salman – are worthy of future study. They illustrate the role of citizen journalism in liberation propaganda campaigns as much as they demonstrate an alternative media tool in covering wars. Perhaps most significantly, the model of liberation propaganda can be tested in future research – wherever there are the necessary conditions of foreign occupation and a national unity engendered by media that seek to deal in 'truth' (even if positioned), rather than deception, as a weapon of that liberation. Such media need to be able to effectively communicate their messages, it must be said.

Among the places we might suggest, where these conditions potentially exist and could be explored, are Kurdistan (in any of the national territories between which it is divided), the Palestinian occupied territories (if a national unity government is achieved) and Iraq, which however currently lacks the necessary condition of undivided nationhood. The ongoing sectarian struggle, feudalism, old rivalries and privilege-driven relations with the occupiers make it difficult to achieve a unified nation.

Nonetheless, in none of these three cases is there currently the necessary condition of the uniting media or medium that could help drive the fight against occupation. This necessary pre-condition underlines the success in the Lebanese case, where the media were able to act openly and effectively. It was possible in this study to examine in considerable detail what precisely the Lebanese version/s of context-specific liberation propaganda looked like. This book thus provides a case study that could form the basis for continuing research in similar kinds of national context.

# NOTES

## 1  Introduction

1. On 25 May 2000, Israeli troops completed their withdrawal from the occupied territories in Lebanon, apart from a small piece of disputed land called Shebaa farms, an area 14 km (9 miles) in length and 2.5 km (1.5 miles) in width at the junction of Israel, Syria and Lebanon. Israel claims it is Syrian land; Lebanon says it is Lebanese land. Syria also says it is Lebanese, but has not yet supplied the United Nations with any documents on the issue (see BBC News, 25 May 2000, and Chassay, *The Guardian*, 10 October 2006).

## 2  Propaganda: Definitions and Techniques

1. The late Geoff Mungham (senior lecturer at Cardiff School of Journalism and expert on propaganda) remarked on the fact that hitherto only von Glahn had written on liberation propaganda. He also noted there was no detailed study of propaganda in a liberation context, as in Lebanon, which is what makes this book novel and unique.

## 3  Ethnography and Journalism Culture

1. Article 4 of the Arab journalists' press code ratified in 1972 and adopted by the Lebanese press syndicate states that 'the press's mission requires objectivity and verifying the accuracy of the information before it is published. Journalists are also bound to get information and facts through legitimate means and to rectify any previously published information in case they turn out to be wrong'. Additionally the

Lebanese press ethical code endorsed in 1974 by the Lebanese Press Federation stated that 'a newspaper is bound to truth and accuracy' (*Al Sahafa Al Loubnania*, issue No. 7, 8.84). No other Lebanese press or media code followed this one.

## 4 Overview of the Arab–Israeli Conflict

1. A *dumun* is equivalent to 1,000 square metres.
2. For more on the massacres committed by Zionist militias against the Palestinians, see Ilan Pappé's book, *The Ethnic Cleansing of Palestine* (2008).
3. On 19 March 1978, the United Nations Security Council adopted Resolution 425, which calls upon Israel to withdraw immediately from all Lebanese territory. It also calls for strict respect for the territorial integrity, sovereignty and political independence of Lebanon within its internationally recognised boundaries. The UN Security Council also decided to establish a peace-keeping interim force for southern Lebanon for the purpose of confirming the withdrawal of Israeli forces, restoring international peace and security, and assisting the government of Lebanon in ensuring the return of its effective authority in the area (Tueini, 1979).
4. The Jewish Agency was established under the League of Nations Mandate for Palestine in July 1922 and 'recognised as a public body for the purpose of advising and co-operating with the administration of Palestine such economic, social and other matters as may affect the establishment of the Jewish National Home and the interests of the Jewish population in Palestine' (Gilbert 1996: 50).
5. According to a poll released by the Beirut Centre for Research and Information shortly after Israel attacked Lebanon in July 2006, 87 per cent of Lebanese people support Hezbollah's fight with Israel, a rise of 29 per cent on a similar poll conducted in February 2006. The level of support from non-Shiite communities for Hezbollah's resistance had also increased: 80 per cent of Christians polled supported Hezbollah, along with 80 per cent of Druze and 89 per cent of Sunnis (Blanford, *Christian Science Monitor*, 28 July 2006).

## 5 The Media in Lebanon

1. Boulos headed Tele Liban's board of directors between September 1996 and 1999.
2. The Arabic edition of Boulos's book was used as a reference in this study, and thus quotations from it have been translated from Arabic into English by the author of this book.

3. The first state-owned television station in the Arab world was Iraqi TV.
4. Radio in Lebanon was established in 1938 by the French Mandate authorities, who controlled it completely until they withdrew in 1946. The newly independent Lebanese Government took it over as a monopoly. As William Rugh explains, 'the French established the precedent of governmental radio, so the Lebanese officials were able to retain it' (Rugh 2004: 195).
5. This ability of the government to set editorial policies comes under the terms of the licence granted to the television station.
6. In addition to this, CLT used to produce local programmes in French, and Boulos was one of their early presenters.
7. The Lebanese civil war erupted on 13 April 1975 (for more details see Chapter Four).
8. The April 1996 military operation was code-named by the Israelis 'Grapes of Wrath'.
9. A confessional political system is one based on religious sectarian grounds and preferences.
10. LL 250 million (Lebanese liras or pounds) was equivalent to US $170,000.
11. Confessionalism being a political system based on religious sectarian grounds and preferences.
12. Al Manar, according to its licence application, is run by an independent board of directors. This board has members (mainly businessmen and bank managers) who have no organisational ties to Hezbollah. However, they support the resistance's operations in south Lebanon.
13. Al Nour, a radio station established by Hezbollah, was later run by a separate board of directors.
14. On 30 July 2006 an Israeli aircraft dropped a massive bomb on a building near the village of Qana in south Lebanon, causing it to collapse on top of dozens of civilians – many of them children – taking cover in the basement. The attack, which left 28 dead and 13 missing, became known as the second Qana Massacre. Qana number two took place 10 years after the first Qana massacre, a full account of which is presented in Chapter Six.

## 6 Tele Liban coverage, April 1996: Grapes of Unity Facing Grapes of Wrath

1. The Israeli Government code-named its operation after the famous novel of John Steinbeck, *The Grapes of Wrath*, relating rhetorically its operation with the theme of 'fighting for existence'.

2. In 2006 Israel again claimed its war was against Hezbollah, not Lebanon; however, after 33 days of war, Hezbollah emerged intact.
3. Head-notes are experiences and memories that the ethnographer carries from the field. They are stories, encounters, conversations, sayings and attitudes that escaped the written field notes or journal and are preserved only in the head of the ethnographer (Sanjek, 1990: 93).
4. Shumur is a village in the western Bekaa valley.
5. Tyre and Sidon are the two main southern cities, 84 km (52 ml) and 48 km (30 ml) south of Beirut.
6. *Assayad* is a Shiite Muslim religious title.
7. The TL anchor–producers who covered the Grapes of Wrath operation from south Lebanon were: Zahera Harb on 13–15 April, 23–25 April and 27 April 1996; Zaven Kouyoumdjian on 16–18 April 1996; Dalal Kandeel on 19–20 April and 26 April 1996; and Rajaa Kamouneh on 21–22 April 1996. Aref Al Abed, Head of News (1993–7), described the teams that covered the events from south Lebanon as suicidal. He praised most the first team that agreed to go south at a time where others were reluctant and were questioning the benefits of doing so (Al Abed, interview with author, 2004).
8. Nabatiyeh is 78 km (49 ml) south-east of Beirut.
9. Katyushas were Soviet-made, multiple rocket launchers with short-range rockets.
10. Tyre, called *Sour* in Arabic, is the fourth largest city in Lebanon.
11. In Lebanon, the word 'martyr' is used to refer to innocent civilians who die from an aggressive military act and thus not just to fighters. The term has been used since 1975 to refer to people who die as a result of state-sponsored oppression, no matter to what religious sect they belong.
12. The prime minister was referring to Hezbollah's relations with Iran. For more information on the link between Hezbollah and Iran, see Hamzeh (2005).
13. The committee was established at the end of Lebanese civil war, in the early 1990s, to co-ordinate the actions of public agencies and NGOs in relation to social affairs.
14. *Hajj* is the pilgrimage to Mecca, which all Muslims try to make at least once.
15. These are massacres committed by the Israeli army against Palestinians in 1948, 1956 and 1992.
16. There was a strong belief among Lebanese officials that the Israeli army was plotting to create a refugee crisis in Lebanon to put pressure

Notes 239

on the Lebanese government to respond to Israel demands to disarm Hezbollah and stop its resistance operations in south Lebanon.
17. South Lebanon and the western Bekaa valley are mainly inhabited by Shiite Muslims and Druze, with minorities of Sunni Muslims and Christians.
18. To know why Lebanese Christians' support for the resistance was an important feature, see Chapter Four on the historical background of the Lebanese–Israeli conflict.
19. Samir Kasir was assassinated on 2 June 2005 in Beirut, a bomb having been planted under his car seat. He was one of the Independence 05 movement in Lebanon's political architecture, the movement formed after the assassination of Prime Minister Rafic Hariri on 14 February 2005.

## 7 Liberation Media: Hezbollah and Al Manar, 1997–2000

1. For full information on Al Manar TV and its structure, see Chapter Five.
2. On 25 May 2000, Israeli troops completed their withdrawal from the majority of the occupied territories in south Lebanon, keeping back a small piece of disputed land called Shebaa farms. This area, at the junction of Syria, Lebanon and Israel, is 14 km (9 ml) in length and 2.5 km (2 ml) in width. Israel claims it is Syrian land, and Lebanon says it is Lebanese land. Syria says it is Lebanese, but has not supplied the United Nations with any written documents on the issue yet.
3. Mohsen is one of only a few researchers who have conducted studies on the media performance of Hezbollah; he has edited two books on the issue and these are listed in the bibliography.
4. In April 1996 Israel launched a military operation against Hezbollah and Lebanon, code-named Grapes of Wrath. The operation lasted 16 days, causing hundreds of Lebanese civilian casualties and infrastructural destruction. The operation ended without achieving its objectives; it was mainly aimed at rooting out the resistance from south Lebanon. On the contrary, Hezbollah and the Islamic resistance gained huge public support in response to the Israeli assaults.
5. See Chapter Six (especially on 26/27 April) for more details of the April Understanding.
6. Lebanon has 18 religious sects. Christians and Muslims constitute, in almost equal numbers, the majority of the population; in addition there is a Jewish minority (see Picard 2002).
7. Swat al Arab was an Egyptian state-run radio station.

8. *Assayed* is a Shiite religious title.
9. Amal was another Shiite movement, headed by House speaker Nabih Beri.
10. For more on the notion of 'us' and 'them', see Said (1978/1995), Said (1981) and Said (2001).
11. On 11 April 1996, Israel's launch of the military operation Grapes of Wrath was marked by the Qana massacre, where the Israeli army bombed the UN headquarters in Qana, killing 106 civilians sheltering in the compound. See Chapter Six for more details of the events of April 1996.
12. The head of the MMU refused to disclose his real name and introduced himself as Haj Maitham. I was told his real name could not be revealed for security reasons.
13. For more information on how Imam Hussein was the role model for Hezbollah fighters, see Qassem 2005: 43.
14. Dayan and Katz (in Tumber 1999) state that 'the most obvious difference between media events and other formulas or genres of broadcasting is that they are, by definition, not routine'. They explain that media events are 'interruptions of routine; they intervene in the normal flow of broadcasting and out lives. Like the holidays that halt everyday routines, television events propose exceptional thing to think about, to witness, and to do' (ibid: 49).
15. Abass Naser moved to work for Al Jazeera as their correspondent in Lebanon.
16. By 'the day of shame and dishonour', Naser is referring to 17 May 1983, when Lebanon signed a peace treaty with Israel under the barrels of Israeli tanks. The treaty was cancelled two years later. For more details, see Chapter Three.
17. On the night of 4 February 1997, two Israeli helicopters collided over one of the northern settlements *en route* to Lebanon, killing all 73 soldiers on board.
18. Throwing rice is a traditional gesture of celebration, welcoming and joy.
19. Beirut airport was re-named Hariri international airport after the assassination of former Lebanese prime minister Rafic Hariri in February 2005.

# BIBLIOGRAPHY

1. Books, journals, theses and websites
2. Newspaper archives
3. Tele Liban news archives
4. Al Manar news archives
5. Interviews and correspondence with the author

The order is letter-by-letter (Al Manar after Allan), not word-by-word, with single-author titles (earliest first) before jointly authored titles.

## Books, journals and websites

Adie, K. (1998), 'Dispatches from the front: reporting war', *Contemporary Issues in British Journalism*; 1998 Vauxhall Lectures, Centre for Journalism Studies, Cardiff University.

Adie, K. (2002), *The Kindness of Strangers*, Headline, London.

Al Abed, A. (2001), *Lebanon and Al Taef*, Centre for Arab Unity Studies, Beirut.

Allan, S. and Zelizer, B. (2004), *Reporting War Journalism in Wartime*, Routledge, London.

Al Manar website (2000), www.almanar.com.lb/NewsSite/AboutUs.aspx?language=en, (accessed 2 May 2000) [The statement was changed shortly after the liberation of south Lebanon on 25 May 2000.]

Alterman, J. (1998), *New Media, New Politics? From Satellite Television to the Internet in the Arab World*, Policy Paper No. 48, Washington Institute for Near East Policy, Washington, DC.

Altheide, D.L. (1997), *Creating Reality*, Sage, Beverly Hills/London.

Atkinson, P. (1992), *Understanding Ethnographic Texts*, Sage University Paper, Qualitative Research Methods No. 25, Sage, Newbury Park, California.

Atwi, M. (2000), *The Zionist Danger over Lebanon*, Dar Al Hadi, Beirut.

Aull Davies, C. (1999), *Reflexive Ethnography*, Routledge, London.

Avalon Project, Yale University Law School, *Balfour Declaration*, URL: www.yale.edu/lawweb/avalon/mideast/balfour.htm (accessed: 12 February 2003).

Bantz, C.R., McCorkle, S. and Baade, R.C. (1980), 'The news factory', *Communication Research*, Vol. 7, No. 1, pp. 45–68.

Bartlett, F.C. (1942), *Political Propaganda*, Cambridge University Press, Cambridge.

Bell, M. (1998), 'The journalism of attachment', in M. Kieran (1998), *Media Ethics*, Routledge, London, pp. 15–22.

Bell, M. (2003), *Through Gates of Fire*, Weidenfeld & Nicolson, London.

Berkowitz, D. (1997), *Social Meanings of News: A Text-Reader*, Sage, London.

Bernay, Edward L. (1928), *Propaganda*, Horace Liveright, New York.

Blanford, N. (2006), *Killing Mr Lebanon: The Assassination of Rafik Hariri and its Impact on the Middle East*, I.B.Tauris, London.

Bleske, G.L. (1991), 'Ms. Gates takes over: an updated version of a 1949 case study', *Newspaper Research Journal*, Vol. 12, No. 4, pp. 88–97, reprinted in D. Berkowitz, (1997), *Social Meanings of News*, Sage, London, pp. 72–80.

Bolak, H. (1997), 'Studying one's own in the Middle East: negotiating gender and self-other dynamics in the field', in R. Hertz (1997), *Reflexivity & Voice*, Sage, London, pp. 95–118.

Boulos, J.-C. (1995), *Television History and Stories*, FMA, Lebanon.

Bowen, J. (2006), *War Stories*, Simon & Schuster, London.

Boyd, D. (1993), *Broadcasting in the Arab World*, Iowa State University Press, Ames, Iowa.

Boyd-Barrett, O. (2004), 'Understanding the second casualty' in S. Allan and B. Zelizer (2004), *Reporting War Journalism in Wartime*, Routledge, London, pp. 25–42.

Breed, W. (1955), 'Social control in the news room: a functional analysis', *Social Forces*, Vol. 33, pp. 326–355, reprinted in D. Berkowitz (1997), *Social Meanings of News*, Sage, London, pp. 107–122.

Bregman, A. (2000), *Israel's Wars: A History since 1947*, Routledge, London.

Bromley, M. and O'Malley, T. (1997), *A Journalism Reader*, Routledge, London.

Campbell, V. (2004), *Information Age Journalism*, Arnold, London.

Carey, J.W. (1989), *Communication as Culture: Essays on Media and Society*, Unwin Hyman, Boston.

Carstens, P., Klinghardt, G. and West, M. (1987), *Trails in the Thirstland: The Anthropological Field Diaries of Winifred Hoernle*, Communication 14, Centre for African Studies, Cape Town.

Casey, B., Casey, N., Calvert, B., French, L. and Lewis, J. (2002), *Television Studies: The Key Concepts*, Routledge, London.

Chomsky, N. (2003), *Middle East Illusions*, Rowman & Littlefield, Lanham, Maryland.

Clifford, J. and Marcus, G. (1986), *Writing Culture: The Poetics and Politics of Ethnography*, University of California Press, Berkeley.

Connelly, M. and Welch, D. (2005), *War and the Media: Reportage and Propaganda, 1900–2003*, I.B.Tauris, London.

Cooley, J. (1973), *Green March, Black September*, Frank Cass, London.

Cottle, S. (2003), *Media Organization and Production*, Sage, London.

Cross, M. (1999), 'Flora Tristan's socialist propaganda in provincial France, 1843–4', in B. Taithe and T. Thornton (1999), *Propaganda: Political Rhetoric and Identity, 1300–2000*, Sutton, Stroud, Gloucestershire, pp. 151–165.

Curran, J. and Gurevitch, M. (2000), *Mass Media and Society*, Arnold, London.

Curry, K. (1999), 'Themes of power and identity in the court festivals of ducal Lorraine, 1563–1624', in B. Taithe and T. Thornton (1999), *Propaganda: Political Rhetoric and Identity, 1300–2000*, Sutton, Stroud, Gloucestershire, pp. 61–76.

Dajani, N. (2001), 'The changing scene of Lebanese television', *TBS Electronic Journal*, No. 7 (Fall/Winter). URL: www.tbsjournal.com/Archives/Fall01/dajani.html (accessed: 9 January 2005).

De Burgh, H. (2005), *Making Journalists*, Routledge, Great Britain.

Denton, R. (1993), *The Media and The Persian Gulf War*, Westport, London.

DeVault, M.L. (1990), 'Talking and listening from women's standpoint: feminist strategies for interviewing and analysis', *Social Problems*, Vol. 37, No. 1, pp. 96–116.

Devore, R. (1976), *The Arab–Israeli Conflict*, Clio Books, Oxford.

Doob, L. (1995), 'Goebbels' principles of propaganda', in R. Jackall (1995), *Propaganda*, Macmillan, Basingstoke, Hants., pp. 190–214.

Durham, F. and Singer, J. (2006), 'The watchdog's bark: professional norms and institutional routines in cable news coverage of Hurricane Katrina', paper presented at the International Communication Association (ICA) Conference, 19–23 June, Dresden, Germany.

Eisenberg, L. (1994), *My Enemy's Enemy: Lebanon in the Early Zionist Imagination, 1900–1948*, Wayne State University Press, Detroit.

Ellul, J. (1965/1973), *Propaganda: The Formation of Men's Attitudes*, Vintage Books, New York.

El-Nawawy, M. and Iskandar, A. (2002), *Al Jazeera: How the Free Arab News Network Scooped the World and Changed the Middle East*, Westview, Boulder, Colorado.

El-Nawawy, M. and Iskandar, A. (2003), *Al-Jazeera: The Story of the Network that is Rattling Governments and Redefining Modern Journalism*, Westview, Boulder, Colorado.

Epstein, E. J. (1973), *News From Nowhere: Television and the News*, Random House, New York.

Ericson, R.V., Baranek, P.M. and Chan, J.B.L. (1987), *Visualizing Deviance: A Study of News Organization*, Open University Press, Milton Keynes.

Ettema, J.L. and Glasser, T. (1998), *Custodians of Conscience*, Columbia University Press, New York.

Farsoun, S. and Zacharia, C. (1997), *Palestine and the Palestinians*, Westview, Oxford.

Firmo-Fontan, V. (2004), 'Power, NGOs and Lebanese television' in N. Sakr (2004), *Women and Media in the Middle East*, I.B.Tauris, London, pp. 162–79.

Fishman, M. (1980), *Manufacturing the News*, University of Texas Press, Austin.

Fisk, R. (2001), *Pity the Nation: Lebanon at War*, Oxford University Press, Oxford.

Fisk, R. (2006), *The Great War for Civilisation: The Conquest of the Middle East*, Harper Perennial, London.

Fiske, J. (1987), *Television Culture*, Routledge, London.

Fowler, R. (1991), *Language in the News: Discourse and Ideology in the British Press*, Routledge, London.

Friedman, T. (1998), *From Beirut to Jerusalem*, Harper Collins, London.

Gans, H. (1979), *Deciding What's News*, Pantheon, New York.

Gieber, W. (1964), 'News is what newspapermen make it', in L.A. Dexter and D. Manning, *White People, Society and Mass Communication*, Free Press, New York.

Gilbert, M. (1996), *Israel: A History*, Doubleday, London.

Giltin, T. (1980), *The Whole World is Watching: Mass Media in the Making and Unmaking of the Left*, University of California Press, Berkeley.

Ginneken, J. (1998), *Global News*, Sage, London.

Von Glahn, G. (1996), 'The case for legal control of 'liberation' propaganda', *Law and Contemporary Problems*, International Control of Propaganda (Summer), Vol. 31, No. 3, pp. 553–588.

Goebbels, J. (1962), *The Early Goebbels Diaries: The Journal of Joseph Goebbels, from 1925 to 1926*, ed. Helmut Heiber, Weidenfeld & Nicolson, London.
Gold, R.L. (1958), 'Roles in sociological field observations', *Social Forces*, Vol. 36, pp. 217–223.
Golding, P. and Elliot, P. (1979), *Making the News*, Longman, London.
Goodall, H.L. (2000), *Writing the New Ethnography*, AltaMira Press, Walnut Creek, California.
Hafez, K. (2001), *Mass Media, Politics & Society in The Middle East*, Hampton Press, Cresskill, New Jersey.
Hall, J. (2001), *Online Journalism*, Pluto Press, London.
Halloran, J.D., Elliot, P. and Murdock, G. (1970), *Demonstrations and Communication: A Case Study*, Penguin, Harmondsworth, Middlesex.
Hammersley, M. and Atkinson, P. (1983), *Ethnography: Principles in Practice*, Tavistock Publications, London.
Hamzeh, N. (2004), *In the Path of Hizbollah*, Syracuse University Press, New York.
Hannerz, U. (1996), *Transnational Connections*, Routledge, London.
Harb, Z. and Bessaiso, E. (2006), 'British Arab Muslim audiences and television after September 11', *Journal of Ethnic and Migration Studies*, Vol. 32, No. 6, pp. 1063–1076.
Hatem, M. (1974), *Information and the Arab Cause*, Longman, London.
Heikal, M. (1996), *Secret Channels*, Harper Collins, London.
Herman, E. and Chomsky, N. (1994), *Manufacturing Consent*, Vintage, London.
Hertz, R. (1997), *Reflexivity & Voice*, Sage, London.
Hippler, J. (2000), 'Foreign policy, the media and the Western perception of the Middle East', in K. Hafez (2000), *Islam and the West in the Mass Media*, Hampton Press, Cresskill, New Jersey, pp. 67–87.
Hobbs, D. and May, T. (1993), *Interpreting the Field Accounts of Ethnography*, Clarendon Press, Oxford.
Hodge, R. and Kress, G. (1993), *Language as Ideology*, Routledge, London.
Hourani, A. (1991), *A History of the Arab Peoples*, Faber & Faber, London.
Hourani, A., Khoury, P. and Wilson, M.C. (1993), *The Modern Middle East: A Reader*, I.B.Tauris, London.
Hudson, M. and Stanier, J. (1999), *War and the Media*, Sutton, Stroud, Gloucestershire.
IIM [Information International Monthly] (2002), 'Grey areas in the Audio-Visual Law', *Information International Monthly*, Issue 5 (November). URL: http://information-international.com/iimonthly/issue5/editorial.html (accessed 6 January 2005).

Iskandar, A. and El-Nawawy, M. (2004), 'Al Jazeera and war coverage in Iraq' in S. Allan and B. Zelizer (2004), *Reporting War Journalism in Wartime*, Routledge, London, pp. 315–332.

Iskandar, M. (2006), *Rafiq Hariri and the Fate of Lebanon*, Saqi, London.

Jaber, H. (1997), *Hezbollah: Born with a Vengeance*, Columbia University Press, New York.

Jaber, M. (1999), *Al Sharit Alubnani Almuhtal* ['The Lebanese occupied zone'], Palestinian Studies Association, Beirut [in Arabic].

Jackall, R. (1995), *Propaganda*, Macmillan, Basingstoke, Hants.

Jensen, B.K. (2002), *A Handbook of Media and Communication Research*, Routledge, London.

Jones, C. (2002), 'A reach greater than the grasp: Israeli intelligence and the conflict in south Lebanon 1990–2000', *Intelligence and National Security*, Vol. 16, No. 3, pp. 1–26.

Jorisch, A. (2004), *Beacon of Hatred: Inside Hizballah's Al Manar Television*, Washington Institute of Near East Policy, Washington DC.

Jowett, G. and O'Donnell, V. (1999), *Propaganda and Persuasion*, Sage, London.

Junker, B. (1960), *Field Work*, University of Chicago Press, Chicago.

Kamalipour, Y. and Mowlana, H. (1994), *Mass Media in the Middle East: A Comprehensive Handbook*, Greenwood Press, Westport, Connecticut.

Kean, F. (2005), *All of Those People*, Harper Perennial, London.

Keith, M. (1992), 'Angry writing: (re)presenting the unethical world of the ethnographer', *Society and Space*, Vol. 10, No. 5, pp. 551–569.

Kennedy, V. (2000), *Edward Said: A Critical Introduction*, Polity Press, Cambridge.

Khalidi, W. and Khaduri, J. (1974), *Palestine and the Arab–Israeli Conflict*, Institute for Palestine Studies, Beirut.

Khoury, N. (1995), *Haret Al Nasara* ['The Christian neighbourhood'], Riyad Al Ryias, Beirut.

Kitch, C. (2003), 'Mourning in America: rituals, redemption, and recovery in news narrative after September 11', *Journalism Studies*, Vol. 4, No. 2, pp. 213–244.

Knightley, P. (2000), *The First Casualty*, Prion, London.

Kontler, L. (1999), 'Superstition, enthusiasm and propagandism: Burke and Gentz on the nature of the French Revolution', in B. Taithe and T. Thornton (eds), *Propaganda: Political Rhetoric and Identity, 1300–2000*, Sutton, Stroud, pp. 97–113.

Kraidy, M. (2000), 'Transnational television and asymmetrical interdependence in the Arab world: the growing influence of the Lebanese satellite broadcasters', *TBS Electronic Journal*, No. 5 (Fall/Winter).

URL: www.tbsjournal.com/Archives/Fall00 Kraidy htm (accessed: 12 January 2005).
Kramer, M. (1989), *Hezbollah's Vision of the West*, Policy Paper No. 16, Washington Institute for Near East Policy, Washington DC.
Krayem, N. (1998), 'Dower wasae'l Al I'elam fi al tasadi llidwan al sahyouni' ['The role of media in resisting the Zionist aggression'], in M. Mohsen (ed.), *Al Hareb Al I'elamieh: Al-I'lam al-Moukawem fi Lubnan* ['Media war: the case of the resistance media in Lebanon'], El-Nada, Beirut, pp. 41–52 [in Arabic].
Lal, J. (1996), 'Situating locations: the politics of self, identity, and other in living and writing the text', in D.L. Wolf, *Feminist Dilemmas in Fieldwork*, Westview Press, Boulder, Colorado.
Lamish, D. and Barzel, I. (2000), 'Four mothers: the womb in the public sphere', *European Journal of Communication* [Sage, London], Vol. 15, No. 2, pp. 147–169.
Lang, K. and Lang, G.E. (1953), 'The unique perspective of television and its effects: a pilot study', *American Sociological Review*, Vol. 18, pp. 168–13.
Lang, K. and Lang, G.E. (1993), 'Theory development: studying events in their natural settings', in K. Jensen and N. Junkowski (1993), *A Handbook of Qualitative Methodologies*, Routledge, London.
Lasswell, H.D., Casey, R.D. and Smith, L.B. (1969), *Propaganda and Promotional Activities*, University of Chicago Press, Chicago.
Lasswell, H., Lerner, D. and Speier, H. (1980), *Propaganda and Communication in World History, Vol. 2: Emergence of Public Opinion in the West*, East-West Center Books, University Press of Hawaii, Honolulu.
Lichtenberg, J. (2000), 'In defence of objectivity revisited', in J. Curran and M. Gurevitch (2000), *Mass Media and Society*, Arnold, London, pp. 238–254.
Makovsky, D. (1996), *Making Peace With the PLO*, Westview Press, Oxford.
Marshall, G. (1970), 'In a world of women: field work in a Yoruba community', in P. Golde (ed.), *Women in the Field: Anthropological Experiences*, Aldine, Chicago (1970), pp. 165–191.
Mead, M. (1977), *Letters from the Field, 1925–1975*, Harper & Row, New York.
Mellor, N. (2005), *The Making of Arab News*, Rowman & Littlefield, London.
Menargues, A. (2006), *Asrar Al Harb Al Lubnaniah* ['Lebanon's war secrets'], Librairie International, Beirut [in Arabic, translated from French].
Mercer, D., Mungham, G. and Williams, K. (1987), *The Fog of War: The Media on the Battlefield*, Heinemann, London.

Merton, R. (1995), 'Mass persuasion: a technical problem and a moral dilemma', in R. Jackall (1995), *Propaganda*, Macmillan, Basingstoke, pp. 260–274.

Miles, H. (2005), *Al Jazeera: How Arab TV News Challenged the World*, Abacus, London.

Miller, D. (1994), *Don't Mention the War*, Pluto Press, London.

Miller, D. (2003), *Tell Me Lies: Propaganda and Media Distortion in the Attack on Iraq*, Pluto Press, London.

Mohsen, M. (1998), 'Al Mouqawama Wallharb Al Nafsieyah' ['The Islamic resistance and psychological warfare'], in M. Mohsen (ed.), *Al Hareb Al I'elamieh: Al-I'lam al-Moukawem fi Lubnan* ['Media war: the case of the resistance media in Lebanon'], El-Nada, Beirut, pp. 55–70 [in Arabic].

Mohsen, M. and Mouzanar, A. (2001), *Sourat Al Muqawamah fi Al I'lam* ['The resistance image in the media'], Strategic Studies Centre, Beirut [in Arabic].

Murden, S. (2000), 'Understanding Israel's conflict in Lebanon: the search for an alternative approach to security during the peace process', *British Journal of Middle East Studies*, Vol. 27, No. 1, pp. 25–47.

Murphy, D. (1976), *The Silent Watchdog: The Press in Local Politics*, Constable, London.

Nast, H. (1998), 'The body as a place', in H. Nast and S. Pile (1998), *Places through the Body*, Routledge, London, pp. 93–116.

Oakley, A. (1981), 'Interviewing women: a contradiction in terms', in H. Roberts (ed.), *Doing Feminist Research*, Routledge, London.

O'Shaughnessy, N.J. (2004), *Politics and Propaganda: Weapons of Mass Seduction*, Manchester University Press, Manchester.

O'Shea, B. (2004), 'Lebanon's 'Blue Line': a new international border or just another cease-fire zone?', *Studies in Conflict and Terrorism*, Vol. 27, pp. 19–30.

Ovendale, R. (1984), *The Origins of the Arab–Israeli Wars*, Longman, London.

Owen, R. (2004), *State Power and Politics in the Making of the Modern Middle East*, Routledge, London.

Palmer Harik, J. (2004), *Hezbollah: The Changing Face of Terrorism*, I.B.Tauris, London.

Panourgia, N. (1995), *Fragments of Death, Fables of Identity: An Athenian Anthropography*, University of Wisconsin Press, Madison.

Pantti, M. and Wieten, J. (2005), 'Mourning becomes the nation: television coverage of the murder of Pim Fortuyn', *Journalism Studies* [Routledge, London], Vol. 6, No. 3, pp. 301–313.

Pantti, M. (2005), 'Masculine tears, feminine tears – and crocodile tears: mourning Olof Palme and Anna Lindh in Finnish newspapers', *Journalism* [Sage, London], Vol. 6, No. 3, pp. 357–377.

Pappé, I. (2008), *The Ethnic Cleansing of Palestine*, Oneworld, Oxford.

Paterson, C. and Sreberny, A. (2004), *International News in the 21st Century*, John Libbey Press, Eastleigh, Hants./University of Luton Press, Luton.

Pavlik, J. (2001), *Journalism and New Media*, Columbia University Press, New York.

Pedelty, M. (1995), *War Stories*, Routledge, New York.

Philo, G. and Berry, M. (2004), *Bad News from Israel*, Pluto, London.

Picard, E. (2002), *Lebanon: A Shattered Country*, Holmes & Meier, New York.

Poole, E. (2002), *Reporting Islam: Media Representations of British Muslims*, I.B.Tauris, London.

Pratkanis, A. and Aronson, E. (1991), *The Age of Propaganda: The Everyday Use and Abuse of Persuasion*, W.H. Freeman & Co., New York.

Qassem, N. (2005), *Hizbullah: The Story from Within*, Saqi, London.

Rabinovich, I. (1985), *The War for Lebanon, 1970–1985*, Cornell University Press, London.

Rampton, S. and Stauber, J. (2003), *Weapons of Mass Deception: The Uses of Propaganda in Bush's War on Iraq*, Robinson, London.

Randal, J. (1993), *Going all the Way: Christian Warlords, Israeli Adventures and the War in Lebanon*, Viking Press, New York.

Ranstorp, M. (1997), *Hizb'ullah in Lebanon: The Politics of the Western Hostage Crisis*, Palgrave, Basingstoke, Hants.

Robins, K., Webster, F. and Pickering, M. (1987), 'Propaganda, information and social control', in J. Hawthorn (ed.) *Propaganda, Persuasion and Polemic*, Arnold, London.

Rodinson, M. (1985), *Israel and the Arabs*, Penguin Books, Harmondsworth, Middlesex.

Rosaldo, R. (1993), *Culture and Truth: The Remaking of Social Analysis*, Routledge, London.

Rugh, W. (2004), *Arab Mass Media*, Praeger, London.

Rutherford, P. (2004), *Weapons of Mass Persuasion: Marketing the War against Iraq*, University of Toronto Press, Toronto.

Ruthven, M. (2000), *Islam: A Very Short Introduction*, Oxford University Press, Oxford.

Saad-Ghorayeb, A. (2002), *Hizbu'llah: Politics and Religion*, Pluto Press, London.

Said, E. (1992), *The Question of Palestine*, Vintage, London.

Said, E. (1995), *Orientalism*, Penguin Books, London.

Said, E. (2000), *The End of the Peace Process*, Granta, London.
Said, E. and Hitchens, C. (2001) *Blaming the Victims*, Verso, New York.
Sakr, N. (2001), *Satellite Realms: Transnational Television, Globalization and the Middle East*, I.B.Tauris, London.
Salman, T. (2001), 'Hezbollah: al tarikh wal ramez' ['Hezbollah: the history and the symbol'], in M. Mohsen and A. Mouzanar, *Sourat Al Muqawamah fi Al Aalam* ['The resistance image in the media'], Strategic Studies Centre, Beirut, pp. 21–39 [in Arabic].
Samuel, E.B. (1998), 'Israel's demoralisation', *Middle East Quarterly*, Vol. V, No. 3 (September), Middle East Forum. URL: www.meforum.org/article/402 (accessed 7 July 2006).
Sanjek, R. (1990), *Fieldnotes*, Cornell University Press, London.
Schlecker, M. and Hirsch, E. (2001), 'Incomplete knowledge: ethnography and the crisis of context in studies of media, science and technology', *History of the Human Sciences Journal* [Sage, London], Vol. 14, No. 1, pp. 69–87.
Schlesinger, P. (1978), *Putting 'Reality' Together: BBC News*, Constable, London.
Schudson, M. (1989), 'The sociology of news production', *Media Culture and Society*, Vol. 11, pp. 263–282, reprinted in D. Berkowitz (1997), *Social Meanings of News*, Sage, London, pp. 7–22.
Schudson, M. (1995), *The Power of News*, Harvard University Press, Cambridge, Massachusetts.
Schudson, M. (2003), *The Sociology of News*, Norton, New York.
Seale, C. (1999), *Researching Society and Culture*, Sage Publications, London.
Seale, P. (1989), *Assad: The Struggle for the Middle East*, Saqi, London.
Sharara, W. (1998), *Dawlat Hezbollah* ['The state of Hezbollah'], Dar Annahar, Beirut [in Arabic].
Shlaim, A. (2001), *The Iron Wall: Israel and the Arab World*, Penguin Books, London.
Simpson, J. (1999), *Strange Places, Questionable People*, Pan Books, London.
Simpson, J. (2003), *The Wars Against Saddam: Taking the Hard Road to Baghdad*, Macmillan, London.
Smith, R. (2005), 'Discipline and profit: an ethnography of the rebirth of Cardiff Bay', MSc thesis, University of Cardiff.
Snow, N. (2003), *Information War: American Propaganda, Free Speech and Opinion Control since 9–11*, Seven Stories Press, New York.
Soloski, J. (1989/1997), 'News reporting and professionalism: some constraints on the reporting of the news', *Media, Culture and Society*, Vol. 11, pp. 207–228; reprinted in D. Berkowitz (1997), *Social Meanings of News*, Sage, London, pp. 138–154.

Swedenburg, T. (1993), 'The role of the Palestinian peasantry in the great revolt', in A. Hourani, P. Khoury and M. Wilson (1993), *The Modern Middle East*, I.B.Tauris, London, pp. 468–502.

Taha, R. (1973), *Al I'lam wal Mar'aka* ['The media and the battle'], Dar Annahar, Beirut [in Arabic].

Taithe, B. and Thornton, T. (1999), *Propaganda: Political Rhetoric and Identity, 1300–2000*, Sutton, Stroud, Gloucestershire.

Tanter, R. (1990), *Who's at the Helm? The Lessons of Lebanon*, Westview Press, Oxford.

Tatham, S. (2006), *Losing Arab Hearts and Minds: The Coalition, Al-Jazeera and Muslim Public Opinion*, Hurst & Co., London.

Taylor, P.M. (1990), *Munitions of the Mind*, Patrick Stephens, Wellingborough, Northants.

Taylor, P.M. (1995/2003), *Munitions of the Mind*, Manchester University Press, Manchester.

Thomas, S. (1996), *The Diplomacy of Liberation*, International Library of African Studies, Tauris Academic Studies, London.

Thomson, O. (1999), *Easily Led*, Sutton, Stroud, Gloucestershire.

Tuchman, G. (1972), 'Objectivity as strategic ritual: an examination of newsmen's notions of objectivity', *American Journal of Sociology*, Vol. 77, No. 4 (January), pp. 660–679; reprinted in H. Tumber (1999), *News: A Reader*, Oxford University Press, New York, pp. 297–307.

Tuchman, G. (1973), 'Making news by doing work: routinizing the unexpected', *American Journal of Sociology*, Vol. 79, No. 1, pp. 110–131.

Tuchman, G. (1978), *Making News: A Study in the Social Construction of Reality*, Free Press, New York.

Tueini, G. (1979), *Peace-Keeping Lebanon: The Facts, the Documents*, William Belcher Group, New York.

Tugwell, M. (1987), 'Terrorism and propaganda: problem and response', in P. Wilkinson and A. Stewart, *Contemporary Research on Terrorism*, Aberdeen University Press, Aberdeen.

Tumber, H. (1999), *News: A Reader*, Oxford University Press, New York.

Viswanathan, G. (2004), *Power, Politics and Culture: Interviews with Edward W. Said*, Bloomsbury, London.

Walsh, J. (1996), 'Qana: anatomy of a tragedy', *Time International* (20 May 1996), Vol. 147, No. 21. URL: www.bintjbeil.com/E/occupation/qana_time.html (accessed: 4 July 2006).

Warner, M. (1971), 'Organisational context and control of policy in the television newsroom: a participant observation study', *British Journal of Sociology*, Vol. 22, pp. 283–294.

Werner, O. and Schoepfle, G.M. (1987), *Systematic Fieldwork: Ethnographic Analysis and Data Management*, Vol. 2, Sage, London.
White, A.B. (1939), *The New Propaganda*, Victor Gollancz, London.
White, D.M. (1950), 'The gatekeeper: a case study in the selection of news', *Journalism Quarterly*, Vol. 27, pp. 383–390.
Williams, K. (2003), *Understanding Media Theory*, Arnold, London.
Wolcott, H.F. (1995), 'Making a study "more ethnographic"' in J. Van Maanen (ed.), *Representation in Ethnography*, Sage, London.
Wolf, M. (1990), 'China notes: engendering anthropology', in R. Sanjek (ed.), *Fieldnotes*, Cornell University Press, London.
Wolfsfeld, G. (1997), *Media and Political Conflict: News from the Middle East*, Cambridge University Press, Cambridge.
Wright, J. (1991), *Terrorist Propaganda: The Red Army Faction and the Provisional IRA, 1968–86*, Macmillan, London.
Yang, M.C. (1972), 'How a Chinese village was written', in S. Kimball and J. Watson (eds), *Crossing Cultural Boundaries: The Anthropological Experience*, Chandler, San Francisco, pp. 63–73.
Zayani, M. (2005), *The Al Jazeera Phenomenon: Critical Perspectives on New Arab Media*, Pluto, London.
Zelizer, B. (2004), *Taking Journalism Seriously: News and the Academy*, Sage, Thousand Oaks, California.

## Newspaper archives

Abdallah, R. (2007), 'Zahera Harb, Qana's reporter in Lebanon...and her footprints in London', *Al Mustaqbal*, 29 March 2007, p. 9.
Abu-Fadil, M. (2000), 'Hezbollah TV claims credit for ousting Israelis', *IPI Global Journalist*, Fourth Quarter 2000, p. 12.
Ahmad, E. (1998), 'Encounter with a fighter', *Al Ahram* Weekly (30 July–5 August 1998). URL: http://weekly.ahram.org.eg/1998/388/re4.htm (accessed: 6 April 2004).
*Al Ahed* (1998), 'Footage from Beir Kalab exposes the enemy's lies' [Translate], *Al Ahed*, 6 March 1998, n.p.
Al Amin, I. (2000), 'Active fighter and a camera that gets anywhere', *Assafir*, 4 February 2000, n.p.
*Al Anbaa* (2000), 'The Israeli soldiers are scared and wanting to withdraw from Lebanon', *Al Anbaa*, 10 February 2000, n.p.
Al Bourji, N. (1998), 'The tanks can not walk over the impossible...', *Al Kefah Al Arabi*, 18 March 1998, n.p.
*Al Hayat* (1999), 'Like a mosquito inside the brain: examples from the Israeli press on the effect of resistance footage on soldiers' morale', *Al Hayat*, 20 May 1999, n.p.

## Bibliography 253

Al Jammal, F. (1996), 'Zahera Harb, congratulations', *Al Sharek*, 27 April 1996, p. 10.

Al Liwaa (1998a), 'Hezbollah media trap in Beir Kalab', *Al Liwaa*, 4 March 1998, n.p.

Al Liwaa (1998b), 'Nasrallah: military filming affects our enemy's morale badly', *Al Liwaa*, 13 July 1998.

Arahman, Abed (2001), 'The resistance media in south Lebanon', *Al Liwaa*, 12 July 2001, n.p.

*Assafir* (JPEG) editions from 1 April 1996 to 30 April 1996, CD-ROM, Arab Documentation Centre, Beirut [copy held by author].

*Assafir* (1996), 'Israeli press comments on filming the resistance operations', *Assafir*, 21 September 1996.

*Assafir* (2006), 'Nasrallah's press conference', *Assafir*, 13 July 2006, n.p.

Atwi, H. (1999), 'Around the clock…' ['Ala Madar Al Saah …'], *Annahar*, 22 July 1999, p. 16.

Atwi, M. (2000), 'Media and the resistance', *Al Sharek*, 27 May 2000, n.p.

Bakhor, G. (2001), 'The camera is stronger than a weapon', *Yedioth Ahronoth*, 17 July 2001, translated [from Hebrew] in *Al Mustaqbal*, 19 July 2001, n.p [in Arabic].

BBC (2000a), 'In focus: Shebaa farms', *BBC News*, 25 May 2000, URL: http://news.bbc.co.uk/1/hi/world/middle_east/763504.stm (accessed on 2 February 2007).

BBC (2000b), 'Hezbollah hails a "great breakthrough"', *BBC News Online*, 30 January 2000. URL: http://news.bbc.co.uk/1/hi/world/monitoring/media_reports/624830.stm (accessed: 7 April 2004).

Ben-Simon, D. (2000), 'Road to Hell', *Ha'aretz*, 17 November 2000. n.p.

Ben Yishai, R. (1998), 'Something is beginning to move in Lebanon', *Yedioth Ahronoth*, 13 March 1998, pp. 10–11.

Blanford, N. (2000), 'Israeli media begin to ask: "Where are the terrorists?"', *Daily Star*, 14 June 2000, n.p.

Blanford, N. (2006), 'Israel strikes may boost Hizbullah base', *Christian Science Monitor*, 28 July 2006, n.p.

*Bmsehneih* (1996), 'A film directed by Hassan Nasrallah', *Bmsehneih*, 20 September 1996. Tel Aviv.

Bziah, S. (1996), 'Even you, God!!', *Annahar Cultural Supplement*, 26 April 1996, p. 6.

Chassay, C. (2006), 'Call for Israel to leave Shebaa farms', *The Guardian*, 10 October 2006. URL: www.guardian.co.uk/israel/Story/0,,1892111,00.html (accessed 2 February 2007).

CNN (1999), 'Lebanon occupation takes centre stage in Israel', *CNN Online*, 2 March 1999. URL: www.cnn.com/WORLD/meast/9903/02/israel.lebanon/ (accessed 21 February 2006).

Fadel Allah, H. (1993), 'The media war in south Lebanon', *Al Majalah*, 11 September 1999, pp. 32–33.

Fisk, R. (2006), 'From my home, I saw what the "war on terror" meant', *The Independent*, 14 July 2006, n.p.

Frucht, L.E. (2000), 'The movement that shaped the Lebanon pullout', *Jerusalem Post*, 8 June 2000, n.p.

Ha'aretz (1997), 'The Lebanese trap', *Ha'aretz*, 7 September 1997, n.p.

Ha'aretz (2000), 'Four Mothers organization dismantled', *Ha'aretz*, 3 June 2000, n.p.

Hamad, S. (2000), 'A storm hit the soldiers' families when informed about their children's death by TV footage', *Al Hayat*, 16 April 2000, n.p.

Jaroudy, H. (1998), 'Zahera, Ala Madar Al Saah' ['Zahera, around the clock'], *Al Liwaa*, 10 November 1998, p. 19.

'K., J.' (1996), 'Kul Al Shashat Janoubiah' ['All channels are ... southerners'], *Dalil Annahar*, 26 April 1996, p. 2 [copy held by author].

Kasir, S. (1996), 'Service public et professionnalisme' ['Public service and professionalism'], *L'Orient Express*, May 1996, p. 32.

Khalifeh, M. and Basil, Z. (1996), 'Reporting ... the edge of death', *Nahar Al Shabab*, 23 April 1996, pp. 16–17.

Khodor, Z. (1999), 'Lebanon's night of terror', *Al Ahram* Weekly (1–7 July 1999), n.p. URL: http://weekly.ahram.org.eg/1999/436/re6.htm (accessed 6 April 2004).

Kifner, J. (2000), 'In the long fight with Israel, Hezbollah tactics evolved', *New York Times*, 19 July 2000. URL: www.library.cornell.edu/colldev/mideast/hizbz.htm (accessed 12 November 2004).

Krayem, N. (2004), 'Al Manar: Qusat al Tassis ...' ['Al Manar: the story of its establishment ...'], *Assafir*, 28 December 2004, p. 5.

Mandour, S. (2001), 'Al Manar fights Hebrew ... in Hebrew', *Assafir*, 30 July 2001, n.p.

Mannion, D. (2006), 'Fighting to tell the truth', *Broadcast* [internet magazine], 4 August 2006, n.p.

Marmal, I. (1998), 'Kamera Al Mouqawama ...' ['The resistance camera: the weapon that doesn't miss its target'] *Assafir*, 10 March 1998, n.p.

Orit, S. (1999), 'A deceiving victory in Lebanon', *Ha'aretz*, 8 October 1999, n.p.

Philips, A. (2000), 'Hizbollah is winning the TV war', *Daily Telegraph*, 12 April 2000.

Segal, N. (2000), 'Hezbollah kills 3 Israeli soldiers, veteran SLA leader in Lebanon', *Jewish Telegraphic Agency*, 4 February 2000, n.p.
Shames, D. (2004), 'Al Manar: from the southern suburb to the southern suburb, a channel that disturbs the Israelis and the Americans', *Assafir*, 24 December 2004, p. 4.
Smaha, J. (1999), 'Media war emphasises the defeat in the psychological warfare with Israel', *Al Hayat*, 20 May 1999, n.p.
Stiener, M. (2000), 'The war enters Israeli homes through TV screens', *AFP* in *Al Sharek*, 8 February 2000, n.p.
Yedioth Ahronoth (1997), 'Hezbollah's media is the new military target', *Yedioth Ahronoth*, 25 April 1997. Tel Aviv.
Yedioth Ahronoth (1998), 'We are less qualified than Hezbollah in propaganda', *Yedioth Ahronoth*, 5 January 1998. Tel Aviv.
Zayat, M. (2000), 'Israel defeat in Lebanon offers juicy material for Israeli media', *Addiyar*, 27 February 2000, n.p.

## Tele Liban news archives

Al Manar Compendium, 1996–2000.
Al Manar TV, *Clips of the resistance*, Beirut [copy of video-cassette held by author].

## Prime-time news programmes (time: 19.30) (in date order)

11 April 1996 Presenter from Beirut Studios: Nada Saliba
11 April 1996 Presenter from Beirut Studios: Tony Salameh
13 April 1996 Presenter from Beirut Studios: Souad Al Ashi
Presenter–producer from Sidon: Zahera Harb
14 April 1996 Presenter from Beirut Studios: Naeemat Aazouri
Presenter–producer from Sidon: Zahera Harb
14 April 1996 Prime Minister Rafiq Hariri, Interview with CNN correspondent Brent Sadler (re-broadcast)
15 April 1996 Presenter from Beirut Studios: Souad Al Ashi
Presenter–producer from Sidon: Zahera Harb
16 April 1996 Presenter from Beirut Studios: Souad Al Ashi
Presenter–producer from Sidon: Zaven Kouyoumdjian
17 April 1996 Presenter from Beirut Studios: Neemat Aazouri
Presenter–producer from Sidon: Zaven Kouyoumdjian
18 April 1996 Presenter from Beirut Studios: Wasef Awada
Presenter–producer from Sidon: Zaven Kouyoumdjian
19 April 1996 Presenter from Beirut Studios: Souad Al Ashi
Presenter–producer from Sidon: Dalal Kandeel
20 April 1996 Presenter from Beirut Studios: Naamet Aazouri

Presenter–producer from Sidon: Dalal Kandeel
21 April 1996 Presenter from Beirut Studios: Tony Salameh
Presenter–producer from Sidon: Rajaa Kamouneh
22 April 1996 Presenter from Beirut Studios: Naamat Aazouri
Presenter–producer from Sidon: Rajaa Kamouneh
23 April 1996 Presenter from Beirut Studios: Nada Saliba
Presenter–producer from Sidon: Zahera Harb
24 April 1996 Presenter from Beirut Studios: Tony Salameh
Presenter–producer from Sidon: Zahera Harb
25 April 1996 Presenter from Beirut Studios: Souad Al Ashi
Presenter–producer from Sidon: Zahera Harb
26 April 1996 Presenter from Beirut Studios: Wasef Awada
Presenter–producer from Sidon: Dalal Kandeel
27 April 1996 Presenter from Beirut Studios: Souad Al Ashi
Presenter–producer from Sidon: Zahera Harb
Al Manar news archives (in date order)
26 December 1996 Re-broadcast of *Hezbollah Media* from Israeli Channel 2 (Tel Aviv), broadcast 25 December 1996 at 19.45
20 October 1997 News Bulletin: 'Killing collaborator Salim Risha'
Presenters: Ali al Mismar and Kawthar Al Mousawi
5 September 1997 Ansariyeh Operation: Uncut footage of Israeli soldiers remains and weaponry

## Prime-time news programme (time: 17.45)

27 February 1998 'Beir Kalab operation'
Presenter: Abdullah Reslan
27 June 1998 'On exchanging detainees and martyrs'
Presenters: Kawthar Al Mousawi and Ali Al Mismar
28 February 1999 'On the killing of Israeli Brigadier-General Eretz Gerstein'
Presenter: Abed Al Hussein Al Dhaini

## Al Manar special report

29 February 1999 Re-broadcast of special report on *Al Manar's coverage of the Gerstein killing* from Israeli Channel 2 (Tel Aviv) broadcast earlier that day

## Afternoon news programme (time: 14.45)

27 April 1999 'On capturing the Sujud Position'
Presenter: Abdullah Areslan

## Prime-time news programme (time: 17.45)
27 April 1999 'On capturing the Sujud Position'
Presenter: Ghada Assaf Nemer
28 April 1999 'On capturing the Sujud Position'
Presenter: Abdullah Areslan
15 May 1999 'On the Beit Yahoun Operation'
Presenters: Kawthar Al Mousawi Noun, Abed Al Hussein Al Dhaini

## Al Manar special report
17 May 1999 Live coverage of the ceremony of capturing the troop carrier M113 in Haret Hreik, Beirut Southern Suburb
Reporting live: Abbas Naser

## Prime-time news programme (time: 17.45)
25 June 1999 On targeting the power stations
Presenter: Abed Al Hussein Al Dhaini

## Al Manar special report
26 June 1999 Hezbollah's Secretary General Hassan Nasrallah's speech
Introduced by Ali Al Mismar

## Prime-time news programme (time: 17.45)
30 January 2000 On killing Akel Hashem, South Lebanon Army (SLA) second-in-command, Commander of the SLA's Western Brigade
Presenter: Ali Al Mismar

## Al Manar special report
1 February 2000 Exclusive interview with Jawad and Hadi, perpetrators of the Akel Hashem assassination

## Prime-time news programme (time: 17.45)
24 May 2000 On liberation coverage
Presenter: Abdullah Areslan
Reporter: Abbas Naser

## Interviews and correspondence with author (with place of interview)
Abou Jahjah, N., Reuters reporter, Tele Liban OB Transmission, Sidon, five-days-per-week programme, 19 April 1996.

Al Abed, A., Head of News, Tele Liban; correspondence from Bahrain, 24 March 2004.

Al Housieni, M., Al Manar producer/journalist; Al Manar headquarters, Haret Hreik, Beirut Southern Suburb, 18 December 2003, not recorded (notes taken).

Al Jammal, M., Head of Hezbollah's central press office; his office, Beirut Southern Suburb, 15 April 2000.

Amhaz, H., Al Manar reporter; Al Manar headquarters, Haret Hreik, Beirut Southern Suburb, 9 January 2004.

Anonymous member of Hezbollah Military Media Unit, Hezbollah media relations office, Haret Hreik, Beirut, 19 December 2003.

Awada, W., Tele Liban news editor; his office, TL headquarters, Telet Al Khayat, Beirut, 19 April 2004.

Boudier, M., Al Manar's Hebrew translator, newsroom journalist and member of the Israeli TV monitoring unit at Al Manar; Al Manar headquarters, Haret Hreik, Beirut Southern Suburb, 10 January 2004.

Dukmak, H., Hezbollah media co-ordinator; his office, Beirut Southern Suburb, 12 January 2004.

Ez-Addine, H., Head of Hezbollah media relations; his office, Beirut Southern Suburb, 12 January 2004.

El Musawi, I., Al Manar's English language news editor; Al Manar headquarters, Haret Hreik, Beirut Southern Suburb, 13 January 2004.

Haidar, M., Al Manar Chairman, Al Manar headquarters, Haret Hreik, Beirut Southern Suburb, 9 January 2004.

Haj Maitham, Head of Hezbollah Military Media Unit, Hezbollah media relations office, Beirut Southern Suburb, 8 January 2004.

Haj Naser, Hezbollah military cameraman; Hezbollah media relations office, Beirut Southern Suburb, not recorded at his request, 8 January 2004.

Hindawi, A., Head of APTV regional operations; his office, Beirut, 4 January 2004.

Hmayed, H., head of clips and propaganda unit for Al Manar; Al Manar headquarters, Haret Hreik, Beirut Southern Suburb, 9 January 2004.

Jammal, M., Head of Hezbollah's central press office; his office, Beirut Southern Suburb, 15 April 2000.

Kamouneh, R., TL Presenter–Producer; her office, Lebanese Foreign Ministry, 17 April 2004.

Kandeel, D., TL Presenter–Producer, her house; Haret Hreik, Beirut Southern Suburb, 6 January 2004.

Kandeel, N., Deputy Head of National Media Council; Lebanese Parliament, Beirut, 15 April 2004.

Kouyoumdjian, Z., TL Presenter–Producer, Future TV, Beirut, 20 April 2004.
Krayem, N. Head of Al Manar TV and Nour Radio Station (1996–9), Al Manar headquarters, Beirut Southern Suburb, 12 April 2000.
Majzoub, N., TL reporter, via e-mail, 5 April 2004.
Mohsen, M., Lecturer in political communication; Lebanese University, Al Saha Café, Airport Road, Beirut, 8 January 2004.
Moukaled, D., Future TV reporter; Future TV offices, Raoushe, Beirut, 16 April 2004.
Mousa, H., Israeli media expert; *Assafir* newspaper offices, Hamra, Beirut, 17 April 2004.
Naim, F., TL Chairman; via phone from Paris, 6 February 2004.
Rahal, H., Head of News, Al Manar (1996–9); *Al Ahed* magazine offices, Beirut Southern Suburb, 10 January 2004.
Raya, M., Hezbollah webmaster; Hezbollah media officials, 5 January 2004.
Rochlin, Y., e-mail correspondence with Hezbollah media officials, 25 February 1998. from within Israel.
Saad, H., TL News Director; her house, Aramoun, south of Beirut, 7 January 2004.
Tabbara, R., former Lebanese ambassador to Washington; his office, Beirut, 25 March 1999.

# INDEX

9/11 see 2001: 11 September
1948–9: *Nakbeh* [war] 68, 84
1956: Suez crisis 69, 70
1967: June [Six-day] War 69, 70–2, 180
1973: October [Ramadan or Yom Kippur] War 69, 72–3
1979: invasion of south Lebanon 1, 74, 99
1982: invasion of Lebanon 77–80, 99, 114, 148, 151
1993: July ('Seven days' Operation) 81
1996: April (Israeli invasion of south Lebanon) 114–15
  11 April (Day 1) 115
  12 April (Day 2) 115–17
  13 April (Day 3) 117–24
  14 April (Day 4) 124–9
  15 April (Day 5) 129–34
  16 April (Day 6) 135–6
  17 April (Day 7) 136–9
  18 April (Day 8) 1, 140–51
  19 April (Day 9) 151–5
  20 April (Day 10) 155–7
  21 April (Day 11) 157–9
  22 April (Day 12) 159–62
  23 April (Day 13) 162–3
  24 April (Day 14) 163–5
  25 April (Day 15) 165–6
  26 April (Day 16) 166
  April Understanding [Israel admits Lebanese right of self-defence] 166–7, 174, 184, 213
1997: 20 October (killing of Salim Risha) 189, 190–1
1998:
  27 February (Beir Kalab operation) 189, 191–3
  June (exchanging detainees and martyrs) 189, 193–8
1999:
  28 February (killing of Eretz Gerstein) 189, 198–202
  27 April (capture of Sujud position) 189, 202–6
  15 May (Beit Yahoun operation) 189, 206–10
  June (attacks on power stations) 189, 211–13

2000:
  January (SLA militias surrender) 189, 219
  30 January (killing of Akel Hashem) 189, 214–16
  23/24 May (liberation of south Lebanon) 189, 217–22
2001: 11 September (attacks on World Trade Center) 47, 124
2006: July (Lebanon war) 4, 90, 144, 170, 222, 230

ABC (American Broadcasting Company) 95, 139
Abdallah, Roula [journalist] 2
Abdullah, Prince 66
Abou Jahjah, Najla [journalist] 122–3
Abraham, Efrat 120
Abu Abbas 138
Abu Khalil, Joseph 86–7
Abu Nidal 77–8
Abu Yasser 192–3
Addine *see* Ez-Addine; Izeddine
Adie, Kate [journalist] 46, 125, 144
Adloun beaches 193
Advision 95, 97
AFP (Agence France Presse) 117, 150, 157, 199
the Ahmad Said war 180
Ahmed, Iqbal [journalist] 197
Al Abed, Aref [head of news] 103–4, 115, 117
  and news management 146, 147
Al Abed, Nour [baby] 142
Al Ahdab, Brigadier Aziz 96
Al Aris, Safi [director] 117
Al Ashi, Souad [presenter] 118, 120, 153, 154
Al Bourji, N. 195

Al Dhaini, Hussein [journalist] 199, 207, 211
Al Hoss, Salim [prime minister] 100, 213
Al Huseini (Housieni), M. 189
Al Jammal, Mouafaq [Hezbollah press officer] 178–9, 182
Al Lakees, Israa 161–2
Allan, S. and Zelizer, B. 47
Al Manar *see* Manar
Alman [village] 159
Al Mashnouk, Nouhad [political adviser] 147
Al Mismar, Ali [journalist] 190, 215
Almouhsen, Hadi and Abed 164
Al Mousawi, Kawthar [journalist] 190, 195, 200–1, 207
Al Murr, Michel [deputy PM] 127
Al Nabulsi, Bahaa al Deen 203
Al Saidi, Naser [finance minister] 212
Amal [movement] 195
ambulance attacked 118–19, 122–3, 140
Amhaz, Hakam [journalist] 191, 200, 212–13, 225
Amitai, Eli [Israeli officer] 200
Amsheet [studios] 96
anonymous Hezbollah expert 178–9
Ansar [Israeli detention camp in Lebanon] 81
Ansariyeh [village] 193–5
anti-Semitism 57–8
Aoun, General Michael 100, 101
April Understanding [Israel admits Lebanese right of self-defence] 166–7, 174, 184, 213

# Index

APTN [news agency]  139
Arabic, broadcasting in  94, 96, 134, 182
Arabic Centre for Information  175
Arab–Israeli conflict  55–7, 149, 169
  1948–9 war  68, 84
  1956 war  69, 70
  1967 war  69, 70–2, 180
  1973 war  69, 72–3
  2006 war  4, 90, 144, 170, 222, 230
  Arab awakening  62–5, 67–8
  Lebanese–Israeli conflict  169
  people's sense of history  31, 209–10, 224, 232–3
  and propaganda  14
  Zionism  58–62
  *see also* Palestinians
Arab League  70, 73
Arab National Congress (1913)  62
Arab peacekeeping force (1976)  97
ARABSAT [satellite]  160
Arab unity  64–5
Arafat, Yassir [chairman of the PLO]  72, 75, 78
Areslan, Abdullah [journalist]  203–4, 212, 220
Argentina  59
Argov, Shlomo [Israeli diplomat]  77
Arida, Alex  93
Arida, Patriarch Antoine  86
Aristotle  23
Arnun [village]  198
Arqoub, Lebanon  74, 75
Asad, Hafez al- [President of Syria]  73
Ashrafieh conference  137, 150
Associated Press (AP)  199
audience  150, 151, 170
authority figures  23–4

journalists  44
Awada, Wasef [chief editor]  118, 142–3, 145
  reporting on Israel  149–50, 166
  reporting on Qana  161–2
Al Awali River  159, 164
Awwad, Tawfiq  86

Baabda palace  148
babies *see* Al Abed, Nour; Deeb, Muhammad
Baher Al Bakar [massacre]  143
balance  48, 144, 229–30
  and objectivity  51
Balfour Declaration (1917)  65–6, 67
Balhas, Saadalh  161
Bandar Bin Sultan, Prince [Saudi ambassador]  157
band wagon [propaganda device]  27, 155, 188, 209
Banks in Lebanon, Association of  156
Barak, Ehud [Israeli foreign minister]  149
  later prime minister  178, 202, 214, 218
Barrett, Oliver Boyd  53
Bartlett, F.C.  5–7, 8, 26, 30, 231
BBC (British Broadcasting Corporation)  139
Begin, Menachem [Israeli prime minister]  73, 79, 88
Beir Kalab [SLA position]  191–3
Beirut  80, 120, 136
  attacked  78, 79, 115, 162
  Heart of Jesus Hospital  162
  Jiatawi Hospital  166
Beirut Airport  74, 222
Beit Yahoun [operation]  206–10
Bekaa valley  84, 114, 127, 238, 239

belief 22–3
Bell, Martin [journalist] 45–6, 125, 144
Ben-Gurion, David [Israeli prime minister] 68, 84, 85–6
Ben-Simon, Daniel [journalist] 202
Beri, Nabih [House speaker] 127, 131, 132, 163, 166
 press conference 148–9
Bernays, Edward L. 30, 231
 vicious propaganda 18
Bet Radio 188
bias 49, 226–7, 230
Bitar, Mrs 164
black propaganda 17, 225–6
Black September [Jordanian civil war] 72, 75
blogs (July 2006 war) 234
Bolak, H. 41–2
Bouize, Fares [foreign minister] 149
Boulos, Jean-Claude 92
Boutros, Fouad [foreign minister] 75
Bowen, Jeremy [journalist] 226
Boyd, D. 93
Bregman, A. 77–8
British Government 19, 47
 Palestine mandate 65, 66–8
 promise to Arabs 65, 66
 promise to Jews 65–6
 strategic interests 62, 66
British Thomson Organisation 95
Bsaleem [power station] 129, 211–12
Budiar, Muhammad [translator] 187–8
Bush, George senior [President of USA] 157
Bute Al Siyyad [village] 138

Cairo Agreement 74
Caleb, J.J. 83
camera crews 133, 135, 140, 167
 Hezbollah 111, 177, 221
 Military Media Unit 182–5, 192–3, 204–6
Campbell, V. 45
Camp David Accords (1978–9) 73
card-stacking [propaganda device] 27, 226
Carter, Jimmy [President of USA] 73, 75
ceasefire 162, 166, 213
 offered by Israel 157–8, 160
Chamoun, Camille 86
Channel 5 see Hazmieh
Channel 7 see Talet Al Khayat
Channel 11 01
Charette (Sharet), Hervé de [French foreign minister] 130, 166
Chatila see Shatila
Chebaa Farms 90
children injured and killed 152, 153–4, 167
 see also Al Abed, Nour; Deeb, Muhammad
Chirac, Jacques [President of France] 133, 157
Chomsky, Noam 69
 and Herman, E. 18
Chouf Mountains 159
Christians 85, 150
 control of certain media 96, 100, 108
 Greek Orthodox 85, 108
  see also Murr TV
 and Israel 84–5, 86–9, 174
 Maronites 76, 83–4, 102, 174
  see also Lebanese Broadcasting Corporation

Christopher, Warren [US foreign minister]  157, 162, 163, 166
Chtaura [town]  163
citizen journalists  126, 234
civil war
  Jordan  72, 75
  Lebanon  57, 76, 81, 83, 89–90
Clausewitz, Karl von  21
Clifford, James  33–4
  and Marcus, G.  40
Clinton, Bill [President of USA]  157, 164
CNN [US station]  139
coast road (Sidon–Beirut)  159–60, 164
  closed  145, 155, 158, 160, 162
collaborators  79, 210
  surrender  195, 216, 221
  see also Hashem, Akel; Risha, Salim; SLA
colour television systems  95
Combs, James E. and Nimmo, Dan D., *The new propaganda*  16
Communist Party  102, 195
Compagnie de Télévision du Liban et du Proche see Tele-Orient (CTL)
Compagnie Libanaise de Télévision (CLT)  93–5
confessionalism in broadcasting  108
Connelly, M. and Welch, D.  19
Consultative Centre for Studies and Documentation  175
context  34
  contextual objectivity  126, 138, 171, 224, 227
  contextual truth  230
  in reporting  47–8
Cottle, S.  49

counter-propaganda  17–18, 181, 188, 193, 200–1
credibility  179, 188–9, 200–1
  undermining  193, 208, 223
  use of cameras  204–6
Cremieux, Adolphe  83
culture  32, 42–3
currency [in news]  48–9

Dajani, Nabil  92
Daouk family [landowners]  64
Davies, Aull  35, 41, 42
Dayan, Moshe  61, 85
Debl [village]  215
Debshe, Lebanon [site of media trap]  182, 183
deception  7, 11–12
  counter-productive  180
  revealed  193
Decree No. 7997 on the media  107
Deeb, Muhammad ('Baby Helicopter')  143, 153–4, 158–9, 162
  his family  163
Deir Yassin [massacre]  68, 143, 151
deliberate propaganda  231
  meaning of 'deliberate'  30
  propaganda need not be  12, 15–16, 134, 135
  propaganda that is not deliberate  169–70
demonising the enemy  187–8
detachment or distancing  34, 37–8, 125, 230
  from events and victims  227, 229, 230
  from personal experience  36–9, 168
  'going native'  171
  rather than neutrality  47

Devore, Ronald 55–6, 57
Diaspora, Jewish 62
Diaspora, Lebanese 150, 155, 164, 170, 178
Diaspora, Phoenician 83
disinformation 11
  *see also* deception
displacement of Palestinian Arabs 61–2, 71–2
Disraeli, Benjamin 58
distancing *see* detachment
diversity in the media 100
Doob, Leonard W. 7, 24
Dreyfus, Alfred 57–8
Drori, Major-General Amir 79
Druze [sect] 75, 83
Dukmak, Haidar [media liaison officer, Hezbollah] 37, 185
Durr, Dr Ibrahim 69

EBU [news agency] 139
editing of footage 125–6
editorial guidance 122
Egypt 70–1
  journalists 52
Eisenberg, L. 82
Eitan, Rafael [Israeli chief of staff] 79
electricity supply damaged 129–30, 136, 211–13
  Beirut 127, 211–12
  Nabatiyeh 126–7
Eliot, George 58
Ellul, Jacques 8–11, 30
  propaganda of integration 9–10, 231–2
El-Nawawy, Mohammed and Iskandar, Adel 47–8, 139, 224
El Nour *see* Nour
emotions 27–8, 167, 169, 202

anger 40, 144
  targeting 135, 188
English, broadcasting in 94, 134
ethnography 32–5, 228–9
eyewitness 46, 47
Ez-Addine, Hassan [head of media relations, Hezbollah] 174, 178, 185, 210

Fadlallah, Hassan [head of news, Al Manar] 108, 109
fairness and objectivity 48, 51, 224
false messages 181
Farsoun, S. and Zacharia, C. 63
*Fatah* ('conquest') [guerrilla group] 72
fear 23, 31, 124, 217
Fedayeen [PLO militia] 74
Feisal [King of Iraq] 66
feminism 40
Ferezli, Elie [deputy House speaker] 150
fieldwork 34, 35–7
filtering information 18
Fisk, Robert [journalist] 222, 224
Fiske, J. 49, 52
footage 125–6
  *see also* images
Four Mothers [movement] 218–19
Fowler, R. 45
Franjieh, Suleiman [President of Lebanon] 96
French, broadcasting in 94–5, 96, 134, 237n.6
French Government 136
  intervention 83, 135, 162
  mandated territories 66, 84
Friedman, T. 72
future research 234
Future Television 107, 108, 147

G7 Summit [Moscow] 156–7
Galilee 78, 82, 173
Gaza 57, 60, 71
Gemayel *see* Jumayyil
Gerstein, Brigadier-General
  Eretz 198–201
Ginzberg, Asher (Ahad ha-Am) 60
Glahn, Gerhard von 20–1, 232
glittering generalities [propaganda device] 27, 168–9
glorifying events 209–10, 226
Goebbels, P. Joseph 7, 24, 168
  his principles of
    propaganda 24–6, 133, 225
  principle 1 (access to intelligence) 25
  principle 2 (one controller) 25
  principle 3 (consequences must be considered) 25
  principle 4 (effect on enemy) 25, 218
  principle 5 (use of information) 25
  principle 6 (must get attention) 25
  principle 7 (true or false, must be credible) 25, 225
  principle 8 (ignore or refute enemy propaganda) 25
  principle 9 (decisions on censorship) 25, 208–9
  principle 10 (use of enemy propaganda) 25–6, 202, 208–9
  principle 11 (black or white propaganda) 26, 225
  principle 12 (use of prestige figures) 26, 197, 213
  principle 13 (timing of propaganda) 26
  principle 14 (use of labels or slogans) 26, 216
  principle 15 (avoid false hopes) 26
  principle 16 (create anxiety at home) 26
  principle 17 (diminish frustration at home) 26, 168
  principle 18 (specify targets of hatred) 26, 123, 144–5, 168, 213
  principle 19 (action or diversion to face strong enemy action) 26, 133
  'propaganda never objective' 7, 31, 228, 231
'going native' 37, 39, 171
Goksel, Timor [UN spokesman] 150
Golan Heights 71, 73
Goodall, H.L. 32–3, 42
Goodenough, Ward H. 32
Grapes of Wrath [military operation] 113–14
Greek Orthodox *see* Christians
Grenada invasion (1983) 178–9
grey propaganda 17, 226
Gur, General Mordecai 74

Habib, Philip [negotiator] 78
Haddad, Saad [head of SLA] 77, 80, 85, 88
Haganah [Zionist group] 68
Haidar, Muhamad [chairman of Al Manar] 36, 109, 110, 178
Haifa (Jaffa) 63
*Hajj* [pilgrimage] 138
Hamade, Marwan [health minister] 151

Hamad, Saad [journalist] 184
Hammersley, M. and
  Atkinson, P. 37, 39, 41
Hammoud, Dr Ghassan 158
Hammoud hospital *see* Sidon
Hamza [*mujahed*] 192, 193
Al Haram Al Ibrahimy
  [massacre] 143
Haret Hreik, Beirut 206, 209, 222
Hariri, Rafic [prime minister] 24,
  102–3, 108, 120, 131
  and ceasefire 166
  and Future TV 147
  on Hezbollah 127–8
  international contacts 136–7,
    157, 163
  international profile 130, 133–4
  on media contribution 228
  and News of Lebanon 160
  reported 116, 130
  and Taif Accord 89–90
Hashem, Akel 189, 214–16
Hass, Amira [journalist] 224
Hatem, Mohammed Abdel-
  Kader 6, 13–15, 23–4
  and psychological warfare 193,
    227
Hayward, J.W. 22
Al Hazmieh [Channel 5
  studios] 95, 96, 98, 99, 102
  mainly Christian 100
  and presidential palace 101
Hebbariyeh [village] 74
Hebrew, broadcasting in 182,
  186–8, 217
Herman, E. and Chomsky, N. 18
Herzl, Theodor [founder of
  Zionism] 57–60
Hess, Moses 58
Hezbollah ('Party of God') 80–1,
  130–1, 137, 177, 209

camera crews *see* Military Media
  Unit
communiqués 120, 208
government view 127, 137
and Grapes of Wrath 113, 173–4
Hebrew Monitoring Unit 186–9
  its audience 177, 217
Media Relations Centre 185–6
  as Central Media Unit 180,
    185
media strategy 176–81, 184, 189,
  227
use of intelligence 199–201
wide support 90, 112
see also *Intiqad*; Islamic Health
  Association; Manar TV;
  Nour Radio
Higazi, Arafat 98
High Relief Committee
  [Lebanon] 127, 135, 156
Hirsch, Baron Maurice de 58
history, sense of 31, 209–10, 224,
  232–3
Hmayed, Hussein [head of
  Political Propaganda
  Unit] 182, 225
Holocaust (Shoah) 67, 68
honest propaganda 14–15, 146,
  168, 227, 231
Hrawi, Elias [President of
  Lebanon] 101, 127, 131,
  136, 148
  goes to New York 161, 164
humanitarian aid 135–6
Hurewitz, J.C. 55
Hurricane Katrina, reporting
  of 126
Hussein, Sharif of Mecca 65, 66
Hussein, Imam [grandson of
  Muhammad] 205
Hussein [King of Jordan] 72, 73, 75

Index 269

images 125, 199
  of attacks 204–5
  of death and injury 126, 134, 152, 184
  editing of footage 125–6
immediacy 48
impartiality 94, 96, 119, 229–30
  not always appropriate 51–2, 159, 224
Independent Communication Channel International (ICNI) 108
Institute for Propaganda Analysis 11, 27–8
  seven propaganda devices 26, 188, 226
integrative propaganda 9–10, 231–2
  as part of liberation propaganda 21
internationalisation of the crisis 155, 156–7
  audiences 178
International Red Cross 194
Intifada ('shaking off') 70, 74
Al Intiqad [magazine] 185
Iqlim Al Kharoub 159
Iraq 66–7
  future research 234
Iskandar, Adel and El-Nawawy, Mohammed 47–8, 139, 224
Iskandar, Marwan 157
Islamic Health Association 196
Islamic resistance 131, 177–8
  see also Hezbollah
Ismaeel, Mariam and Ibrahim 165–6
Israel 68–9, 151, 187–8
  as the enemy 122, 130
  as a friend 78–9, 145
  news media 182–4

northern Galilee attacked 127, 213
Israeli forces 178, 183–4
  1940 to 1970s 68, 71, 73
  1970s incursions into Lebanon 1, 74, 99
  1982 invasion of Lebanon 77–80, 99, 114, 148, 151
  1990s 'security zone' 115, 172, 177, 198
  checkpoints 206, 220
  1996 attacks see 1996, April
  2000 withdrawal from Lebanon 90, 177, 219–21
  air raids 162–4
  army radio 188
  morale 217–19
  soldiers' mothers 178, 183, 187, 217–19
  Special Forces 193–4
  target roads and bridges 164–5, 211
  target TV and radio stations 170, 184, 222
  warships 145, 164
  see also Lebanon, 'security zone'
Israeli Government 211
  ceasefire 157–8, 160, 162, 166, 213
  official statements 130, 179, 180–1
  reported sceptically 149–50
  subverted by media traps 182
  policy towards Lebanon 84–90, 139
  policy towards Lebanon, admits right of self-defence (April Understanding) 166–7, 174, 184
  propaganda 78, 80
  seen to have lied 182, 191–3

Israeli TV  188, 217
　re-broadcasts Al Manar
　　TV  186–7, 193, 200–1, 219
　see also Radio Israel
Izzedine, Wissam  93, 98

Jaber, Hala, *Hezbollah*  173–4
Jaffa (Haifa)  63
Jalloul, Mahmoud
　[cameraman]  117
Al Jamhour [power station]
　211–12
Jarjouaa [village]  203
Al Jazeera TV  47
Jerusalem  63, 67, 71
Jewish Agency  84, 86
Jewish Colonisation
　Association  64
Jews  63–4
　already in Palestine  56, 63
　in Israel  57
Jezzine [town]  190, 191
*al Jihad*  210
jingle removed at time of crisis  160
Al Jmiajmeh [massacre]  113
John Paul II [pope]  153
Jordan  66, 68
　and the Palestinians  72, 75
Jorisch, Avi, *Beacon of Hatred*  222–3
Jounieh, church explosion  102
Jourat Al Balout [transmitter]  139, 141
journalism culture  38, 42–4
　context  47–50
　news values  45, 48–9
　objectivity  45–7
　partial truths  51–3
journalists  36–7, 46, 52, 119, 232
　camera crew  133, 135, 140, 167
　citizen journalists  126, 234
　helping civilians  165, 171
　needing no instructions  128, 134, 225
　as voice of victims  167–8, 170, 224
　see also war reporting
Journalists' Syndicate in
　Lebanon  180
Jowett, Garth and O'Donnell,
　Victoria  16–17, 22, 227
　analysing a campaign  29
　analysis of propaganda  169–70, 225–6
Jumayyil, Amin [President of
　Lebanon]  89, 100
Jumayyil, Bashir [President of
　Lebanon]  87–9
Jumayyil, Peir  87
Jumblat, Walid [Druze
　leader]  131, 149
June [or Six-Day] War (1967)  69, 70–2, 180

Kahlani, Avigdor [Israeli
　minister]  194–5
Kamouneh, Rajaa
　[presenter–producer]  146, 150, 158
Kandeel-Yaghi, Naser [deputy
　head, National Media
　Council]  146, 154–5, 160
Kasir, Samir [journalist]  170
Al Kataeb Phalangist party  86, 87
Katyusha rockets  130, 150, 173, 211
Katz, Elihu [media scholar]  184
Kellen, Konrad  11
Kfar Qassem [massacre]  68
Kfour [bomb attack]  199
*Khamseh ala Sabaah* [current affairs
　programme]  140
Khiam [Israeli detention centre in
　Lebanon]  221

Khoury, Ibrahim [chairman of
    Tele Liban] 36
Khoury, John 98
Kibia [massacre] 68
Kohl, Helmut [German
    chancellor] 157
Kontler, Laszlo 7
Koran (Qur'an) 207
Kouyoumdjian, Zaven
    [journalist] 123, 135,
    238n.7
  and massacres 140, 142,
    143–4
Krayem, Nayef [chairman of Al
    Manar and Al Nour] 180,
    181, 183, 187, 205–6
  on broadcasts to Israel 217–18,
    219
Kurdistan, future research 234
Kuwait 67

Lahed, Antoine 77, 214
Lahed militia *see* SLA
Lahed Radio 121, 126
  communiqués 122, 130
Lahed TV 200, 216
landowners 64
Lasswell, Harold 11
Lavon, Pinhas [Israeli defence
    minister] 85
Law 382 on the Media 102,
    106–8, 185
leader-symbols 23–4
League of Nations 65, 67, 84
Lebanese army 75, 135,
    160, 165
  alongside Hezbollah 194, 197,
    198
  divided politically 101
  on same side as Hezbollah 117
  use of TV news 116–17

Lebanese Broadcasting
    Corporation (LBC) 100,
    101, 102, 108
  studios attacked 222
Lebanese Forces [militia] 87, 89,
    102
Lebanese Government 76,
    79, 90
  and Hezbollah 90, 111–12, 127,
    137, 203
  and Israel 89, 107, 162
  and the media 92, 105,
    160–1
  attitude in time of crisis 128,
    155, 169
  involvement 97–8, 105–6
  licensing 106–8
  non-interference 122,
    134
  non-regulation 126
  programme content
    restrictions 93–4
  supports satellite
    broadcasts 150, 154
Lebanese High Relief
    Committee 127, 135, 156
Lebanese Law 382 on Audio-
    Visual Media 102, 106–8,
    185
Lebanese Media Group
    (LMG) 110
Lebanese National Movement
    (LNM) 76
Lebanese unity 81–2, 155, 233
  with Hezbollah 90, 194
  and the Israeli invasion 137,
    156
  journalists' aim 161, 168,
    212–13, 227, 233–4
  and the media 124, 135, 160–1,
    213

Lebanon 84
 civil wars 57
 Israel admits right of
  self-defence (April
  Understanding) 166–7, 174,
  184
 and the Palestinians 72, 74, 75,
  76
 'security zone' [Israeli-
  occupied] 80, 115, 177, 198
  attacked 115–16, 162, 163
  checkpoints 206, 220
  detention camps 81, 221
  pressure on civilians 81, 121–2
  resistance 74, 81
  socialist parties 75–6, 80
  *see also* Lebanese Government;
   Lebanese unity
 legal constraints 93–4, 119
 legend and myth 23–4
 Levine, Major-General
  Amiram 219
 liberation 6
  of south Lebanon 217–21
 liberation propaganda 9–10, 21,
  181, 225–7, 230–3
  as defined here 30–1, 39
 licensing of media 106–8
 Lichtenberg, J. 50
 Liebes, Tamar [media
  scholar] 184–5
 Litani River 76–7, 84
  area south of 80, 127
 Lloyd George, David 66
 Lubrani, Uri 130

 McCary, Michael 116
 Maitham, Haj [head of Military
  Media Unit] 183, 202–3, 208
 Major, John [British prime
  minister] 136, 157

Majzoub, Nadine [reporter] 117,
  124–5
 interviews injured child 153–4,
  158–9
Makari, Farid [information
  minister] 128, 150, 154
Al Manar TV 108–12, 172, 185,
  189
 aims of its journalists 232
 audience 177, 178, 186–7, 217,
  223
 and hatred 222–4
 Hebrew broadcasts 186–8, 217,
  219
 and Military Media Unit 183
 and objectivity 224
 Political Propaganda
  Unit 181–2, 225
 and propaganda 110, 168, 225–7
  counter-propaganda 181
 re-broadcast by Israeli
  TV 186–7, 193, 200–1
  which it re-broadcasts 186–7,
  200–1
 Resistance Dept 182
 studios attacked 170, 184, 222,
  233–4
Mannion, David [ITV news
  editor] 144, 230
Mansour, Albert [information
  minister] 102
Mansouri [massacre] 118–19,
  122–3
Marmal, I. [cameraman] 193
Maronites *see* Christians
Maroum, General Kobi 173
Al-Mashrek Television 102
massacres 68, 79
 *see also* Jmiajmeh; Mansouri;
  Nabatiyeh; Qana; Suhmur
mass society 10

media traps 182, 189
  Beir Kalab 191–3
  Debshe 182–3
  Sujud 202–6
Mellor, Noha 52
Merhej, Bechara [MP] 211
Merton, R. 24
Military Media Unit
  [Hezbollah] 111, 177,
  182–5, 192–3
  at Beir Kalab 192–3
  at Beit Yahoun 207–8
  at killing of Akel Hashem
    214–16
  at Sujud 202–3
Miller, D. 13
Ministry of Information 96, 136
Mohsen, Professor
  Muhammad 176–8
Montefiore, Sir Moses 83
Mossad [Israeli intelligence] 86,
  87, 190, 191
mothers of Israeli soldiers 178,
  183, 187, 217–19
motives 13, 24
Mouad, Rene [President of
  Lebanon] 101
Moukaled, Diana [journalist] 147
Mount Haramon, Lebanon 74
Mount Lebanon 129, 136
Mreijeh, Beirut, air raids 162
Mugabgab [Maronite leader] 86
*mujahedeen* 190, 192, 194–7, 206–7,
  209–10
  Jawad and Hadi 215–16
Mungham, Geoff 78–9, 80
Murr Television (MTV) 108
Murtada [*mujahed*] 192–3
Muslims' control of certain
  media 96, 99
myth and legend 23–4

Nabatiyeh [town] 120–1, 126–7,
  135
  massacre 142
  propaganda 148, 155
Naim, Fouad [TL
  chairman] 102–5, 115, 117,
  122, 146
Al Najat church, Jounieh 102
Najem, Dr Jawad 140
*Nakba* or *nakbeh* ('catastrophe')
  [expulsion of Arabs] 68,
  207
name-calling [propaganda
  device] 27, 168–9, 188, 216
Napoleon Bonaparte 62
Naser, Abass [journalist] 209–10,
  220, 221
Naser, Haj [cameraman] 205
Nasrallah, Assayed Hassan
  [Secretary General of
  Hezbollah] 80, 120, 131,
  183, 221
  future research 234
  his sons 194–6
  as public figure 24, 189, 194–7,
  210
Nasrallah, Hadi [*mujahed*] 194–6
Nasser, Gamal Abdel [President of
  Egypt] 70–1, 72, 73
Nast, H. 39–40
National Broadcasting Network
  (NBN) 107, 108
nationalism 2, 55, 67, 70, 227
National Liberal Party 99
native 42
  'going native' 37, 39, 171
  Palestinians 59–61, 66
NATO (North Atlantic Treaty
  Organization) 13
Nazi Party propaganda 7, 24
  *see also* Goebbels

Nemer, Gada Assaf
 [journalist] 203
neutrality 159, 229
 not expected 138
 and objectivity 45
 and patriotism 146
News of Lebanon [TV
 channel] 160
newspapers and magazines 97,
 184–5, 217, 219
news reports 98–9
 carrying dual messages 116–17,
 120
 factual, not fabricated 171, 224
 introduction [opinion] 152, 212
news values 45, 48–9
newsworthiness 117
New Television (NTV) 102, 108
Nour Al Abed [baby] 142
Al Nour (El Nour) [radio
 station] 110, 180, 184, 185

objectivity 38, 159, 224, 229–30
 and bias 226–7
 contextual 126, 138, 171, 224,
 227, 230, 233
 and fairness 224
 in journalism culture 45–7
 negotiable 224
 'objective truth' 168
 and propaganda 3, 228
 in reporting 45–7, 125, 167–8,
 228–30
 Fouad Naim 146, 168
 risk factors 51
OB (outside broadcast) unit 115,
 121, 198
 at Sidon 117–18
observer as participant 35
occupation 224
Occupied Territories *see* Gaza;
 Golan Heights; West Bank;
 *see also* Lebanon, 'security
 zone'
October [Ramadan or Yom
 Kippur] War (1973) 69,
 72–3
Orit, Shohat [journalist] 202
O'Shaughnessy, Nicholas 19–20
Osterhaus, William E. 98–9,
 102
Ottoman Empire 62–5
Ouzai, near Beirut 196

Palestine 55–6, 59–60
 biblical 83
 British mandate 65, 66–8
 displacement of Arabs 61–2,
 71–2
 future research 234
 partition 67–8
Palestine Liberation Organisation
 (PLO) 70, 72, 78
 Black September [Jordanian
 civil war] 72, 75
Palestinians 57, 61–2, 68
 displacement 61–2, 71–2
 and Lebanon 74–6, 90
 sense of history 31, 56, 209–10,
 224, 232–3
partiality sometimes
 expected 51–2, 159, 224
participant observation 34–5,
 35–7
partition of Palestine 67–8
patriotism 47, 144, 227
 and neutrality 146
 and the Qana massacre 144–8,
 167
Pedelty, Mark 44
Peel Commission 67, 84
perception 22

Peres, Shimon [Israeli prime minister]  87, 132, 142–3, 166
   reported  61, 157
Phalange Party  79, 82, 86, 87–8, 99
   Al Kataeb  87
   militia  76
Philo, Greg and Berry, Mike  181
Pinsker, Leon  58
plain folks [propaganda device]  27, 161, 188, 197
political propaganda  8–9
populist media  177, 185
power over information  18
power stations  136, 211–12
Pratkanis, A. and Aronson, E.  8, 22–3
professionalism  38, 46, 49–51, 229–30
   hybrid  37
   in practice  2, 117, 119, 125, 170
   war reporting  53, 125, 224
propaganda  3–5, 6–8, 12
   of agitation  9
   analysing a campaign  29
   black, grey or white  17
      black  225–6
      grey  226
      white  145, 225, 227, 231
   counter-propaganda  181, 188, 193
   of the deed  24, 116
   defined  5–6, 30
      by Bartlett  8, 131
      by Doob  7
      by Ellul  8–11
      by Institute for Propaganda Analysis  11
      by Jowett and O'Donnell  16, 169–70
      by Lasswell  11
      by NATO  13, 132
      by Pratkanis and Aronson  8
      by Taylor  15
      by Thomson  12
   'deliberate'  231
   need not be deliberate  12, 15–16, 134, 135
   not deliberate  169–70
   failure of  28–9
   images  145–6, 148
   of integration or unity  9–10, 151, 231–2
   internal and external  29
   liberation  181, 225–7, 230–3
   subversive  9–10, 21, 232
   targets  29, 170
   third wave  186
   and truth  179
   of truth  14–15, 146, 168, 227, 231
   *see also* Goebbels, P. Joseph; Institute for Propaganda Analysis
*Propaganda Fide, Sacra Congregatio de*  6
psychological propaganda  193, 227
Public Diplomacy  18
public-service broadcasting  104–6

Qana [massacre]  1, 112, 140–2, 145
   bereaved  161, 163, 164
   coverage  143–4, 145–7, 167–8
      of aftermath  6, 152–5, 161–2, 165–6
   graveyard  162
   propaganda  146–51, 155
Qur'an (Koran)  207

Rabin, Yitzhak [Israeli prime minister]  86–7

Radio Al Nour *see* Nour
Radio Israel 121, 122, 126, 188, 217
  Arabic service 188
  reliability of news 109
Radio Lebanon 97
radio-monitoring unit 121
radio stations 100, 106
  Ministry of Information 96
  *see also* Lahed Radio; Nour; Radio Israel; Radio Lebanon; Voice of Lebanon
Rahal, Hussein [head of news, Al Manar] 191, 216
Ramadan [October or Yom Kippur] War (1973) 72–3
Randal, J. 79, 84–5, 89
recency 48
reflexivity 40
  self-reflexivity 39–42
refugees, Lebanese 120–1, 124, 135, 137
  refusal to become 121, 147–8
  regret they left 129
  return home 167
refugees, Palestinian 57, 61–2, 71–2
religion motivating journalists 227
reporters *see* journalists
reporting *see* news reports
resistance, use of the term 130–1, 137
Reslan, Abdullah [journalist] 192
Reuters [news agency] 122–3, 139, 199
revolution 20–1, 232
rhetoric 23, 26, 91, 122, 169
Rhodes, Cecil John 58
Risha, Salim [SLA officer] 190–1
Rizk brothers 95
  Charles Rizk [TL chairman] 99
  Edmond Rizk [information minister] 101, 102
Roseneil, Sasha 40
Roshco, Bernard 48
Rothschild, Baron Nathaniel 58
Rugh, William 92, 100

Saatchi & Saatchi [advertising agency] 102
Sabra [refugee camp] massacre 79, 151
Sadat, Anwar el- [President of Egypt] 73
Sadek, Nesrine 139
Sadler, Brent [broadcaster] 139
Said, Ahmad [broadcaster] 180
Said, Edward [writer] 60, 69, 181
  and Hitchens, C. 61, 69, 70
Sakr, Naomi 108
Salam, Saeb [Lebanese prime minister] 74
Salemeh [TL journalist] 157
Salman, Hanadi [blogger] 234
Salman, Talal [publisher] 194
Salti, Rasha [blogger] 234
El Salvador 44
Samaha, Michael 100
Sarid, Yossi [Israeli minister] 149
Sarkis, Elias [President of Lebanon] 97
satellite broadcasts 160, 223, 233
  government decision 150, 154
Saudi Arabia 136
Sawaya, Klaude 98
Schudson, M. 43, 49, 51
'security zone' [Israeli-occupied] 115, 177, 198
  checkpoints 206, 220
Segal, Naomi [journalist] 214
self-censorship 131

self-reflexivity 39–42
semantics 19
sensational reporting 135
September 11 attacks (2001) 47, 124
Sfeir, Mar Nasrallah Boutros [cardinal bishop] 128, 131, 153
Shalak, Samar 138
Shamir, Yitzhak [Israeli foreign minister] 78
Sharet *see* Charette
Sharett, Moshe [Israeli prime minister] 84–5
Sharon, Ariel [Israeli defence minister] 78, 79, 88
Shatila [refugee camp] massacre 79, 151
Shia Muslims 80, 178, 225
  and television 108
  *see also* Hezbollah; Manar TV
Shlaim, Avi [writer] 71
Sidon [city] 82, 116, 117, 118
  Al Wastani 162
  Hammoud hospital 119, 123, 143, 153–4
  refugees 120, 136
  TL studio 140, 145
Sinai Peninsula 70, 71, 72, 73
Six-Day [or June] War (1967) 69, 70–2, 180
Skaf, George [TL chairman] 101
SLA (South Lebanon Army) ['Lahed militia'] 77, 206, 214, 216, 219–20
  captured or wounded 207, 208
  and Salim Risha 190–1
  surrender 195, 216, 221
  *see also* Lahed Radio
Snow, Nancy 11, 19

sociological propaganda 8–9
Soloski, J. 51
Stren [Zionist group] 68
subjective language and images 125
sub-propaganda 17
subversive propaganda 9–10, 232
  as part of liberation propaganda 21
Suez crisis 69, 70
Suhmur [massacre] 115
suicide attacks 224
Sujud [operation] 192, 202–6
Sunni Muslims and television 108
  *see also* Future TV
Sursock, Emile [landowner] 64
Swat al Arab [radio station] 180
Sykes–Picot Agreement (1916) 65
symbols [propaganda devices] 31, 197
sympathy 135, 138
Syria 66–7, 85, 101, 162

Tabbara, Riyad [Lebanese ambassador to USA] 151
Al Taif Accord 89–90
Taha, Riyad [journalist] 180
Taif Accord (1989) 100–2
Taithe, B. and Thornton, T. 17, 188
Talet Al Khayat [Channel 7 studios] 93, 96, 98, 102, 139
  mainly Muslim 99–100
  taking sides 100
Tanter, R. 78
target *see* audience; propaganda
Tawalba, Hassan 52
Taylor, Philip M. 15–16, 179, 227

Tele Liban (TL) 97–106
  aims of its journalists 232
  April 1996 coverage 103–4,
    116–17, 163
    see also 1996, 11–26 April
  Channel 7 and Hezbollah 109
  and the civil war 99–100
  emergency team 137–8
  international team 136
  studios under attack 170, 222,
    233–4
  and the Taif Accord 100–2
  target audiences 150, 170
  under Naim 102–6
Télé Lumière 108
Tele-Management 95, 97
Tele-Orient (CTL) 95–7
television in Lebanon
  1940s to 1970s 92–9
  the 1980s 99–101
  early 1990s 101–6
  later 1990s 107–12
  Law 382 on the Media 106–8
  see also Manar TV; Tele Liban
    (TL)
terrorist groups 137
testimonial [propaganda
  device] 27, 188
third wave propaganda 186
Thomson, Oliver 11–12, 28–9
Thomson Company [French] 110
Thomson Organisation
  [British] 95
Tiger militia 76
TL see Tele Liban
transference [propaganda
  device] 27, 188, 213
Transjordan 66
translators 187–8
treason 119
triangulation 39

Tripoli, Lebanon 84
truce see ceasefire
trustworthiness 23, 103–4
truth 179, 229–30
  contextual 230
  and credibility 179
  'objective' 168, 230
  positioned 168, 224, 230
  and propaganda 179
  propaganda of 14–15, 146, 168,
    227, 231
truthfulness 189
Tuchman, Gaye 50
Tuieni, G. 75, 76–7
TV5 [French channel] 139
Tyre [city] 77, 84, 132–3
  inhabitants 121, 127
  Najem hospital 118, 133, 140, 141

UK see British Government
Um Abbas 138
United Nations (UN) 67, 70
  General Assembly 75, 161
  Resolution 242 (1967) 71, 90
  Resolution 425 (1978) 77, 81, 90
  Tyre HQ 132
  UNIFIL 77, 90, 129, 132, 133
    aid convoys 135, 138
    Qana HQ 129, 162
    soldiers 123, 140–1, 143, 167
United Television (UTV) 108
unity 213
  see also Lebanese unity
USA 151, 222–3
  journalists 50–1
US Government 47, 116
  aid to Israeli forces 73, 75
  intervention 135, 136, 162,
    163–4
  propaganda 18–19
  and terrorist groups 137

Ussishkin, Menachem 83

vicious propaganda 18
victims 174, 224
　journalist as voice of 167–8, 170, 224
　Vietnam War (1955–75) 178–9
viewers' trust 103–4
vocabulary 125
Voice of Lebanon [radio] 97
voluntary reporters *see* citizen journalists

Wakim, Jacques 96
war reporting 44, 46–7, 125
　and contextualisation 48
　and propaganda 52–3, 155
Weizman, Ezer [Israeli defence minister] 77
Weizmann, Chaim 65–6, 82–3
West Bank 57, 60, 71
Western governments and propaganda 13, 18–19
Western news media 45, 46, 50–2, 137

Whaley, Barton 11
White, A.B. 8
white propaganda 17, 145, 225, 227, 231
Williams, Kevin 52, 159
Wolcott, H.F. 42–3
World Zionist Conference (1897) 59
Wozniak, Major-General Stanisław 132

Yeltsin, Boris [President of Russia] 157
Yom Kippur [or October] War (1973) 69, 72–3

Zabarie [soldier's mother] 219
Zalmnobites, Tel [journalist] 183
Zbqeen [village] 138
Zelizer, Barbie 43–4
Zionism 58–62
　and Lebanon 82–3, 84
　opposition to 63–4
'Zionist forces' 190